Crossing Borders: Post 1980 Subcontinental Writing in English

For Amrit,
   It is always good to meet,
        Jashn

Crossing Borders
Post 1980 Subcontinental Writing in English

Edited by
JASBIR JAIN

Institute for Research in Interdisciplinary Studies, Jaipur

RAWAT PUBLICATIONS
Jaipur • New Delhi • Bangalore • Mumbai • Hyderabad • Guwahati

ISBN 81-316-0251-6
© Contributors, 2009

No part of this book may be reproduced or transmitted in any form or by any means, electronic or mechanical, including photocopying, recording or by any information storage and retrieval system, without permission in writing from the publishers.

Published by
Prem Rawat for **Rawat Publications**
Satyam Apts, Sector 3, Jawahar Nagar, Jaipur 302 004 (India)
Phone: 0141 265 1748/7006 Fax: 0141 265 1748
E-mail: info@rawatbooks.com
Website: www.rawatbooks.com

New Delhi Office
4858/24, Ansari Road, Daryaganj, New Delhi 110 002
Phone: 011 2326 3290

Also at Bangalore, Mumbai, Hyderabad and Guwahati

Typeset by Rawat Computers, Jaipur
Printed at Chaman Enterprises, New Delhi

for Dayaji
who was always crossing borders

We faced each other across the table at the Hotel
Rawat, Krishna and myself, flown in from a
different clime.

Mini Nanda led me by the hand to him.

. . . .

At that moment in time I was Krishna's votary
paying him obeisance for still being alive in
this murderous age, retaining a philosophy to guide
the blind, trying to reconstruct a world where crazed
homuncules run amok directionless allowing splintered
minds and bodies to drown in their own blood
and muck in bombed and burning cities.

Jean Arasanayagam
(Extract from "The Visionary: Two Poems for Daya Krishna, Poem 2")

Contents

Preface / xi

Introduction: Borders, Border Theories
and Crossing Borders / xiii

NAYANTARA SAHGAL
Rejecting Extinction / 1

SHYAMALA A. NARAYAN
Indian English Literary Criticism: Crossing
Linguistic Boundaries / 9

JASBIR JAIN
Terrorism at the Feet of Buddha: From Taliban
to LTTE and the In-Between / 23

AVINASH JODHA
Eclectic Cartography: Spaces of Memory and
Belonging in Sorayya Khan's *Noor* / 38

CHARU MATHUR
Terror vs Terrorism: Reordering the World / 50

PURABI PANWAR
Violence and Life in a Metro City:
A Look at *Maximum City* and *Sacred Games* / 58

USHA BANDE
The Politics of Honour/ Horror:
An Analysis of Mukhtar Mai's *In The Name of Honour* / 66

Contents

SUDHA SHASTRI
New Arrivals: *The Barn Owl's Wondrous Capers*, Graphic Novel / 82

SAVYASAACHI JAIN
One Crossing, Many Journeys / 94

KEKI N. DARUWALLA
Love Across the Salt Desert / 107

JEAN ARASANAYAGAM
The Journey / 115

SUNITI NAMJOSHI
Summer Days / 130

E.V. RAMAKRISHNAN
Terms of Seeing: Four Poems / 131

JEAN ARASANAYAGAM
Crossing Borders / 136

SOMDATTA MANDAL
History and/or a Sense of Place:
Reading Amitav Ghosh's *The Hungry Tide* / 139

KINSHUK MAJUMDAR
Crossing Cultural Boundaries:
A Study of Amitav Ghosh's *The Hungry Tide* / 152

MADHURI CHATTERJEE
Home and the Travelling Self: Amitav Ghosh's
The Hungry Tide and Vikram Seth's *From Heaven Lake* / 164

NIDHI SINGH
Identity Under the Shadow of Violence: *The Shadow Lines* / 174

SIMRAN CHADHA
Ethnic Nationalism and the Pluralistic Space of the Nation
in the Fiction of Michael Ondaatje / 181

MINI NANDA
Mending the Fault Lines: Same Culture, Separate Nation / 194

E.V. RAMAKRISHNAN
Poet as Witness: Ethnicity and the Discourse of the
Nation in the Poetry of Jean Arasanayagam and Agha Shahid Ali / 205

NISHAT ZAIDI
Centre/Margin Dialectics and the Poetic Form:
The Case of Agha Shahid Ali / 222

VIJAYA SINGH
Hell is the Absence of the Beloved:
Agha Shahid Ali and the Poetry of Impossible Mourning / 236

ANSHOO SHARMA
Transcending Borders of Patriarchal Hegemony:
Dattani's: *Where There's a Will* / 247

PAYAL NAGPAL
Alternative Sexual Constructs in Mahesh Dattani's
Seven Steps Around the Fire and *On a Muggy Night in Mumbai* / 256

Contributors / 267

Preface

Crossing Borders: Post 1980 Subcontinental Writing in English is a collection of some of the papers presented at a seminar organized by Institute for Research in Interdisciplinary Studies (IRIS) from 20th to 22nd September, 2007. This seminar became possible with the collaboration, support and sponsorship of various agencies and institutions, and the cooperation of several individuals. In this collaborative effort we were crossing borders all the time.

But seminars do not only require ideas or funds, they also require individuals – intellectuals willing to share their time and thoughts, willing to interact and give of themselves. For this, we express our gratitude to Nayantara Sahgal, Girish Karnad, Jean Arasanayagam, Suniti Namjoshi, E.V. Ramakrishnan, Mukul Kesavan, Savyasaachi Jain, Shyamala Narayan, Somdatta Mandal, Sharmishtha Panja, Purabi Panwar, Usha Bande and all the other scholars who joined us. IRIS members presented papers, made the posters, introduced the authors, looked after the transport and carried out the various mundane tasks of seminaring in perfect unison and harmony.

The theme, as we floated the concept note, was concerned with "Borders, Border Theories and Crossing Borders: Post 1980 Subcontinental Writing in English". Both the implication and desire were directed at a horizontal relationship amongst the literary expressions of the subcontinent. We share our borders with each other – India, Pakistan, Sri Lanka, Bangladesh, Bhutan and Nepal. China and Afghanistan are also near neighbours. It is true that some of these countries find no representation here but it is hoped that in some future venture the gaps will be filled. What we had in mind was the

SAARC constellation. The language limitation and the exclusion of translated texts were in large measure practical strategies to facilitate work at the same wave-length. Yet, it is impossible to adhere rigidly to any such restriction because culture is a wide term and envelops us from all sides.

As each writer has defined the theme from her or his own perspective, we have a wholesome discussion of the kinds of borders and the nature of border crossings. One may ask why "Crossing Borders" then. We do want to assert the positive aspect of crossing borders and wish to retain the initiative with the human will – as a way of growth, self-evolvement and reaching out to the 'other'.

IRIS stands beholden to the contributors to this volume, especially to Nayantara Sahgal, who has allowed us to include the inaugural address she delivered. We also acknowledge the permission which Keki Daruwalla, Suniti Namjoshi, Jean Arasanayagam and E.V. Ramakrishnan have given us to include their creative work. Keki Daruwalla's story was first published in his first volume of short stories *The Sword and the Abyss*; Jean Arasanayagam's "The Journey" is from *All is Burning* and E.V. Ramakrishnan's poems from his collection *Terms of Seeing*.

This volume is dedicated to the memory of Professor Daya Krishna. This was perhaps the last seminar where he was briefly present and the dinner hosted by the Rawats, perhaps his last public appearance, where he sat at the centre table surrounded by a host of admirers and friends. He was a person always open to ideas, willing to cross all kinds of borders, disciplinary, ideological and generational. We miss the discussions we had with him over the years that we have known him. This volume pays our homage to him.

Introduction: Borders, Border Theories and Crossing Borders

Borders are significant markers of nation formation and go on to create communities and identities. They mark territorial limits, define cultural practices and signify ownership and belonging. Metaphorically, they signify a moral restraint between the acceptable and the non-acceptable patterns of behaviour. One may be 'bordering' on insanity or immorality in the course of meeting challenges.

Gloria Anzaldúa in identifying the Chicano people as border people was primarily concerned with the in-between status of the Mexican border people, Mestiza, people with a mixed heritage of languages and cultures, marked by greater flexibility and plurality. The title of her 1987 book, *Borderlands/La Frontera* brought together the dual nature of the border which was both a closure and an opening, a borderland as well as a frontier. The subtitle of the book *The New Mestiza* projects the new mestiza consciousness, representative of plurality and flexibility and a mixed heritage, which discouraged separatism. People living on the borders become aware of 'flowing' cultures. We find this on all our borders – international, national and regional. Travelling towards and to Nepal, this is more than obvious. Nepalese people and people of the Terai region in Bihar keep on an on-going traffic and even if they are citizens of one country, effectually they belong to two. They can own leaders and movements on both sides.[1]

At the time of writing this I am reading a travelogue by the well-known film actor of yesteryears Balraj Sahni, *Mera Pakistani Safarnama* (Punjabi). Sahni's origins were in west Punjab. He grew up in Rawalpindi and Lahore and when he went back in 1962 to this area, he went as an outsider, a non-citizen and a stranger. Yet in the midst of the frequent reporting to the police stations and moving only within permitted areas, he searched for the past. The pleasure he experienced in listening to the languages and words of his childhood memories was immense. He felt pulled towards the sounds of the language he had been missing in Bombay. Here is an example of languages and memories transcending borders, even if the physical presence is elsewhere.[2]

Balraj Sahni also traces the history of the formation of the district Gujarat in Punjab. It is a land inhabited by the same Gujjar community which was later to spread out to Gujarat in Western India. The conjecture is that with the Muslim invasions the migrations were directed towards the plains. These people, in Pakistan and in Kathiawar, still share commonalities of dress and customs. National boundaries are no barrier to the flow of cultures, histories and languages. And perhaps it is by identifying these flows that one may work towards reduction of conflicts. This also forces on us the recognition that the concept of purity or fixity is a myth. Fundamentalist positions pride themselves on purity, the separation of the essence from adulterations. But neither cultures, nor languages and not even lineages are 'pure' in the sense of 'absence of interaction' or 'cross-fertilization'. Purist attitudes tend to ignore histories, migrations, fluctuations of power centres, seismic changes and human weaknesses.

As national identities are in a process of re-forming themselves due to immigrant new populations and the extension of citizenship, it has become even more urgent to shift the debate from fixity in identity to an encompassing of the nation's pluralities. Over the last few decades, multiculturalism, diversity and globalization have been the areas of discussion. These concepts recognize legal steps initiated by the nation state/s or the economic forces that seem to be interconnected and global but they, in large measure, marginalize the role of the individual initiative. There is a deep connection between how individuals think and how nations form themselves, how laws are made or resisted and how dialogue opens out discussion. In 1999, Nurjehan Aziz brought out a collection of essays significantly titled, *Floating the Borders: New Contexts in Canadian Criticism* (Toronto: Tsar, 1999). The essays were mainly concerned with the different 'new' Canadians – Indian, African, Sri Lankan, Chinese, Caribbean and even Italians and East Europeans – and examine the inflow of different cultures that have shifted locations to form a new conglomeration as nostalgia, fear and the desire to belong to the new homeland contest with each other for expression. There is much to be said for this kind of culture formation, but only if borders are crossed and exclusivities transcended.

Language, in itself, is a border which works both ways: it acts like a barrier when cultures need to express themselves in an alien language, but when these alien languages become a bridge enabling a crossing then cultures travel and enrich themselves as well as others. Kunzang Choden's *The Circle of Karma* is one such work which travels in more than one sense. It opens out to the reader the gendered nuances of a family in the Himalayan kingdom of Bhutan and completes a circle not only of karma but of travelling away and returning. It carries the Bhutanese culture, deeply inhabited by Buddhist traditions, to the outside world and establishes links with it.

It is not easy to encompass all the major trends of contemporary writing within the limits of this anthology – and definitely not when the writing we focus on is in English. Themes, concerns, attitudes invariably get entangled with the issue of language as the writer's cultural and class background and readership encroach on the aesthetic dimensions of the literary artifact. Thus, even in the crossing of borders, some new boundaries and exclusions creep in. The act of defining inevitably implies some exclusion. But within the wider context of geographical spaces, at least four different trends are perceptible. These are the concern with ethnic violence and power struggles, from Afghanistan to Sri Lanka, in metropolitan cities and remote islands and in the underworld which unites the land mass through its arm supplies and ideological infiltrations; the inevitability of migration, exile, homelessness and refugeedom as new power centres replace old ones; then hidden beneath these forces is also the individual need for recognition and identity; a fourth trend, though weak in comparison to the others, is the search for truth, for forgiveness and for connections. Somewhere in this process the notion of 'home' has undergone a change; somewhere the individual finds comfort in non-recognition, and somewhere in the background is also the feeling of temporariness, of living only in the present whether it is a community ghetto, an imprisoned space, a chawl, a refugee camp, or war and civil strife. One is caught up in the 'moment to moment' strife: a kind of artificial sustenance, a mouth-to-mouth act of resuscitation. Terms like eternity and illusion have receded into the background.

Is there hope in this temporariness? Is it likely to throw up a more meaningful relationship between people? Is it going to have a cathartic effect? These are some of the questions border crossings have thrown up. As one reads the literature of the subcontinent, it is possible to discern some differences as well, reflecting the difference in histories and political attitudes, and the presence or role of religions. It is possible to note the concern with power centres which suppress and throttle and those which dissipate and undermine, between the totalitarian and democratic forms. As one reads these authors it is possible to perceive the difference in the way they relate to their subject and to the imagined readership; the responsibility which some of them take upon themselves to arouse the conscience of the world, to draw attention to the consequences of power struggles and the scholarly excavations which some others display, or the non-emotional objective portrayal of gruesome details. These differences raise issues of aesthetics – what goes into the making of good art? What is it that goes to make a classic?

This volume includes both creative and critical writing and generates its own inner debates regarding the nature of border crossings and the human initiative in crossing them. Two discourses run as parallel strands – the need to hold on to a moral, ethical and political location, and the need to move into unexplored regions so that different worlds can find connections. Different interpretations, different initiatives, a constant re-examining of the ground one occupies, an ongoing need to reach out, to choose, to rebel, to restate positions, to invent new genres, to get under the surface of seen realities – all these are worked out in various way as ideas, histories, forms and institutions are placed under the scanner.

Literature is a way of debating these issues and criticism is an assessment and evaluation of the way we are heading. Caught in the tumultuous issues of the present, which way do we go? Borders act in multiple ways. They allow infiltration, invasion, taking over; they become in-between spaces; they define identities and nations; they exclude and dehumanize the 'Other', create polarities and power struggles, prevent fertilisation of ideas; introduce inequalities. Borders also become fringes, margins, peripheries. Crossing borders in humanistic discourses becomes a search for expanses, for commonalities, a sharing and restoration of values. Crossing borders compels a recognition of the 'Other' as 'Oneself'. By claiming an initiative, it renders it possible for positive interaction – not only conflictual, exclusivist positions. Our hearts reach out to cultures and languages which we recognize as familiar – for instance the sprinkling of Urdu/Persian words in Hosseini, or the element of unquestioning love as in the case of Fokir (in *The Hungry Tide*), or a fight for truth, a search for forgiveness – acts and quests which insist that we need to go across in order to recognize ourselves. Finally the issue is of how we survive, what we need in order to survive and the ethicality of our relationships. Unfortunately, no matter what we think and feel, the question whether we have a choice or not, remains open as systemic violence threatens us and issues of religious, racial and political differences still crowd our horizons. *Crossing Borders* is an attempt at learning to accept change, to recognize difference and place it outside a power relationship, so that instead of hierarchical structures, equal relationships become possible.

Notes

1. During a visit to Nepal in March 2008, I was keen to learn more about Nepalese writers and the kind of writing they were doing. Some members of the Society of Nepali Writers in English were generous enough to share

their work with me and make available back numbers of a literary journal, they bring out. Poetry is written far more frequently than prose. The back issues also had several short stories, of which a fairly large number were concerned with the instability of the political situation. Several poems also dwelt on similar issues – and the common man's fear and aversion to the power game. Culturally (and also where political history was concerned), they shared a lot with India. A poem by Basanta Lohani speaks of the 'inside mind' – the world of enlightenment which could make the world a better place (*Of Nepalese Clay* Vol. 2, October 2001, pp. 2–3). Laxmi Prasad Devkota's series of sonnets on Gandhi, *Bapu and Other Sonnets*, (Kathmandu: Mahakavi Laxmi Prasad Devkota Study and Research Centre, 2006) provide another indication of shared history.

2. See Balraj Sahni, *Mera Pakistani Safarnama* (Delhi: Arsee Publishers ed. used 2006). pp. 93–96.

1
NAYANTARA SAHGAL

Rejecting Extinction

We start life as readers, not as writers. It is the chords that other writers have touched in us and awakened in us through words written perhaps in another country, another language, another century, that have given us entry into worlds not remotely like our own, and involved us in feelings and experiences we would otherwise never have had – long before we ourselves began to write – that have much to do with what we ourselves write later. In this sense there is a world of literature where we meet and touch and influence each other, and it is far removed from the actual world we live in which divides and separates us in so many ways. The world of letters teaches us not only to recognize our common humanity but also to value our diversity and to realize that our differences are worth preserving. The actual world, to our sorrow, has often taught us very different lessons. If literature has any function it is to convey our differences to each other through our individual visions, and in doing so there is no 'clash of civilizations', only a comradeship between civilizations. So I am making a distinction here between the freewheeling life of the imagination that we inhabit as writers, and life on earth where we are confined to, and operate within, specific circumstances of location and community and nationality – or of displacement from these – all of which factors have been responsible for shaping us and making us what we are.

I think it is very hard for a writer to speak in terms of generalities, like the themes this seminar will be addressing. One can only speak of what one knows from one's personal experience. In that respect I run counter to your theme of Borders and Crossing Borders – in other words a literature brought about largely by the experience of migration. I have not migrated, nor have I been part of the cross-cultural experience as it is understood today. I think of myself as having been invaded, occupied and colonized because these are not just words to me, nor a chapter in a history book. They have overshadowed my lifetime, and whatever culture-crossings have taken place in me have been a result of these and not of decision or choice. Today's border crossings – whether of necessity or choice – strike me as being largely one-way traffic. It is my culture that must cross and change and merge. Traffic does not flow the other way. And in the process it is as if past history is best forgotten. A few years ago Mr. Naipaul was invited to a writers' get-together at Nimrana in Delhi. On the last day there was to be a discussion for which the agenda had been laid down and the topic was colonialism and other related issues. It fell to me to make the opening remarks and as soon as I started Mr. Naipaul said he was tired of colonialism and didn't want to hear any more about it. So that was that. Forgive me for not using his title but I am a republican and my tongue lapses into mister. Personally I don't think recent history can be brushed aside so casually when many living imaginations and situations worldwide are still products of it. Therefore I was interested to see from the program that this seminar will be exploring the Concept of Self as it emerges through interaction with politics and memory.

Again, contrary to much of today's thinking, I have a hard time believing this is One World. It is certainly a better connected world but the nation state is very much, and very aggressively, with us. Nations are not about to pool their resources or surrender their identities or give up their separate deadly stockpiles of weapons of mass destruction. Some nations think nothing of making war on other sovereign nations and occupying them. And as always, it is the powerful that lay down the agenda that others must follow. So as long as there are nations there are going to be national literatures, each arising out of its own soil and its own collective consciousness. Jawaharlal Nehru, a writer himself, has expressed India's collective consciousness in these words: 'For we are very old and trackless centuries whisper in our ears.' This sentence vividly evokes a distinct and unique identity, not to be confused with other national identities which are as distinct and unique. Art, of course, crosses national borders, but nothing has yet eliminated borders. It seems to me they are here to stay for a long time. And much as I would like to believe otherwise, the global arrangement I am looking at is still the one that empires brought into being by those 300 odd years of European exploration, conquest and colonization that mythologized Europe as the centre of the worlds, inhabited by a master race, and bestowed upon it the monopoly of civilization – all of which gave it the right to impose its mindset on the rest of creation. Those empires wound up long ago but new empires of occupation have taken their place, and so far as essential human affairs are concerned, the West is still in charge, politically, military financially, and therefore, culturally. Absurd imperial terms like the Middle East, the Near and Far East are still in use though they were concocted to indicate how Near or Far these areas were from the British Foreign Office in Whitehall, and had nothing to do with their actual position on the map as East or West Asia. Then, in the kind of globalization we have been conscripted into, we are required to subscribe to the curious economic philosophy that the world is a supermarket and the purpose of our life on earth is to go shopping. It is this mindset that tells us cross-cultural connections are more relevant today than roots, and this may well be true according to the prevailing fashions and priorities that govern us. But fashions need not be taken seriously when they are laid down for us by think-tanks and experts thousands of miles away. It makes more sense to evolve one's own criteria, relevant to ones own circumstances.

If I fit anywhere among the subjects you are going to explore it would probably be under writing as resistance. At one time or another I have been on the wrong side of the establishment – whether of the accepted power structure; or of accepted conventional morality; or of what was considered to be the sort of books Indians should be writing about India. I was brought up by rebels against the established order – people who had committed their lives to overthrowing British rule. Later, when I began to write, and was being published in Britain and America, my American agent told me, 'Honey, readers don't want to read about people like themselves. They want contrasts.' I had something quite different in mind which I proceeded to do. I wrote novels with contemporary Indian political settings, novels which in sequence have turned out to be about the making of modern India. When I have set a novel in the past, as I did *Mistaken Identity*, the 1920s setting related to what anguished me then about contemporary India, which in this case was the growing tide of Hindu fundamentalism. When I went back to the early 1900s in a part of *Rich Like Us*, it was to highlight the nightmarish contemporary theme of the novel, in this case the dictatorship known as the Emergency of 1975. My fiction did not rise out of the proverbial heat and dust seen through the lenses of the Raj or the post-Raj, because inside of me there was an Indian, buried for centuries, who was struggling to come out, looking and behaving like an ordinary human being as villainous or as virtuous as any other – and not like an ethnic curiosity or an exotic oriental specimen. Just as we had come to know the English, Irish, French, Russians and other by reading their literatures – which means seeing them as they saw themselves – so others would have to see us as we saw ourselves, and not expect us to fit into their imaginings of us.

In common with all writers who write from their soil I did not feel surrounded by the presence or constant awareness of another culture to measure myself up against. At one time I was advised against politics as material for fiction. Arranged marriage, joint family, quaint customs, local colour, maharajas etc., were the favoured themes. But one does not pick and choose one's material. One works with the material one has and in my case politics was my natural material. I had no other, having grown up in a climate filled with the sound and fury, and overflowing with the passion of the fight for freedom when every issue, from the cloth you wore, to the school you went to, to the company you kept, was a political issue, and when politics was not something 'out there' but an intimate part of family life. But leaving aside my own case, politics which is only another name for the conditions we live under – is very much the material of fiction, as it is of all art. The artist, above all, is a political animal, acutely sensitive to the environment she lives in. We would not have understood the times we have lived through but for the political consciousness of European, Asian, African, American and Latin American writers. In our own time politics has become increasingly inseparable from private life, and the line between public and private has been a continually disappearing one all over the world as vast numbers of people have had to face the consequences of political events in their personal lives.

Politics is about power, and not only in the public domain. For me it has been a constant presence in gender relations, in the unequal equation between husband and wife which takes the wife's subordinate role for granted. I notice as I look back on my writing that the hesitant and powerless women of my earlier novels – who are not even convinced of their right to be individuals – get more confident in the later novels, and in the last two they step out to become confident individuals. I suppose this has something to do with my own stumbling progress from virtual voicelessness as a wife to acquiring a voice and persona of my own.

Asian writing comes out of several continents now and its cross-currents of racial experience have added a new dimension to literature. Black immigrant literatures have enlarged the vistas of writing in English, transformed the English language and spun new life and lyricism from it. But it is a special genre occupying its own imaginative space, and it does not conflict with, nor can it take the place of those who write from home. Staying home makes for its own kind of writing. It is where we are located on the map that gives us our particular angle of vision along with the insights and, above all, the point of view that flow from it. This gut vision grows out of the cauldron of ideas, emotions, and physical sensations – sounds, sights, smells, food, drink – that assail us every day of our lives. As opposed to the recurring migrant theme of exile, and the pains, problems and rewards of adjustment, the daily business of living in India literally assaults us with our own realities: the ugliness of caste, corruption, female fœticide and religious fundamentalism, and alongside these, computers, satellites and a sexual revolution. We live in co-existing time zones, among tremendous contrasts, and with paradoxes of a kind that allow us to defecate without shame in public but forbid us to kiss in public. To whom can this tumultuous scene possibly matter but to the lives that are affected by it, the people who enjoy or must suffer its consequences, and those among us who feel compelled to do battle against it? The ultimate battles for a new world must be fought on one's own soil and part of every battle is putting it into words. Our stories are gut-bound to our own society. They mirror what concerns us: the things we take pride in as well as our fears and anxieties. They question our values and the direction we may be taking. In this respect my own fiction bears witness to my faith in secular political ideals, cultural and religious pluralism, and the rightness of non-violence. My last novel *Lesser Breeds* revives the decades when non-violence was used for the first and only time in history as a weapon in a fight for freedom. I meant *Lesser Breeds* to be a tribute to a heroic period, and to the continuing relevance of non-violence, but now I think of it more as an epitaph. With military might growing mightier all around us, including our own, what chance would Satyagraha have against it?

The value of staying rooted, as opposed to migration, is that it preserves the wholeness of a point of view that has not had to time itself in order to make itself understandable to another society. This organic wholeness matters, if only because the world we are living in is not even-handed on the question of identity. It is taken for granted that some identities have a right to exist while others must be surrendered. Taken far enough this would be cultural genocide. So it makes good sense to reject this form of extinction and for us, or any culture, to hold on to what makes it original and exceptional on a scene that is fast becoming standardized, and in danger of being reduced to a monoculture. By what makes us exceptional I do not mean the religious fundamentalism, here or among the Diaspora, that masquerades as culture. Point of view is crucial to life and literature, the pivot on which a story turns. It is the very spine of the story. Narrative depends on it. Style is the frills you clothe it in. Character, action, inaction, what happens or doesn't happen, are the result of it. And in its larger meaning, as an angle of vision that derives from its own history, geography and regional memory, it ensures that a culture – along with the literature that can arise only from it – will remain alive. The only differences worth keeping among peoples are cultural, and if this diversity is reduced to a one-culture hegemony, then literature itself cannot survive. Great things happen, great creative energy is released in life and ideas, in language and literature, in art and science, only when cultures interact and flow into each other.

It is a mark of great literature, whether written on home ground or elsewhere, that it has a resonance beyond its time and borders. There are states of mind and feeling that reflect the human condition everywhere. One does not have to migrate to feel exiled or alien. As a child in British India I felt like a foreigner in my own home town, Allahabad, because it had so few reminders of anything Indian. All the roads were named after British generals and governors, the cinema showed English films, and every establishment catered for a British clientele. I had to learn my own language outside school and discover

India outside my stifling colonial confines. Some of this is reflected in *Lesser Breeds* when a nationalist family hires a teacher in the 1930s to un-teach their daughter what she is being taught in her convent school. He wonders how to do this and discovers he can do it simply by shifting her point of view to give her an entirely different perspective of the same event.

In reverse, a migrant can feel securely rooted to the ground where he has settled because it is human nature to put down roots, and natural to adapt to one's surroundings and be influenced by them. So there is no hard and fast divide between the condition known as exile on the one hand and roots on the other. Nor can storytelling be divided into these categories. But if one thing distinguishes home-grown writing from writing elsewhere, it is the home-grown sensibility for which there is no substitute. And that is a priceless possession, not to be argued out of or given up, at least as long as there are nation states and national literatures.

My own background has set me down in a shifting landscape between exile and roots in spite of having stayed rooted. Some years ago I described my imagination as schizophrenic and invented my own definition of schizophrenia as a state of mind and feeling that is firmly grounded in a particular subsoil, but above ground has a more fluid identity that does not fit comfortably into and single mould. Nowadays I also feel like a stranger in a world whose political arrangements, economic priorities and military solutions are not of my choosing. What I am and what I write is the end result of these bits and pieces.

Earlier I referred to having been on the wrong side of conventional morality. In 1994 I made a border-crossing of my own when I published a personal correspondence titled *Relationship* that tracked the growth of a relationship outside marriage. It seemed important to bring a woman's experience – my own – to light in a country where family honour is sacrosanct, silence is the law for women, and any attempt to break it brings on merciless punishment. Border crossings of this kind need to be made. Sometimes courage fails, as in a case I know of a Sri Lankan writer who told me she had, after much agonizing, changed the ending of a story she had written because her husband was shocked and upset that the heroine leaves her husband for her lover. To avoid upsetting her husband, endangering her marriage, and ruining her reputation, she re-wrote the ending. I asked her if the artistic outcome of the story did not require its own natural ending. She agreed it did but said she could not take the risk. If these are still the impossible terms most women have to surrender to in life and literature, then surely we who write must reject them by having our say through fiction, poetry and autobiography.

Recently I was interested to hear from a social activist who was interacting with rural women on the subject of domestic violence, that she had used an extract from *Relationship*, translated into Hindi, in a discussion with them. It had led to a lively question and answer session. My border-crossing into forbidden territory has more than served its purpose if it has found a response among rural women with whom I can share this common ground.

2

SHYAMALA A. NARAYAN

Indian English Literary Criticism: Crossing Linguistic Boundaries

In *A History of Indian English Literature* (published by the Sahitya Akademi) M.K. Naik declared: 'It is obvious that Indian English literature ... is legitimately a part of Indian literature, since its differentia is the expression in it of an Indian ethos' (4). All other literary critics, such as K.R. Srinivasa Iyengar and C.D. Narasimhaiah, have emphasized the importance of considering Indian Writing in English as a branch of Indian literature. It logically follows that it can be best analysed in the context of Indian literature. This paper proposes to examine the work of critics who cross linguistic boundaries, and attempt their literary analysis in the larger context of writing in various Indian languages. Literature is a cultural as well as a linguistic construct, so literatures written in different Indian languages, sharing the same culture, have a lot in common, and it would be fruitful to analyse literature across linguistic frontiers. Jasbir Jain, Meenakshi Mukherjee, Krishna Rayan, E.V. Ramakrishnan and K. Satchidanandan are among the critics who have made the attempt.

Indian literature is one though written in different languages. That is the motto of the Sahitya Akademi. Though this declaration of Dr S. Radhakrishnan tends to oversimplify the situation, it cannot be disputed that certain commonalities exist in the literature produced in the different languages of India, including Indian English literature. The question of a national literature becomes particularly complex in the case of India, with so many languages and linguistic and literary traditions. Sisir Kumar Das sums up the situation well in his Preface to *A History of Indian Literature 1911–1956*. He observes:

> The present essay ... strongly defends the uniqueness of each literature in the country, and looks at each one of them as distinct expressions of experiences of each community. No attempt has been made to subordinate the uniqueness of any one of them either by a hegemonic construction, nor by the imposition of "values" claimed to be exclusively Indian. It recognizes, both from the ideological position of the author as well as the methodological compulsions, the plurality of Indian life. On the other hand it also contests the idea of "heterogeneity" that completely subordinates commonalities in cultures and the relationship between the self and the other. Commonalities among Indian literatures are many, and they are not mere coincidences. Empirical studies of Indian literature, both synchronic and diachronic, indicate very clearly and strongly, the areas of commonality, and more significantly the existence of continuous movements among individual literatures, towards certain points of convergence, thematic, generic, ideological and so on.... . Indian literature, then, has been treated here not as a homogeneous whole ignoring the splendid diversities among them; nor as disparate entities ignoring the factors of history and geography that have made them interact with one another. Indian literature is a complex of literatures, related to one another, at times by geographical proximity, at times by a shared history. (xiv)

Some scholars and writers (such as Mukul Kesavan)[1] feel that the very idea of an Indian literature is misleading. Shormishtha Panja points out that:

> While a number of influential scholars argue that there is a single Indian literature they are hard put to define it with any degree of plausible specificity. They invariably fall back either on generalities that would be true of any literature, not just Indian, or they reduce the marvellous plurality of Indian literatures and unselfconsciously and hegemonically confine it within a single religious framework. (5–6)

Poet and critic K. Satchidanandan puts it even more strongly:

> The construction of a monolithic Indian culture, character or literature is thus an act of civilizational violence that inevitably involves a negation of heteroglossia, a silencing of ethnic diversity and religious pluralism and a bulldozing of diverse cosmologies and world views that together constitute the federation of Indian cultures. This is not to deny certain shared patterns of literary evolution, linguistic kinships

and intercultural ties developed over centuries of co-existence. The foreign observer looking from a distance does find a semblance of cultural unity in India, but coming closer one begins to see hundreds of Ramayanas and Mahabharatas, dozens of philosophical systems and religious cults that were never called Hindu until the nineteenth century, ... (10)

Critics like Jasbir Jain and Meenakshi Mukherjee have not tried to construct a monolithic Indian literature; they have a different critical agenda, to analyse Indian English literature in the context of Indian literature. This entails breaking down the barriers between Indian literature written in English and that written in other Indian languages like Bangla, Hindi or Punjabi (the Bhashas). Satchidanandan himself adopts this approach in another article in the book: "Historicizing Sarojini Naidu", when he looks at Naidu's work in the context of poetry in Indian languages like Urdu, Bangla and Telugu:

> Imagine Sarojini as a poet of Urdu *ghazals* or Hindi *Chhayavadi* poetry, Telugu *bhavakavita* or the early semi-mystic and nature oriented Bengali poetry of Tagore, and any reader will immediately know where to place her. (60)

His essay, "Signing in Different Scripts: Literatures in Independent India" (27-48) surveys literature written in various Indian languages, including English.

E.V. Ramakrishnan employs the comparative approach when studying modernism in Indian poetry, in *Making it New: Modernism in Malayalam, Marathi and Hindi Poetry* (1995). The book provides a fine overview of modernism in three Indian languages; Ramakrishnan reveals the commonalities (born of shared cultural elements and a common encounter with the west) and the differences which arise from local cultural factors, determined by history and geography. Though the book is written in English (making it accessible to many Indian critics) he does not examine Indian English poetry (perhaps the fact that he is himself an Indian English poet of repute might have proved inhibiting). He clearly shows the pitfalls of applying western literary theories:

> If regional literatures from India are fed into prefabricated canon manufactured in metropolitan countries and universities they may merely serve as illustrations of theories that have no relevance to the actual conditions in which they are produced. The present study is an

attempt to read the poetry written during the modernist phase in three Indian languages in a comparative Indian context. (v)

The companion volume, *The Tree of Tongue: An Anthology of Modern Indian Poetry* (1999) enables the reader who does not know Malayalam, Marathi and Hindi to have access to the texts through their English translations, some of them by Ramakrishnan himself.

Krishna Rayan's *The Burning Bush: Suggestion in Indian Literature* (1988) analyses texts (short stories, poems, novels) in Asamiya, Bangla, Gujarati, Hindi, Kannada, Kashmiri, Malayalam, Marathi, Oriya, Punjabi, Sanskrit, Sindhi, Tamil, Telugu, and Urdu. But his aim in analysing these diverse texts was more to test the validity of his theoretical apparatus, than to investigate the commonalities of different Indian literatures. In his own words:

> The crucial stage in the enquiry therefore consists in verifying whether a suggestion-based critical approach is applicable to literary texts in different Indian languages and whether the results achieved are found to contribute enough to our understanding of the texts to validate the approach. (7)

However, his experience serves to pinpoint a major problem of working with translations:

> An individual investigator can only study the texts at second hand in translation except when he is conversant with the language of the original.... I have been able in the case of each text to check my comments over with the author or the translator, and when neither was available, with a critic or scholar of standing in the language. Even so, access to the verbal and prosodic nuances of the original has remained necessarily blocked, except when, as with the Kannada poems, I had myself roped to a guide and tried to share the experience of a direct encounter with the language of the original. (7)

Earlier critics like C.D. Narasimhaiah and M.K. Naik had laid emphasis on judging in the Indian context. Narasimhaiah had organized a seminar in Mysore in 1984 "Towards the Formulation of a Common Poetic for Indian Literatures". But he was suspicious of modern critical theories like structuralism, deconstruction etc. His forte was a close reading of the text, not theory, so he never resolved the theoretical issues concerned. His concept of "Indianness" in literature is unsatisfactory. As Shormishtha Panja points out, he elided Hinduism and Indian:

Quoting from Aurobindo's *Savitri, Amarakosa*, a book of lexicography and *Sabdamanidarpana*, a book of grammar, he says that the essence of Indianness as expressed even in these very disparate works is the fact that "everything is geared to the recognition of the spiritual behind the material in Indian life." Where then should one place the work of the Progressives in Hindi and Urdu literature and the *Utttar Adhuniks* in contemporary Bengali literature? Or those Indian English novelists who insist on the sheer materiality of existence? ... What is striking about all the essays in this volume [*The Function of Criticism in India*, 1986] is that almost all of Narasimhaiah's examples from Indian literature are from Hindu texts. All the sacred tests and mantras that he quotes are Hindu. Yet Narasimhaiah himself is completely impervious to his Hindu bias. (5)

M.K. Naik's critical practice, using the most appropriate tools from Western and Indian critical theory, provides a better guide. He has published a few comparative studies, such as an analysis of Whitman's "What is Grass" and B.R. Tambe's Marathi poem "A Blade of Grass" (*A Critical Harvest*, 131–140). In *Indian English Literature 1980–2000* he compares Raja Rao's *Kanthapura* (1938) with N.S. Phadke's Marathi novel, *Zanzavat* ("The Tempest", published in 1948), and examines the treatment of the theme of untouchability in English and Marathi:

> Another comparison between the two literatures is equally revealing. Mulk Raj Anand's *Untouchable*, which came out in 1935, was possibly the earliest attempt to deal with the lives of the depressed classes, not only in Indian English literature but in modern Indian literature in general, also. It is significant that a similar attempt in Marathi (reputedly one of the richest of Indian literatures) came only half a dozen years later. This was *Upekshitanche Antarang* ("The Mind of the Spurned") by S.M. Matey published in 1941. (250)

Naik repeatedly urges the importance of evaluating Indian English literature in the context of literature in other Indian languages:

> Indian literature written in several languages, is a vast joint family (so typical of the Indian ethos blessed with many brothers, some of whom are veritable Methuselahs). Tamil, the oldest of the living Indian languages, boasts of a literature which is more than two thousand years old... . The youngest of these brothers is Indian English literature – a baby not even two hundred years old. (*A Critical Harvest* 55)

Meenakshi Mukherjee's *Realism and Reality: The Novel and Society in India* (1985) is the first book which attempts to read Indian literature across linguistic boundaries; it investigates the birth and development of the novel in India. (It does not deal primarily with Indian English literature; her earlier book, *The Twice: Born Fiction* published in 1971 did that.) She does not 'try to write a history of the novel in India', she attempts to see the novel in a broader perspective:

> The general belief, even in our faculties of literature, is that while an isolated study of the Tamil novel or Indo-Anglian fiction can be a legitimate academic activity, any attempt to study the Indian novel in a broader perspective is bound to be a futile endeavour. This book is an attempt to refute that argument. It is my contention that the novel in India can be seen as the product of configurations in philosophical, aesthetic, economic and political forces in the larger life of the country. Despite obvious regional variations, a basic pattern seems to emerge from shared factors like the puranic heritage, hierarchical social structure, colonial education, disjunction of agrarian life and many others that affect the form of a novel as well as its contents. (viii)

She analyses in detail texts she has read in the original, such as *Pather Panchali*, Bankim Chandra Chatterji's *Indira*, Manik Bandopadhyay's *Putul Nacher Itikatha* (Bangla) and Premchand's *Godan* (Hindi); U.R. Anantha Murthy's *Samskara* in the much acclaimed translation by A.K. Ramanujan is also taken up for study. She shows that it is important to 'take a holistic view of the novel in India as a genre nursed by, if not born out of, the tension between opposing systems of values in a colonial society, and modified by certain indigenous pressures' (vii).

The essays in *The Perishable Empire: Essays on Indian Writing in English* (2004), which won the Sahitya Akademi Award, are not confined to literature written in English. For Meenakshi Mukherjee, Indian English literature and literature written in the Bhashas are both constituents of Indian Literature. As she says in the Preface:

> The present volume is an attempt to consider the complex and evolving relationship between English and India through literary texts that emerged out of this contact from the mid-nineteenth century to the end of the millennium. I have tried to take into consideration in this study the layered context of the other Indian languages surrounding English, and the intricate socio-economic pressures that impinge on literary production. (ix)

Mukherjee is aware of their unequal treatment. Contemporary Indian English literature gets more attention than writing in other Indian languages, while early work is neglected:

> While the early novelists in the Indian languages are constantly being subjected to renewed critical assessment, their English counterparts have rarely been resuscitated for critical reading.... The reasons for this selective amnesia and the asymmetrical destinies of the English- and Indian-language novels of the colonial period need to be explored. (7–8)

Meenakshi Mukherjee observes that western education and English literature influenced writing in all the Indian languages:

> The educated Indian saw all Western literature in a timeless continuum. This college curriculum exposed him simultaneously to several centuries of European classical texts and canonical literature from Britain, and 'colonial editions' of popular fiction of the time also became available to him outside the classroom. He responded to both enthusiastically and without much fastidiousness about literary status or chronology, although it is possible to detect a difference in the way such reading was processed by the Indian language novelist and Indians who wrote novels in English. (5)

She notes the commonalities among the writers, as also the variation in response.

The early novelists in the "vernacular" and the novelists in English belong to roughly the same social segment across the country – upper caste urban Hindu male (women like Swarnakumari Debi or Krupa Satthianadhan were rare exceptions) and must have read the same English books – both canonical and popular. Yet the language in which they wrote seemed to automatically determine the way this reading would be processed for creative purposes. Indian English novelists displayed their acquaintance with the classics of Western literature more readily than did Indian-language novelist, parading this knowledge as validation, as it were, of their status in the eyes of the putative reader. They never mentioned the popular writers except to denounce them, and took care to align themselves only with the best in ingenious ways. Using epigraphs from Byron, Scott, Cowper, Moore, Shakespeare or Coleridge at the beginning of chapters was a common practice (18).

The Perishable Empire is primarily about Indian Writing in English, in accordance with its subtitle. There is no sustained analysis of Bhasha literature; texts written in other Indian languages are cited for illuminating comparisons. For example, when talking about the specificity of Bhasha writing, as contrasted with the homogenising tendency of Indian English literature in her essay "The Anxiety of Indianness", she refers to the work of Mahashweta Devi:

> While reading her, we know exactly where Lohri is situated – at the intersection of three districts of Chotanagpur – Ranchi, Palamau and Sarguja – and this is not a gratuitous piece of information. (171)

Jasbir Jain has made the most sustained contribution to criticism across linguistic boundaries. In addition to excellent studies of Indian English authors like Nayantara Sahgal, Anita Desai and Shashi Deshpande, she has written three books which explore the growth of the novel in India. *Beyond Postcolonialism: Dreams and Realities of a Nation* is the sequel to two books tracing the novel from 1857 to 1905, and from 1905 to 1950 (in Punjabi). *Feminizing Political Discourse: Women and the Novel in India 1857–1905* examines literary works written in Bangla, Urdu, Punjabi, Malayalam, Hindi, and English. She demonstrates that the novel has roots in the native tradition, even if the encounter with the west provided an impetus to it.

Beyond Postcolonialism: Dreams and Realities of a Nation considers various issues relating to colonialism and postcolonialism by examining fiction in many Indian languages. Jain declares:

> My focus has been on writers who have problematized this dislocation, not where they are located, whether it is Mumtaz Shah Nawaz, Attia Hosain, Intizar Husain, Manzoor Ehtesham or Abdus Samad – writers for whom dislocation is a constant happening and a constant reminder of all traumas. It is primarily because of this that the two ends of my frame are constituted by *Pahla Girmitiya* and *Sookha Bargad*. (17)

Jain examines the dreams and realities that have engaged the attention of the writers from 1947 to the present, across languages and regions, focusing on the concerns of gender, caste, religion, nation-building and aesthetics both at home and in diasporic writing. Her aim is:

> to work, not for parallel accounts of literary developments in the different languages, but to identity their common concerns along with

the differences that exist because of linguistic or regional traditions, and the different politico-economic and caste histories; to explain the everyday revolutions which are taking place everywhere; and to work for an integrated concept of Indian writing across languages. (12–13)

She examines the term "postcolonialism" with reference to fiction in various Indian languages, and finds that it is not very useful:

Postcolonialism in Indian writing, right from the outset, has been a borrowed term, adopted or disputed by critics, used by those on the margins, perhaps even owned temporarily. But it has failed to reflect the continuity of literary traditions across languages. (40)

She finds three dominant tropes in the contemporary Indian novel:

The dominant tropes of the contemporary Indian novel are a reworking of the meaning of karma and dharma, terms which we have inherited and need to review afresh because they work at more than one level: the individual, the community and the nation. In themselves, they can limit one, but they also have the capacity to expand and acquire relevance for social and political relationships. Another dominant trope is that of belonging – *where* does one belong in terms of language, region, religion, nation? And *how* does one belong? Jyotirmoyee Devi, Abdus Samad, Laxman Gaekwad, Manzoor Ehtesham – all ask the same question. A third trope is the preoccupation with violence and hatred. These raise their own political questions. There is violence of different kinds in the committing of 'sati' (Sahgal's *Rich Like Us*), of persecution (Mahasweta Devi's "Draupadi"), social discrimination (Gurdial Singh's *Marhi da Diva*), communal riots (Tharoor's *Riot*). There is the violence born out of aggression, hatred and the myopia of the authorities. (18)

Another collection of critical essays by Jain, *Writing Women Across Cultures*, also transcends barriers of language. The period ranges from the late nineteenth century to the present, from Bankim Chandra Chatterjee to Meera Syal. Non-English texts include Tagore's *Ghare Baire*, Mahasweta Devi's short story, "Draupadi", Krishna Sobti's Hindi novel *Ai Ladki*, Dalip Kaur Tiwana's *Katha Kaho Urvashi* (Punjabi), M.K. Indira's *Phaniyamma* (Kannada) and Dalit autobiographies like Kaushalya Baisantri's *Dohra Abhishap* (Hindi), Baby Kamble's *Jeevan Hamara* (Marathi), and Sharan Kumar Limbale's *Akkarmashi*.

The advantages of this strategy, of reading literature across linguistic barriers, are obvious – literature is analysed with regard to the context which brought it into existence. What E.V. Ramakrishnan said about Bhasha literatures applies equally to Indian English literature: if we adopt reading practices manufactured elsewhere, literary texts 'may merely serve as illustrations of theories that have no relevance to the actual conditions in which they are produced' (v). But there are also drawbacks. No individual can know all Indian literatures at first hand. *Realism and Reality* presents a good argument regarding the social factors which influenced the growth of the novel, but the examples are confined to Bangla, Hindi and Kannada. What about other languages? Meenakshi Mukherjee briefly mentions early works in Tamil, Malayalam and Gujarati.

A similar feeling of incompleteness arises when reading Jasbir Jain's work. *Feminizing Political Discourse* examines the Indian fictional tradition by analysing works in Bangla, Urdu, Punjabi, Malayalam, Hindi, and English, but what about Tamil, Gujarati or Marathi? *Beyond Postcolonialism* has a wider sweep, covering more languages.

If we think of literary criticism as a collaborative enterprise, as 'the common pursuit of true judgment' (in the words of T.S. Eliot adopted by F.R. Leavis), the critic working across linguistic boundaries will find it difficult to get "collaborators" as they may not know the same languages. The critic has no option but to study the literary works in translation. Jasbir Jain is fully aware of the problems of working through translations, and reveals her strategy:

> I have tried to use translations with honesty and discretion. Wherever there has been more than one translation, I have referred to all of them. At the same time, I am aware that I am likely to have missed out on a great deal. Translations have their own limitations. At times, no other work of the writer is available to support one's findings, at others, no biographical details are there. I also have a request to Indian publishing houses that translations should be particular to mention the date of first publication of the text in the language of origin. The best of them, highly respected ones, very often forget to do so. This lapse is going to cause havoc in cross-language literary histories. Literary histories also often do not mention the date of first publication. At times, even literary monographs skip over them. I have tried to trace the dates of the first publication in most cases through various channels and apologise in advance for all likely lapses which may have occurred in the process. (*Beyond Postcolonialism* 10–11)

Many important literary texts are not available in translations. Though attempts have been made by different agencies such as the Sahitya Akademi, Katha and the National Book Trust, and individual scholars, one cannot get a comprehensive view of Bhasha literatures. And it is a well known fact that much is lost in translation – what the critic reads is not the author's work, but the work mediated through the sensibility of the translator. In spite of these difficulties, attempts have been made to view Indian literature in its totality. Sisir Kumar Das (1936–2003) completed two volumes (VIII and IX) of *A History of Indian Literature*. Another volume in this project, *A History of Indian Literature 500–1399*, appeared posthumously in 2005. In the Preface, he admits the difficulties of working with a team of scholars from various Bhashas, 'Some scholars declined to complete the promised work after keeping me waiting for long, some did their work after great persuasion and some could not be persuaded at all' (*A History of Indian Literature 1800–1910*: xi).

Many other scholars have been aware of these problem; as the late Sujit Mukherjee pointed out in the "Preface" to his *A Dictionary of Indian Literature*:

> My area of interest was Indian Literature in general, not confined to any particular language. Quite often I found that when I needed any preliminary information on an Indian author or literary work of an earlier century – and even of more recent times – I would have to work my way through several works before I could get what I was seeking. There was no single reference work I could consult.

A Dictionary of Indian Literature, the first volume of which appeared in 1999, covers Indian literatures in twenty Indian languages, starting with the Vedas and Upanishads up to 1850. It is a great loss that Sujit Mukherjee passed away before completing the second volume. However, he has published many other seminal works which facilitate a comparative approach to Indian literature. Three decades ago, he attempted a history of Indian literature in *Towards a Literary History of India* (1975) and *Some Positions on a Literary History of India* (1980). *Translation as Discovery and Other Essays on Indian Literature in English Translation* (1982) has a good bibliography of Indian novels in translation, and his posthumous essays *Translation as Recovery* (2004) are equally useful to researchers in this area.

The Sahitya Akademi's six volume *Encyclopaedia of Indian Literature* (1987–1994) has entries pertaining to all Indian languages, not just

Sanskrit. Earlier histories, such as Maurice Winternitz's three volume *History of Indian Literature* (first published in German, 1913–1920) dealt only with ancient Indian literature in Sanskrit, Prakrit and Pali, ignoring the Tamil heritage. *Masterpieces of Indian Literature* published by the National Book Trust in 1997 to commemorate 50 years of Indian Independence, provides the English-knowing reader with a lot of information about works and writers in nineteen Indian languages. The first two volumes contain entries about the masterpieces of Asamiya, Bangla, English, Gujarati, Hindi, Kannada, Kashmiri, Konkani, Malayalam, Manipuri, Marathi, Nepali, Oriya, Punjabi, Sanskrit, Sindhi, Tamil, Telugu and Urdu literatures. The format of the entries is interesting: after mentioning the genre, time, locale, date of first publication and the main characters, there is a note on the author. A descriptive account of the work comes next, and the entry ends with a critique. The third volume contains an annotated bibliography, brief additional pieces, a glossary and an index. As Sukumar Azhicode, the Chairman of the National Book Trust puts it in his Foreword, '*Masterpieces of Indian Literature* is mainly concerned with the setting up of the bridges of understanding among the various literatures in India ... this three-volume treasure chest unfolds the cream of the great works in the literatures of India' (xiv).

Anthologies of translated texts can also help the reader formulate a map of Indian literature. *Modern Indian Literature: An Anthology* covering literature of the period 1850 to 1975 was published by the Sahitya Akademi under the general editorship of K.M. George in three volumes, in 1992, 1993 and 1995. Sahitya Akademi also brought out *Medieval Indian Literature* in four volumes. Individual efforts too have facilitated an acquaintance with Indian literature: a good example of this is *Staging Resistance: Plays by Women in Translation* edited by Tutun Mukherjee (New Delhi, OUP, 2005), a collection of eighteen plays by women, from ten different Indian languages: Bangla, Gujarati, Hindi, Kannada, Malayalam, Marathi, Punjabi, Tamil, Telugu and Urdu. All the plays included in this collection are being published for the first time in English translation, and can help us chart out the course of women's perspectives in Indian drama. *Image and Representation: Stories of Muslim Lives in India* edited by Mushirul Hasan and M. Asaduddin (OUP, 2000) contains 34 short stories from 11 Indian languages, including English.

Anthologies of critical essays by diverse hands which treat common themes in Indian literature also further this agenda. For example,

Narrative of the Village: Centre of the Periphery edited by Jasbir Jain grew out of a seminar on "The Village as Protagonist", and includes papers which approach the theme through literary constructs, films and folk cultures. Works in Bangla, Hindi, Malayalam, Marathi and Urdu are analysed, in addition to work in English. Books like *Creating Theory*, an anthology of critical essays by creative writers, also transcends linguistic boundaries. The editor Jasbir Jain's introductory essay, "Connections", maps Indian literary criticism from the nineteenth century to the present, across languages. The essays deal with basic theoretical concerns of contemporary Indian literature: the place of western influences, the validity of western parameters, the importance of literary tradition, the usefulness of the Indian oral tradition for the modern writer, the claims of history, the importance of the local, and whether universal values are possible or desirable.

One fact which emerges from all this is the importance of translation. Departments of English in India could help the process by prescribing a third Indian language as a compulsory paper for students of M.A. Scholars who take interest in a number of Indian languages are needed. Till good translations of all major Bhasha works are available, crossing linguistic boundaries in criticism will remain an isolated phenomenon. And a true analysis of literature in any Indian language, including English, will remain incomplete as long as the literary terrain in India remains poorly charted.

Note

1. In an informal discussion with the present writer (Jaipur, 21 September 2007) Mukul Kesavan observed that the concept of a national literature for India, on the lines of a national bird, a national animal etc., is silly.

Works Cited

Das, Sisir Kumar. *A History of Indian Literature 500–1399: From the Courtly to the Popular*. New Delhi: Sahitya Akademi, 2005.

—. *A History of Indian Literature 1800–1910, Western Impact: Indian Response*. Vol. VIII. New Delhi: Sahitya Akademi, 1991.

—. *A History of Indian Literature 1911–1956, Struggle for Freedom: Triumph and Tragedy*. Vol. IX. New Delhi: Sahitya Akademi, 1995.

George, K.M., Chief Editor. *Masterpieces of Indian Literature.* New Delhi: National Book Trust, 1997.

Jain, Jasbir. *Beyond Postcolonialism: Dreams and Realities of a Nation.* Jaipur: Rawat, 2006.

—, ed. *Creating Theory: Writers on Writing.* Delhi: Pencraft, 2000.

—. *Feminizing Political Discourse: Women and the Novel in India 1857–1905.* Jaipur: Rawat, 1997.

—, ed. *Narrative of the Village: Centre of the Periphery.* Jaipur: Rawat, 2006.

—. *Writing Women Across Cultures.* Jaipur: Rawat, 2002.

Mukherjee, Meenakshi. *The Perishable Empire: Essays on Indian Writing in English.* New Delhi: OUP, 2000.

—. *Realism and Reality: The Novel and Society in India.* Delhi: OUP, 1985.

Mukherjee, Sujit. *A Dictionary of Indian Literature: Beginnings to 1850.* Hyderabad: Orient Longman, 1999.

Naik, M.K. *A History of Indian English Literature.* New Delhi: Sahitya Akademi, 1982.

—. *A Critical Harvest: Essays and Studies.* New Delhi: Creative Books, 2005.

Naik, M.K., and Shyamala A. Narayan. *Indian English Literature 1980–2000: A Critical Survey.* Delhi: Pencraft, 2001.

Panja, Shormishtha, ed. *Many Ideas, Many Literatures.* 2nd ed. Delhi: Worldview, 2001.

Ramakrishnan, E.V. *Making it New: Modernism in Malayalam, Marathi and Hindi Poetry.* Shimla: Indian Institute of Advanced Study, 1995.

—, ed. *The Tree of Tongues: An Anthology of Modern Indian Poetry.* Shimla: Indian Institute of Advanced Studies, 1999; Poems in Hindi, Gujarati, Malayalam, and Marathi, trans. into English.

Rayan, Krishna. *The Burning Bush: Suggestion in Indian Literature.* Delhi: B.R. Publishing Corporation, 1988.

Satchidanandan, K. *Authors, Texts, Issues: Essays on Indian Literature.* Delhi: Pencraft, 2003.

3
JASBIR JAIN

Terrorism at the Feet of Buddha: From Taliban to LTTE and the In-Between

This paper concerns itself with violence, its overspills and the challenges it poses: to the nation state and to the continuation and sustenance of human value structures. In the above contexts it sets out to explore contemporary fiction, namely Michael Ondaatje's *Anil's Ghost,* Khaled Hosseini's *The Kite Runner,* Temsula Ao's short fiction in *These Hills Called Home* and Amitav Ghosh's *The Hungry Tide,* works which problematize the impact of violence and the scars it leaves behind. The whole subcontinent, right from Afghanistan to Sri Lanka, right through Pakistan, India and Bangladesh, is caught up in this complex play of power and violence in everyday life. The concern is also with the contradictions which coexist between religion/spirituality and violence and between cultural commonalities and political anger and factionalism. The human ability to hold opposites together is amazing just as the ability to hang on to hope in the face of disaster, to erase cultural pasts in order to preserve what one begins to believe is true and important for identity formation. Is this resilience, transformation or submission to the power of others? Is it survival or myopia?

South Asian countries, over the centuries, have had shifting geographical boundaries and power centres. Cultures and religions have travelled from one end to another. Seventy per cent of Sri Lanka's population still believes in Buddhism. These are dominantly Sinhalese and claim to be of Aryan origin, having migrated from eastern parts of India during the fifth century. Buddhism travelled to the country during the 2nd century BCE. Afghanistan, similarly has been open to Buddhist influence in certain phases of its ancient history. For more than three centuries it was part of the Gandhara Empire.[1] It was during these years that Buddhist statues and sculptures were built all over the place. Over the centuries they remained intact and were preserved both for historical reasons and as an attraction for travellers, despite the changed religious affiliations of the people. But in March 2001 the Bamiyan statues were dynamited, just as in 1992 the Babri Masjid was demolished in Ayodha. Are these destructions an attempt to change histories and re-form identities at both individual and collective levels or simply manifestations of unthinking power? The Taliban announced a destruction of even the Buddha statues in museums, undermining both a sense of continuity and human memory.

As I sit down to write this paper, headlines in the news magazine and newspapers are increasingly about violence. In an article "Abyss of Reason" in a recent issue of *Outlook*, Mariana Babbar quotes Farook Saleem, a political commentator, 'As our national defense strategy seems to have collapsed, our own proxies, the Taliban and the Jihadis, are now waging a war on Pakistan itself'.[2] Despite this, both support for the militants and fear of them continue to coexist because of reasons of strategy and the power to be exercised through them in Afghanistan and Kashmir.[3] In another political commentary in the same issue of *Outlook*, Pankaj Mishra asks the question whether the Indian state is a biased institution as it ignores crimes against Christians and tribals while persecuting Muslim suspects.[4] Headlines in *The Times of India* report violence amongst the Bodos and Muslim immigrants.[5] Pictures of Christian refugees living in relief camps in Orissa crowd the pages. Terror creates fear and leads either to submission or resistance.

The civil war in Sri Lanka has continued over nearly three decades. It is a conflict between the Sinhalese majority and the separatist organization Liberation Tiger of Tamil Eelam. And in Afghanistan the country has passed through a coup against King Zahir, a takeover by his cousin Prince Daoud in 1973, whose own rule as President lasted barely five years, when he too was ousted and assassinated by the army in April 1978, invasion by the Russians, take over by the Mujahideens, supercession of this power by Taliban, the direct entry of America post 9/11. There is little to differentiate between the many militant groups or even between the intentions of the two outside powers – Russia and America – except for ideology.[6] Loyalties and political groupings oscillate between the various factions and the outside influences like Pakistan, United States and Russia who have used them and are using them for their own purposes – preservation of their borders, hold of their power and ideology and larger political goals push them towards this.[7]

The impact of civil wars cannot simply be measured in terms of the dead or of economic loss. Amongst the many casualties of genocidal warfare, ethnic and religious conflicts are a permanent dislocation and disorientation. Violence demands a heavy price: loss of trust and faith and freedom; a permanent inhabitation of fear, a continuity and inflaming of the feeling of hatred and revenge bringing about a temporariness in relationships as the areas of refuge go on shrinking.

As a counter argument, one can state that if violence and conflict can travel across groups, communities and countries, why is it not possible for humanistic impulses to travel across barriers of race, caste, religion and politics? Freud linked aggressive social behaviour with the sexual instinct,[8] one that is sadistic in its import. A natural fall out of this violence would be the dominance of a masculine, patriarchal culture, leading to a process of control and erasure of all that does not fit in with it. Even Hitler had his willing executioners and critics like George Steiner have wondered at the coexistence of a sensitivity to music and the ability to carry out executions without a second thought in Hitler's Germany, 'artistic sensibility and the production of art are no bar to active barbarism' (Steiner 45). Freud points out 'It is clearly not easy for men to give up the satisfaction of this inclination to aggression. They do not feel comfortable without it'.[9] One of the ways of controlling this aggression is to be conscious of guilt – a bad conscience.[10] Though Freud's theory of sexuality has been questioned and supplemented by several psychologists, the debate on aggression and its correctives has not received the same kind of attention. Violence and its counter-measures have ordinarily been placed in religious discourses or personal value systems. This brings me back to Buddhism which advocates compassion and a reaching out as well as the transcendence of the ego. The writerly imagination, by stepping out of itself, achieves both in differing degrees.

Ondaatje's *Anil's Ghost* (2000), is different from the rest of his work. In this he returns to Sri Lanka as a background after a gap of several years. The only other work which uses Sri Lanka as a background is his autobiographical record *Running in the Family*. The obvious theme in *Anil's Ghost* is Anil's return as a forensic expert to the land of her birth, now torn by civil strife. But as she exhumes the dead bodies, she also uncovers a whole lot of related pasts and histories of exclusion, suppressed knowledge(s) and erased histories. In the process she realizes that courage is of different kinds – one like hers which insists upon voicing her findings, the other of Sarath who stands in for her to bear the consequences of her courage; then Gamini's who prepares his brother's body and Ananda's courage who lives with his sense of loss. There is also the courage of the genuine seer who goes into self-exile in the hills.

Anil returns to her homeland with the sensibility and the purposefulness of an outsider. But her contact with living human beings compels her to get involved. As the novel works its way through fear and destruction and acts of violence, it becomes a saga of missing people, bomb blasts and broken bones. The past comes forward to yield its ghosts. Surprisingly, in the midst of this brutality, the human capacity to search for truth manages to survive. The ability to sacrifice is summoned from its hidden recesses in order to demonstrate the integrity of human desires and values, which are indispensable for the act of survival in an environment of fear and suspicion.

The scene which really shocks one and remains to haunt the reader is the moment of Gamini finding his brother's body among the seven bodies he is writing a report on. 'Ever since he had picked up the third photograph, all he could hear was his heart banging'. Slowly he comes back to the present:

> There were things he could do. He didn't know. There were things he could do perhaps. He could see the acid burns, the twisted leg. He unlocked the cupboard that held bandages, splints, disinfectant. He began washing the body's dark-brown markings with scrub cotton. He could heal his brother, set the left leg, deal with every wound as if he were alive, as if treating the hundred small traumas would eventually bring him back to life.[11]

He recalls the history of every scar that Sarath had acquired during his boyhood days, he lingers over his memories of their relationship and of Sarath's wife, a woman both the brothers had loved.[12] And with each memory his brother's character rose before his very eyes, a man 'who in his sarong would stroll into the garden or into the verandah with his tea and newspaper. Sarath had side-stepped violence because of his character, as if there had never been a war within him'. As he looks at his brother's body and washes and tapes up the wounds, he recalls the hundreds of other cases 'where every tooth had been removed, the nose cut apart, the eyes humiliated, with liquids, the ears entered ... .' Sarath's body was dressed in a shirt with giant sleeves: 'Gamini knew why ... . Below the elbows the hands had been broken in several places'.[13]

The connection with Anil's departure is immediately clear. Anil, when she goes to the authorities with the evidence of their involvement in the violation of human rights, finds that her evidence is questioned, the body of the Sailor substituted and all preparations made to trap her in her statement as her evidence subverts the state's power. Sarath comes to her help and manages to send her Sailor's body as well as smuggle her out of the country.

The skeleton of Sailor, the dead man, strangely enough is the connecting link between the different personal narratives and the main reason for Anil's involvement in a world she had tried to leave behind. Anil's suspicions are aroused when she finds this recently buried skeleton in a site which could not have harboured it and she begins to look for answers to her many questions. Has the man been buried where he died or has his body been brought here? Is it a recent murder or an old skeleton? Whose body is it? In her endeavours to identify the dead body she travels, seeks help, locates Ananda with Sarath's help in order to reconstruct the face, watches him patiently reconstruct the face, living through Ananda's many moods, withdrawals and closing-ins. All this in pursuit of truth, with the aim of charging the government for its complicity in the violence.

But when the face is reconstructed it is a peaceful one: it embodies peace not a person. It is the Buddha in him – the way Ananda wants the dead to be – at peace, not unhappy, or in pain and struggling. It is the face of the universal man, difficult to label with any particular identity. But the search continues and yields the man's identity. Sailor was a man called Ruwan Kumara, a toddy tapper, later a miner and a rebel sympathiser.[14]

Anil's efforts at facing the truth and confronting the authorities with it place her in a position where she is interrogated as if she were a criminal. Her truth is dismissed as untruth, for it would disturb the fragile (and surface) peace which the authorities have sought to create. Anil escapes but Sarath pays with his life for having assisted her. One is compelled to ask – has it been worth it? Anil's insistence on exposing the truth and Sarath's knowingly walking towards his death? Perhaps, yes. This resistance defines all that is worthwhile in life. Martyrdom has many faces and this unheroic martyrdom insists upon the human.

Of the many endings of the novel – Anil's escape, Gamini's dressing of Sarath's body, the bomb blast 'killing the President' – the ceremony of the *netra-mangala* is the most significant. Ananda reconstructs a damaged Buddha statue but with the eyes yet unformed, the statue is not Buddha. Ananda and his nephew climb upto the face, amidst the chanting of *slokas* and set about the task with patience and devotion. Ananda paints the eyes without looking at the face – it is not possible to stand the penetrating vision of the eyes. But the face when completed is no longer the face of a god – distant and composed – instead it is a human face with a 'pure sad glance'. Somewhere during the course of the novel the distance between Sailor and Buddha is transcended. But ghosts are never finally done with. Memories become the ghosts that haunt Ananda, remain with the reader and the woman Anil who would always carry 'the ghost of Sarath Diyasena' (305).

The refugee is one who gets caught between two sets of circumstances, lives in a temporariness, and has no idea about a tomorrow. The journey itself is the trial by fire. Less than half-way through Khaled Hosseini's *The Kite Runner*, the narrator Amir and his father decide to 'elope' from their own home. The atmosphere was full of distrust and hostility, 'You couldn't trust anyone in Kabul anymore – for a fee or under threat, people told on each other, neighbor on neighbor, child on parent, brother on brother ... .'[15] The journey is slow, arduous and fear-ridden with death facing them at every turn – in the bus, in confrontation with the Russian soldiers, hidden in the airless basement and in the tank of a fuel tank full of the stench of gasoline.

Hosseini's second novel *A Thousand Splendid Suns*[16] marks the transition from the phase of the civil strife and the change of invaders more graphically and that too from an urban location like Kabul, but *The Kite Runner* with the personal narrative of discrimination, jealousy and power play as its main strand and war as a dislocating force, works through a discourse of guilt and forgiveness. Bamiyan features in both. In *A Thousand Splendid Suns,* Laila, her father Babi and her childhood friend Tariq, make a day trip to Bamiyan: 'The two Buddhas were enormous, soaring much higher than she had imagined from all the photos she'd seen of them ....' As they climb up, the two thousand-year-old history of the statues – the adjacent caves, the monks who dwelt there, the frescoes they painted – is unfolded by Babi for the younger people. Babi had planned the trip so that the children could experience peace and learn of their rich heritage.[17] It is exactly this heritage that the Taliban sets out to destroy. The museums are destroyed with all pre-Islamic statues being broken and paintings ripped off the walls. The universities are closed and books burnt in heaps.[18] These acts are marked by violence which seeks to destroy human memory and layered identities. The human beings relationship to the past is of crucial importance, all the more so in times of strife.

Relationship to the past as well as to Bamiyan is also present in *The Kite Runner*. Bamiyan locates the margins. Hassan and his father Ali who are Hazaras and as such a discriminated-against community, go back to Hazarajat, a village just off Bamiyan. Forced by his own loneliness, Rahim Khan goes to the village to bring them back.[19] The past – inheritance, memories, actions – continue to inhabit the human mind. The guilt which Amir harbours in his own mind is intensified by a series of events: the nagging thought that he has shied away from helping Hassan when Assef had raped him, that Hassan is a better human being than him. There is also the realization that he has falsely accused Hassan of theft and is thus responsible for their (Hassan and Ali's) self-exile. There is also the guilt that he with his lack of physical courage and stamina, his travel sickness and his inclination to creative writing is something of a disappointment to his father. At some point he is conscious that Rahim Khan is aware of his guilt. The past refuses to let go. Rahim Khan summons him to Pakistan and much against his will he is pulled back, nudged by Rahim Khan's words: 'There is a way to be good again' (168).

The return is a confrontation with the truth and a widening of his understanding. Hassan is his half-brother and Sohrab, Hassan's son, is the only grandchild Baba will ever have. Much against his own wishes, he is pushed by Rahim Khan's will to go to Afghanistan through the war-torn area and experience a different kind of refugeedom – poverty, fear, remnants of the past as a street beggar turns out to be a university professor who has known Amir's mother, the bombarded orphanages and the violence of the Taliban. The past catches up with him as the man who has taken away Sohrab is the one who was Hassan's rapist, the one whose act had sown the seed of guilt. In the test of physical strength, Amir is no match for Assef, who has shaped his ideology on Hitler's lines and is tough both physically and mentally. Finally it is Sohrab, who like his father before him, comes to Amir's help with his slingshot.

Assef's recounting of his cruelties as a Talib is horrifying in its triumphant tone:

> Door to door we went, calling for men and the boys. We'd shoot them right there is front of their families. .... I'd sweep the barrel of my machine gun around the room and fire and fire until the smoke blinded me ... . You don't know the meaning of the word 'liberating' until you have done that, stood in a roomful of targets, let the bullets fly, free of guilt and remorse, good, and decent ... . It's breathtaking.[20]

A non-religious man, Assef has suddenly become passionate about his single-minded mission – a cleansing mission, removing the garbage from Afghanistan – massacring Hazaras, stoning adulterers, raping children, flogging women – a mission with the aim of purity and monolithic nation-building. Somewhere it is also the enjoyment of power, the ability to strike fear in others.

Amir's personal sense of guilt is multiplied by several things – his father's illicit relationship with Ali's wife, Sohrab's orphanhood and his own ability to take him to the States because of immigration problems. Sohrab's desperation at being abandoned leads the boy to attempt suicide. The uncertainty takes away not only whatever childhood he may still have retained after hunger, poverty and being made an object entertainment dressed up as a girl with heavy make-up and jingling bells, travel as a fugitive from the long arms of the Talibs, but it also destroys his trust in others. Amir had assured him, he'll take him along and now the legal hassles leave him little choice. Sohrab closes in, locking up his mind and heart in silence, a silence he doesn't break even when he travels to the States, starts living with them in a strange land, among strange people. Afraid and alone, Sohrab's silence is a total withdrawal from life:

> *Silence* is pushing the OFF button. Shutting it down. All of it. Sohrab's silence wasn't the self-imposed silence of those with convictions, of protestors who seek to speak their cause by not speaking at all. It was the silence of one who has taken cover in a dark place, curled up all the edges and tucked them under.[21]

And then, Soraya spots kites and Amir buys one and starts flying it – after a gap of more than a quarter century.

> I looked at Sohrab. One corner of his mouth had curled up just so.
> A smile.
> Hardly there.
> But there.[22]

Amir who has been asking for forgiveness in silence and penitence, says to himself, 'For you a thousand times over'. He clings to this little indication of Sohrab's response – 'Only a smile. A tiny thing. A leaf in the woods, shaking in the wake of a startled bird's flight'.[23] Amir accepts it with open arms with all pretences having fallen away and the courage to face the truth.[24] Amir travels twice through Pakistan, once with his father on their way to America and then to and fro to Kabul to bring Sohrab to safety. This journey, taken under duress, is a transformative journey where guilt, repentance and recovery all come together to change his attitude and way of thinking and he learns to move away from pretence a little closer to the true values of his inherited past.

The Kite Runner and *A Thousand Splendid Suns*, both like *Anil's Ghost* are narratives of deep compassion, novels where the violent rupture with the past has to give way to a slow return by the thinnest of connections. Different kinds of borders are crossed in Hosseini's two novels: the physical borders of national boundaries, of culture, of discrimination and of relationships. In *A Thousand Splendid Suns*, Miriam takes upon herself the responsibility of Laila, her husband's second wife. As each political change takes place, people hope for a better, and more peaceful future, they hope the Mujahideens will free them of the communists; the Talibs of the faction-ridden and corrupt Mujahideens and the Americans of the Talibs. In fact, in describing the Taliban's exit, Hosseini uses words very similar to George Bush's hate speeches, 'soon after the attacks, America bombed Afghanistan, the Northern Alliance moved in, and the Taliban scurried like rats into the caves' (*The Kite Runner* 316). Has the homeland been distanced because of insecurity, violence and a hostile, cramping environment? Civil war, continued insurgency, inability to imagine the borders of the nation from one's own location destroy different kinds of abstractions – and the idea of homeland is one such.

It is the failure of this imagination – the inability to imagine a homeland – which is manifested in Temsula Ao's short fiction in *These Hills Called Home*, stories about the Nagas. It also manifests itself in the ideological conflict regarding Sunderbans in Amitav Ghosh's *The Hungry Tide*. Ghosh has woven an intricate web of issues around Sunderbans, its inhabitants, the new refugee population, and the cultural politics. There are at least three different narratives being told: the outer framework of Nilima summoning Kanai to Lusibari, the relationship that develops between Piya and Fokir, and the embedded narrative of Nirmal's love for freedom and imagination. In fact this diary forms the central core of the novel and its presence is registered right at the beginning.

Nirmal is one person who resists restrictions and wants to reach across; Nilima likes to work with systems and defined boundaries. She is bypassed when the packet of writing is bequeathed to Kanai. As Kanai begins his journey, he dips into the narrative (which strangely enough is not italicised in its first presentation though through the rest of the novel the passages from the diary are italicised) and a passage reads, 'There are no borders here to divide fresh water from salt, river from sea'.[25] The land here is in a constant state of flux, subject to the pressure of tides. The absence of visible borders is no restrictions on crossing them. When Nirmal reads out the travels of Frances Bernier and his description of having been caught in a storm, Horen immediately exclaims; 'They crossed the line by mistake and ended up on one of Dokkhin Rai's islands' (147). Yet again when Nirmal, Kusum and Fokir make their way to the islands, Kusum reveals that they had crossed the line Bon Bibi had drawn to divide the tide country, a line,

Nirmal realizes, as real to her as 'a barbed wire-fence might be to me'. Suddenly the flow of time is woven into the geographical space. Nirmal wonders whether the 'very rhythms of the earth were quickened here so that they unfolded at an accelerated pace?'[26]

Other borders are also crossed when Nirmal attends the puja in honour of Bon Bibi, and realizes that the mantras were Arabic invocations – 'it was a strange variety of Bangla, deeply interpenetrated by Arabic and Persian' – an invocation passed on from generation to generation through the oral tradition.[27] The final border is crossed when Fokir shelters Piya from the storm with his own body, 'she could feel the bones of his cheeks as if they had been superimposed upon her own; it was as if the storm had given them what life could not; it had fused them together and made them ones'.[28]

Underneath the nostalgia for deities like Bon Bibi and the sense of wonder at the marvels of nature is the consciousness of danger from the world of nature – storms, tigers, crocodiles and land being swept away from under one's feet – on the one hand, and on the other from the aggressive human animal who seeks to control and impose his authority. There is no easy option. The traces of the colonial past are evident in Lusibari, even in its name, which carries the mark of ownership by a foreign woman named Lucy, and the political need to evacuate the refugees is another reality that needs to be faced. There are no absolute categories possible in discussing the issues of violence and aggression.

All violence, even if it is not of the same kind, leaves its scars. Violence is experienced both by the doer and the sufferer. And it changes both. If Assef is brutalised, Amir recovers a lost heritage (*The Kite Runner*). Miriam's ghastly murder of Rashid is a release for Laila (*A Thousand Splendid Suns*). These are all acts of personal transformations – not only in Hosseini's work but also in Ghosh's *The Hungry Tide* and Ondaatje's *Anil's Ghost*. They are brought about by people like Sarath and Fokir. Compassion, a way of reaching across, a way of releasing the self from its prisons, however is not enough unless it is accompanied by a political consciousness of preservation and solidarity.

The responses of the ordinary people to the political happenings are one of bewilderment, non-comprehension and hope that perhaps the tide will turn. Such responses are reflected in Hosseini's work. Again, political action is comprehended through one's own self-interest and long term gains, a way of seeing which is not always rational or just. Violence too has its causes which deviate from value system, but at times represent a self-assertion of a body of people. The factors which distort right causes are several: factionalism, corruption and playing into the hands of expansionist imperialists. The contest at one level is between identity and power, and at another level between national concerns and outside intervention, as the birth of many terrorists organizations testifies.

Terrorism becomes a closed trap in which the individual is caught. Temsula Ao's short stories bear a testimony to this, especially "An Old Man Remembers" and "Shadows", both included in *These Hills Called Home*.[29] In the latter story Imli becomes a victim of inter-tribal rivalry in the underground movement and is done to death in a merciless manner. The facts of the way he was murdered are suppressed for fear that it would lead to more violence. The underground rebels cut themselves off from all access to justice and community grieving. Additionally they lend themselves as easy victims to jungle rogues and terrorist groups from adjacent borders. Desertions are common but rehabilitation, if not impossible, is difficult. Horto, the man responsible for Imli's, death becomes insane and wanders around as a man without any identity, 'They could not say whether he was Naga or a Kachin or a mainland Burmese' (85). Finally, Horto dies a gruesome and violent death as retribution comes full circle.

"An Old Man Remembers" is a tale of loss and grief. Sashi, a former underground rebel, now lives in the village. After his term in prison, he had never talked about his underground experience. But now that his closest friend and comrade in the movement is dead, he feels that the tale has to be passed on, especially when his young grandson asks him about it. Young Mao, he feels, was something of an inquisitor. Sashi's tale is one of straying in and out of the underground movement. Each time the friends try to come out of it, they get trapped by circumstances. Yet they continue to watch on the quiet for an opportunity to escape. During one of their escapes they come across some soldiers of the Indian army, end up killing them and setting the abandoned farm on fire – a fire in which the dead bodies are also burnt. As he examines the past, the full realization of what had happened to them comes to him. He stands outside himself, willing to criticize, not demanding pity, fully prepared to expose himself to judgment, 'we were not yet sixteen when we became such ruthless killers' (108). The return home, when it happens, is full of desolation. Life is lived on the fringes of society in fear and guilt.

The past lives on, refusing to be done with. In the midst of this, is it possible to select the moments of sustenance, the shared normalcies and create a counter-discourse to violence? Violence appears to be systematic but so is the resistance to it. In between these two opposing forces is a whole area of relationships – Miriam and Laila, Amir and Sohrab, Anil and Sarath, Sashi and Imli. There is compassion, there is sharing and there is a going across: all acts of transcendence of borders and hatred and obsessions with the present. Loyalties, allegiances, single-mindedness characterize both sets of approaches. Religion, in some form or the other also plays a role as does faith. In May 2002, a mountainside sculpture of Buddha was carved out of a mountain in Sri Lanka. It was an effort at a reproduction of the Buddhas of Bamiyan. A 300 metre statue was also discovered by archeologists in Bamiyan on Sept. 8, 2008.[30] Perhaps it is these forces of faith, at a human level, that help to build bridges so that the crossings are possible and easier.

Notes

1. The statues are believed to have been sculpted during the fifth century, a period when Afghanistan was part of the Gandhara Empire. See internet ref http://www.en.wikipedia.org/wiki//Buddhas_of_Bamiyan#History. Accessed 7 October, 2008. Also see http://www. commondreams.org/headlines01/0301-04.htm.
2. *Outlook*, 6 October 2008, Farook Saleem also points out that more people have died in such acts of violence in the last five years, than in the Indo-Pak war.
3. Ibid.
4. See Pankaj Mishra "India: A Massacre Justified By Philanthropy", *Outlook*, 6 October, 2008, pp. 48–49.
5. *The Times of India*, 7 October, 2008. Jaipur edition.
6. My inferences have been derived mainly from my reading of *The Rise of Taliban in Afghanistan: Mass Mobilization, Civil War, and the Future of the Region* by Neamatollah Nojumi (New York: Palgrave, 2002) and *The Clash of Fundamentalisms* by Tariq Ali (London: Verso, 2002).

7. See Tariq Ali, p. 207. Ali's contention is that US aid was given to the 'opponents of pro-Soviet people' in order to create conditions for USSR intervention. He quotes from Zbigniew Brzezinski's interview published in *Le Nouved Observateur* 15–21 January, 1998, where Brzezinski comments 'What is more important to the history of the world? The Taliban or the collapse of the Soviet Empire? A few crazed Muslims or the liberation of Central Europe and the end of the Cold War?' (p. 208). Also see internet references http://www.en.wikipedia.org/wiki/sri_lankan_civil_war, accessed 7 October 2008.
8. Refer "'Civilized' Sexual Morality and Modern Nervous Illness" (1908) in *Sigmund Freud: Civilization, Society and Religion*. Vol. 12 (New Delhi: Shrijee's Book International, 2003) p. 27. The Editor's Introduction to "Civilization and Its Discontents" (1930), in the same volume also reiterates this. See p. 258.
9. See "Civilization and Its Discontents" *Sigmund Freud: Civilization, Society and Religion*" p. 318.
10. Ibid., pp. 330–338.
11. Michael Ondaatje, *Anil'sGhost* (New York: Vintage, 2000), p. 287.
12. Ibid., pp. 251–253.
13. Ibid., pp. 288–290.
14. Ibid., p. 269.
15. Khaled Hosseini, *The Kite Runner* (London: Bloomsbury, 2003, 2004), p. 98.
16. Khaled Hosseini, *A Thousand Splendid Suns* (London: Bloomsbury, 2007).
17. Ibid., pp. 132–135.
18. Ibid., 250–251.
19. *The Kite Runner* pp. 178–181. Also see p. 294 where Amir comments upon the destructions of the statues, an act which reflects an act annihilation of the past.
20. Ibid., p. 242.
21. Ibid., p. 315.
22. Ibid., p. 323.
23. Ibid., p. 324.
24. Earlier he had told his father-in-law not to address Sohrab as the 'Hazara boy' (p. 315).
25. Amitav Ghosh, *The Hungry Tide*. (New Delhi: Harper Collins, 2004, 2005) p. 7.
26. Ibid., pp. 223–224.

27. Ibid., p. 246.
28. Ibid., p. 390.
29. Temsula Ao, *These Hills Called Home* (New Delhi: Zubaan with Penguin, 2006).
30. See http://www.en.wikipedia.org/wiki/Buddhas_of_Bamiyan#History.

Works Cited

Ali, Tariq. *Clash of Fundamentalisms*. London: Verso, 2003.
Ao, Temsula. *These Hills Called Home: Stories From a War Zone*. New Delhi: Zubaan & Penguin, 2006.
Babbar, Mariana. "Abyss of Reason". *Outlook*, 6 Oct. 2008.
Freud, Sigmund. "'Civilized' Sexual Morality and Modern Nervous Illness," in *Sigmund Freud: Civilization, Society and Religion*. Vol. 12. New Delhi: Shrijee's Book International, 2003.
—. "Civilization and Its Discontents" in *Sigmund Freud: Civilization, Society and Religion*. Vol. 12. New Delhi: Shrijee's Book International, 2003.
Ghosh, Amitav. *The Hungry Tide*. New Delhi: Harper Collins (2004), 2005.
Hosseini, Khaled. *A Thousand Splendid Suns*. London: Bloomsbury, 2007.
—. *The Kite Runner*. London: Bloomsbury (2003), 2004.
Mishra, Pankaj. "India: A Massacre Justified by Philanthropy," *Outlook*, 6 October 2008.
Nojumi, Neamatolloh. *The Rise of Taliban in Afghanistan: Mass Mobilization, Civil War and the Future of the Region*. New Delhi: Palgrave, 2002.
Ondaatje, Michael. *Anil's Ghost*. New York: Vintage, 2000.
Steiner, George. "Cry Havoc", *Extraterritorial* (1971). Harmondsworth: Penguin, 1975.

Internet Sources

http://www.en.wikipedia.org/wiki/Buddhism_in_SriLanka.
http://www.en.wikipedia.org/wiki/Sri_Lankan_Civil_War
http://www.commondreams.org/headlines01/0301-04.htm
http://www.en.wikipedia.org/wiki/Buddhas_of_Bamiyan#History.

4

AVINASH JODHA

Eclectic Cartography: Spaces of Memory and Belonging in Sorayya Khan's *Noor*

> The sole *raison d'être* of a novel is to discover what only the novel can discover.
>
> Hermann Broch[1]
>
> My face is coming .... I am looking for the join.
>
> Toni Morrison, *Beloved*

'The death of the novel' has been emphatically declared and agreed upon by all the major avant-gardes of the later half of the twentieth century and these declarations carry a tone of finality that dissociates the death of novel from Barthes's rhetorical declaration of 'the death of the author.' If the novel is dead, is dying or has already been buried, it is imperative to ask before the final obituaries are read out why the skies seem to be finally closing down on a genre that has survived more than four centuries of unprecedented upheavals?

Milan Kundera looks into the issue squarely and points out, 'Man has now become a mere thing to the forces (of technology, of politics, of history) that bypass him, surpass him, possess him. To those forces, man's concrete being, his "world of life" has neither value nor interest' (Kundera 4). Kundera refers to history as a train that is 'easy to board, hard to leave' (Kundera 8) Such is the charm of this train that everyone – politicians, writers, artists seek to come aboard. It is essential to question the obligation of the novel to history, to politics and to polemic concerns. Can the novel allow itself to be consistently fathered by history? How far and how long can the novel hope to survive the relentless infringement of history and politics that seem to wrest life out of it?

The novel in its essence is an act of multiple transgressions; in fact all art in the greatest of its manifestations has been transgressive. The novel has to posit a challenge to the totalitarian subsuming of human life in the tantalizingly uncompromising grand narratives of power – of history, of politics, of religion and of 'progress'. Sorayya Khan's *Noor* is situated in a specific historical context – the partition of Pakistan and Bangladesh in 1971. Khan gets into the spaces of Pakistan and Bangladesh and the war that left countless haunting tales of brutalities and genocide. History provides her a definite frame and her negotiation of history with her commitment to the spirit of the novel can be an interesting subject of critical inquiry to comprehend some of the ways in which contemporary writing has handled the challenges that appear to force the novel genre into oblivion.

Noor opens with an epigraph from Agha Shahid Ali that reads, 'Your history gets into the way of my memory' and the very next page presents history at its naked best, reduced to a matter of fact skeleton that states that 'On 12 Nov. 1970, a cyclone hit East Pakistan. One million people died.' Next up it offers the exact dates of the beginning of the civil war between West and East Pakistan, the date of India's entry into the war and the end of the war with East Pakistan becoming Bangladesh. However this neat historical reference rounds off with an unabashed, unfaltering statement of the number of the dead, 'Between 300,000 and three million people died.' 2.7 million people might or might not have died but history can account for all of them with its miracle of fairly rounded off figures.

Noor doesn't set out to set the records straight. It is a far cry from parallel, unofficial, marginal, authentic eyewitness histories of the gory carving of Bangladesh. Bangladeshi poets, writers, artists and filmmakers have dealt with the traumatic events of the independence of Bangladesh fuelled by the mad logic of General Yahya Khan's conviction 'kill three million of them and the rest will eat out of hands.'[2] The historical and artistic renditions of the events concentrate primarily upon bringing out the true story of the mass murders, rapes and brutalities relying heavily upon eyewitness accounts.[3] However together at best they succeed in exposing the Pakistani establishmentarian and historical lies.

Sorayya Khan draws maps that do not strain to comply with or defy the colonial cartographs of Pakistan and India and the postcolonial cartography of Pakistan and Bangladesh. In fact she manages more by circumventing the claws of history and grounding her work in the interstices of individual and collective memory. *Noor* enters the war tentatively but with the unmistakable certainty of the adolescent Noor who enters the dreams of her mother Sajida the very night she is conceived:

> The suspended girl focused her attention on Sajida. The velvet texture of her big black eyes poured into her plea.
> 'Ammi,' she called in the high-pitched voice of a young child registering an all-consuming need for her mother ... . The force of what was said stunned Sajida. The 'Ammi' that grew from the strange girl was different. It had an urgency all its own, absent in the wails of her young sons who took the word for granted ... . The cry evoked a private set of memories Sajida had grown to forget ... . Sajida trembled. Because her past, unclear and unspoken, forever lingered just beyond her touch, Sajida immediately recognized the visit from her future. (2–3)

Sajida knows that her child will be different and she instinctively decides to protect her child, to make Noor her 'secret' (8). But what she doesn't know even as she absorbs colours around her with a never before hunger (7) is that her daughter will lay bare all secrets not only of her private world but of the world outside, unravel the past both private and public, express the unspoken through her insistent colours.

Who is Noor? Is she a retarded child, a curse that has to be lived with? Is she the names the doctors give her? Is she a guilt that can never be overcome? Noor is a memory in corporeal form, a memory that simultaneously incriminates and heals, wounds and seeks atonement, endearment. Within few hours of her birth Noor metamorphoses from a beautiful child into a baby with flat, uncertain features with only the vague certainty of the name the doctor gives to her condition – Mongoloid. Hussein feels dazed as her face brings to him the memory of General Z's daughter and his own retarded cousin (21). But Noor's face opens a geographic space for Ali, a space and the embedded memories that he had strived so hard to keep at bay:

> Ali, in an earlier life and another land, had seen children like Noor, a shade from black, in the hold of death. When Noor's face collapsed

into what it would be, he leaned closer, and strangely recalled
something of the war he'd seen. The soiled maternity ward, new blood
drying upon old, the sticky sweat of desperate work, evoked a moment
in his other life. Although the day was dry and cloudless, Ali smelled a
flooding pit of mud and he heard rain, unforgiving streams falling in
deafening sheets. (20–21)

Noor's face and her medical condition with the inborn disabilities
put her life and that of her family into an intricate web of complexities.
Her slowness to learn basic things, heart rending cries and food
idiosyncrasies, painful as they are, bring everything 'normal' into an
interesting perspective. They compel her family to acknowledge and
experience an alternative way of seeing and of being.

Noor's life cannot be choreographed like that of her elder brothers
and other children. She demands a space of her own and an effort of
will and of love from her family to find access to her special nature.
Looking at his daughter in the 'first minutes of her life' Hussein is
more than surprised:

Hussein was struck by her darkness. Not her skin but eyes were deep
and endlessly black, like the abandoned well of his childhood in his
great grandfather's house .... His daughter's eyes were fixed on him, as
if his baby girl had been born with the ability to focus, and mere
moments after birth, already had something of consequence to share.
(19)

Noor is special, she has her own abilities. She cannot register
physical pain or the change in seasons but she is acutely sensitive
towards her own emotions and feelings and those of the others in her
family. She absolutely dotes on her father, waits endlessly for him
each day as he returns from work and does not acknowledge her
presence. She wonders at the miracle of her father's love attempting
to feel its intimacy by merely witnessing it bestowed on her
brothers (35).

More than anything else Noor has a unique gift – her inborn
instinct for colours as if it is a physical manifestation of her mother's
hunger for colours in the days of her pregnancy (7). She latches upon
colours with her first set of crayons with an astounding certainty,
beginning with a predilection for blue; filling sheet after sheet with
blue. While the others in the family are ecstatic over Noor's gift,
Hussein cannot take it:

He'd known, since the day Noor arrived, the moment he'd seen her features, freshly flat on her face, that she was abnormal. But when he saw what she had made, sheets filled simply and perfectly with blue, he couldn't abide it. He believed the drawings reflected his daughter's mind, amorphous and unformed, so much so that the ugliness of what she'd spilled onto paper was the very essence of who she was. (31)

Hussein's inability to accept the fact of his daughter's difference from other children makes him blind to his daughter's gift. What he sees as 'emptiness' and 'ugliness' turns out to have a subtlety and beauty that captivates the other members of his family. Laying out Noor's drawings side by side Sajida discovers 'movement' in Noor's blue (31). Nanijaan instinctively feels that her granddaughter's drawings were 'invocations to God' and that in them 'something of beauty was unfolding' (49). Her single colour paintings raise the cyclone in Sajida's and Ali's memories (84, 93); and bit by bit, painting after painting she unfolds the space of Bangladesh and the war in the mind of her mother who carried only hazy images of her childhood landscape in her memory and more so into Ali's mind who had painstakingly banished these memories into the nailed compartments of deliberate forgetfulness.

Sorayya Khan's *Noor* impinges into the settled borders of nation states and into the banished spaces of personal and collective memories at multiple levels. Ali sees the vast stretches of a left behind, forgotten Bangladesh right in the heart of Islamabad, opening into his granddaughter's face and her drawings almost as real and as haunting as the abandoned houses of the East Pakistanis all over the city (37). Ali goes out of his way to avoid these houses with their pervasive sense of 'being there and not being there' as they remind him of East Pakistan and the war. But his fear finds a manifestation in the architecture of the house he himself builds. A perfect square with adjacent rooms on all sides, practically without any windows on the outside walls, the house looks 'stark, uninviting, a virtual fort' (40); almost a perfect replica of Ali's state of mind. Looking at the house Nanijaan has a feeling that 'her son's choice of house of house spoke to the dark secrets all men of war shared' (39).

Noor gets into the *windowless fortresses* of Ali's house and his mind, in person and through her drawings. She draws her paintings sitting inside the open courtyard in the centre of Ali's home and her delicate, persistent strokes crumble the impenetrable walls of Ali's world. As Noor's paintings shift from depictions of abstract to more concrete images, Sajida realizes:

> There was no question now. Noor's drawings were no longer simple words to be alphabetized on a wall. They were windows into another world, far away and distant, which might have ceased to exist without Noor. Sajida had always expected that her children would humble her with their lessons; she hadn't considered that one of them would teach the past, bring it back and put it in front of her with an exactitude that was astonishing. (117–118)

Such is the *exactitude* of Noor's depictions that Ali sees the thin grey of the Bangladeshi landscape, the thunder of monsoons, the rituals of war and the myths of superiority and manhood carried out in rapes and brutal torturing of women, women with severed breasts and men with hacked penises, vacant eyes and bloated bodies, babies caught up in rifle bayonets, pits of mud, blood and bodies, the macabre dance of war and naked inhumanity fiercely contending to outdo each other in the game of death.

Noor's paintings in their exact depictions of the past open *windows* to the past and posit questions to the present. Her calligraphic drawing of the letters of the word 'Allah' asks Nanijaan the position of God in her household (49); her drawing of a fine Italian shoe asks questions of love to her father Hussein and reminds him of his betrayal (98–99); and as her accuracy in painting grows so do her questions, they grow bigger, acquire bigger landscapes and implications. Noor's painting of the river *Sitalakhya* leads Nanijaan to peer after years into the maps with a magnifying glass and all that she discovers is a 'thin scribble in the pale green of the map,' but she discovers something else instantly:

> It came to her. Indeed, she had questions. They could not be answered by books, intricate maps or anything else she might read. Something entirely different was demanded. She would have to stand in front of her youngest son, her favorite of all, and find the words. What did Ali do in East Pakistan? What did he see? What did this boy *find* so far?
>
> (146–147)

She does find words to ask Ali these questions and when she knows that her son has killed people she has more questions to ask – *What does it feel like, to kill someone? Where do you put that knowledge during the day? At night?* (151). Ali's outrage at his mother's questions is only partial because he knows that he has waited all his life for someone to ask him these questions. Stirred into life by Noor's drawings, Ali's memories have a crucial significance as they are not merely accusatory visitations from the past; on the contrary, Ali knows that more than ever before now his past has arrived to seek the intimacy of acceptance, to reveal meanings that have so far eluded him:

> It occurred to Ali that Noor's drawing was a manifestation of what he'd locked away so carefully years ago in the cabinets of his mind. In the presence of a granddaughter he loved so much and her meticulous drawing of the Sitalakhya the day he'd buried a woman, he understood what had happened. His past had arrived. Soon it would be its own gallery, for all to see. However faint there was a measure of relief in that. (141)

Sorayya Khan makes Noor a harbinger of memories, her every single evocation of memory brings questions that could never be asked in the past and are evaded in the present. Even Ali who appears to be the target of the questions that are asked by Nanijaan, Sajida and Noor has his own questions. As the exiled memories of the war come back to him, he looks at them with the distance of time, no more threatened by the immediacy of the horrors, he reflects at them attempting to come to an understanding of his own reasons to rush into the war, the ensuing madness, the delusion and disillusionment where every grand notion of honour, patriotism, courage is reduced to a singular instinct to survive in the face of an overwhelming, paralyzing fear:

> Ali couldn't remember. He wasn't certain that, in the beginning, he'd needed or even had a reason to go to war. He'd rushed into it, an adventure of a lifetime … . After he landed in East Pakistan at the Dhaka airport, it took one day before he asked himself, *this is my country?*, another day to know he wasn't fighting the war *for* his country, another day yet to realize he wasn't fighting for Nanijaan or, for that matter, any family. On the fourth day he felt like a mercenary.
> … In the end, he'd fought and killed for an unremarkable reason: to save himself. (183–184)

These are realizations that may seep through the grandest of the rhetorics of war into the conscience of any soldier mustering courage enough to face and to own up his past. Ali, compelled by Noor's drawings, revisits his past in the most gruesome of its details. He looks into the skin of the horrors, no longer desirous of an escape. Sorayya Khan intertwines Ali's memories of the war into the narrative of the novel in the italicized sections. These sections are crucial as they, brick by brick, form a bridge between the Ali who was lost in the war and the Ali who came back with a vacuum in his heart. Most of these sections in all their exactitude of details round off with a question from Ali – *Did you know that?*

More than any display of superior knowledge of war, the insistence of the question reveals the burden of knowing, the pain of disillusionment and the pressing need to be humanized through sharing, understanding and acceptance. These are questions that cross the borders of the specifics of time and space and they have a magnitude that encompasses entire humanity in its existential dimensions.

History does not ask questions. It wounds and incriminates or extols and celebrates forever encapsulated by the inexorable logic of binaries, either or, either you are the victim or you are the victimizer. A novel may be historical or counter-historical but it cannot afford to be judgmental if it hopes to survive this era that is marked by a plethora of histories. Sorayya Khan visited Pakistan and Bangladesh and researched before writing her novel. She met and interviewed Pakistani soldiers who were a part of the war and also heard the accounts of the victims in Bangladesh. Any dedicated disciple of history may ask how many Pakistani soldiers did really adopt Bangladeshi children and bring them home. Did Sorraya meet a character like Noor? Or can there be an individual like Noor with the miracle of an ability to paint pictures from other people's memories? Why didn't Sorayya choose to tell the story of a real victim, for instance the story of a raped woman or a brutally murdered intellectual?

The questions valid as they are, are as misdirected. There are no obvious answers in the offering. The novel in the insistence of its focus upon human life brings to light what fails to transpire through the most exact of the histories. It delves into the concrete domains of human existence, into its unexplored, unrealized possibilities. *Noor*, both as a novel and character, carries a special inheritance and shares natural ties with a family of fictions that has embraced and sustained the essence of the novel genre in its veins. This intimate web of relationships can be traced in the figures of Beloved in Toni Morrison's *Beloved*; Saleem Sinai in Rushdie's *Midnight's Children*; Sufia Zinobia in *Shame*; and Remedios the Beauty in Marquez's *One Hundred Years of Solitude*.

Each one of them is special, a miracle of miracles, and yet more real than the real itself. They carry within their faces and their being the eclectic cartography of human existence. The irregularity of their faces and gestures sometimes corresponds to the indiscriminate drawings of geo-political borders: Saleem Sinai with his horned temples and elongated nose has a map face, Noor's flat face and drooping features resembles the landscape of Bangladesh with its miles and miles of flat land. But beyond the visible irony of the cartography of nations on their faces they bring together lost maps, maps of silence, maps forgotten by nations in their eagerness to be born.

Noor is not good with letters and words but she can paint pictures that no words may reach; Saleem can turn himself into a radio and tune into the voices of the other midnight's children; Sufia blushes and blushes more absorbing the unfelt, unrecognized invisible shame of others; Remedios remains blissfully oblivious of her own beauty or the customs of the world around her; Beloved has milk teeth and she falters as she speaks. Homi Bhabha refers to the significance of her broken words:

> Her words are broken, like the lynched people with broken necks; disembodied, like the dead children who lost their ribbons. But there is no mistaking what her live words say as they rise from the dead despite their lost syntax and their fragmented presence. (Bhabha 17)

The *lost syntax* of Beloved's speech breaks the silence of the past of slavery and it causes the 'unspeakable thoughts to be unspoken' (Bhabha 10). Noor fears visible borders but her paintings render even the deepest of the divides palpable. By their insistence, even as Hussein tears some of them away, they compel a breaking of the silence in Ali's private space of the war that had been both private and public.

Noor, Beloved, Saleem, Sufia and Remedios at one level become the metaphors for the novel; their compulsive bringing into life of the others' forgotten memories reflects the novel's resistance to forgetting and forgetfulness. They, like the novel, dwell in the domains of human possibilities. They bring to the fore alternate perspectives that reach beyond the horizons of history and bring into light the invisible perforations created by history's intrinsic inability to account for what is human.

Sorraya Khan's *Noor* reveals a rich cross border literary lineage and inheritance but it does not limit itself to a redundant reenactment of a powerful tradition. *Noor* carries this tradition into its veins but it paves a path of its own. Rushdie's Saleem Sinai engages himself in the mammoth task of negotiating the handcuffs of history that turn his life into a vast theatre staging the drama of partition. *Midnight's Children* exposes the multiple perforations in history, in all its ironies and political mockery; it signals the ever present absence of human love that finds a manifestation in the hole that appears in Adam Sinai's heart. A similar hole in the throat of Prudencio Aguilar and gaps created by multiple solitudes, demand attention in Marquez's *One Hundred Years of Solitude*. The terrible loneliness of the three sisters' home in *Shame* and the shadows of the past in *Beloved* indicate the insistent presence of similar absences.

Noor steps into these holes, the absences signaled by Marquez, Rushdie and Morrison, into the realization of the possibilities of filling them in with sharing, acceptance, love and belonging. What appears in flashes in the figures of Sufia in *Shame* and Remedios the Beauty in *One Hundred Years of Solitude* gains a full life in *Noor*. Noor like *Beloved* demands an intimate acceptance of the past that arrives in a physical form:

> My face is coming I have to have it I am looking for the join I am loving my face so much. I want to join I am loving my face so much my dark face is close to me I want to join. (Bhabha 18)

Noor too *wants to join* as she does on the last page of the novel in her embrace with Sajida and Ali as a deep and immense moan rises from his belly and fills his house. However, belonging in *Noor* moves beyond the claims of a banished past and emerges as the central concern in Sorayya Khan's narrative. Ali in his complete disillusionment with war sees in Sajida the string of humanity and hope and immediately steps into the role of a father (120). Nanijaan dyes her hair black to resemble her adopted granddaughter's pitch black complexion and at once ties herself with Sajida in the bonds of sisterhood (72). She accepts Noor with equal pride like Sajida and Noor immediately finds place in the family tradition with her first word – 'Nanijaan' (29). These relationships speak of ties deeper than those of blood as they have their roots in the willingness to love and share.

Noor captures the spirit of the novel. The novel stops short the onward march of history and takes time to reflect like Nanijaan who deliberately reduces her pace, no longer in a hurry to reach somewhere but on the contrary to arrive slowly at an understanding of the loose ends of her family's past – *what has been and may have been possible* (159). As she braces herself for death she moves gradually into the acceptance of the fact that her son Ali did kill people in East Pakistan and at the same time she realizes the significance of Ali's gift from Bangladesh – Sajida, his decision to remain unmarried, his silent penance, his love for Sajida and her children unconditional and whole.

Noor emphasizes the significance of second chances – Sajida gives Hussein a second chance and lets him in again in her life, Nanijaan and Sajida give a second chance to Ali in their acceptance of his past, and life too gives Ali a second chance, in the form of Sajida and Noor, to exorcise his past and live in the security of what he missed most in the war, security of love and belonging. The novel in all the eclecticism of its cartography gives humanity a second chance to step out of the sweeping tide of history and search for maps of love and belonging lost in the margins of history. *Noor* carries the waft of a promise that chances for the novel and humanity are yet far from over.

Notes

1. Milan Kundera in *The Art of the Novel* brings into consideration the lectures given by Edmund Husserl in 1935 on the "Crisis of European Humanity". Husserl revealed the 'one-sided nature' of European sciences that reduced the world to a mere object of technical and mechanical investigation and thereby put the 'concrete world of life' beyond their horizon. Kundera sees in the history of the novel a remarkable insistence to keep this 'concrete world of life' under permanent light and he quotes Herman Broch's statement to emphasize his own convictions about the purpose of the novel genre.

2. Pakistani General Agha Mohammed Yahya Khan reportedly made the comment to the journalist Robert Payne on February 22, 1971. This comment also apparently led to the controversy regarding the real number of victims that is often put between 300,000 and three million. Pierre, Stephen and Robert Payne (1973), *Massacre*, (New York: Macmillan). See Bangladesh Atrocities www.wikipedia.com

3. The first of the novels written on the war was Anwar Pasha's *Rifle Roti Aurat* (1973) that was written during the war. The novels that have a direct focus on the war are Shaukat Osman's *Jahannam Hoite Bidai* (1971), *Nekre Aranyo* (1973) *Dui Soinik* (1973), Rashid Haider's *Khanchai* (1975), and *Andha Kathamala* (1982), Shaukat Ali's *Jatraa* (1976), Selina Hossain's *Hangor Nodi Granade* (1976), Mahmudul Huq's *Jiban Aamar Bone* (1976), Syed Shamsul Haq's *Nil Dangshon* (1981) and *Nishiddho Loban* (1981), Harun Habib's *Priyo Joddha Priyotoma* (1982) etc. Some writers have also dealt with the bleak scenario of Bangladesh in their novels like Rashid Karim's *Prem Ekti Lal Golap* (1978), *Ekaler Rupkatha* (1980) and *Sadharon Loker Kahini* (1982). Some other accounts of the war have been *Ami Virangana Balchhi (I am the Heroine of War, Speaking...)* – memoir by Nilima Ibrahim. *Ghum Nei (Sleepless Nights)* – memoir by Nasiruddin Yusuf, *Ami Bijoy Dekhechi (I have witnessed the Victory)* – memoir by M.R. Akhtar Mukul, *A Tale of Millions* – memoir by Major (R) Rafik Ul Islam, *Ekattorer Dinguli (Days of 71)* – memoir by Jahanara Imam (1986), *Maa (The Mother)* – novel by Anisul Hoque (2003), *Jochhna o Janani'r Galpo (The Tale of Moonlight and the Motherland)* – novel by Humayun Ahmed (2004). See www.bangladeshinovels.com. and Bangladesh Atrocities www.wikipedia.com.

Works Cited

Bhabha, Homi. *The Location of Culture*. London: Routledge, 1994.
Khan, Sorayya. *Noor*. New Delhi: Penguin Books India, (2003) 2004.
Kundera, Milan. *The Art of the Novel*. (1968) London: Faber and Faber, 2005.
Márquez, Gabriel García. *One Hundred Years of Solitude*. (1967) New Delhi: Penguin Books India, 1996.
Morrison, Toni. *Beloved*. London: Chatto & Windus, 1987.
Rushdie, Salman. *Midnight's Children*. London: Vintage, 1995 (1981).
—. *Shame*. London: Vintage, 1995 (1983).

5

CHARU MATHUR

Terror vs Terrorism: Reordering the World

War against terrorism was declared by the US President George Bush in response to the horrific events of September 11, 2001. It began with Al Qaeda being identified as the terrorist group responsible for the attacks. And since Afghanistan and its rulers, the Taliban, were harbouring the leaders of Al Qaeda, Afghanistan became the main target of the US anti-terrorist mission. The country and its people are no threat to the United States, but they are the ones taking the full weight of America's indignation. Afghanistan has been substituted for terrorism because it is accessible to military power and terrorism is not. More than seven years later the war goes on unabated, with shifting aims, new targets, expanding scope and refurbished strategies. Since the attack that took place on American soil is supposedly an attack on the freedom and civilization of the whole world, the war to combat terrorism is global in scope. The President's declaration, 'either you are with us or with the terrorists', amounts to laying down the law for the world, painting it in black and white with no shades of grey. Therefore Asia, and specifically Afghanistan, in this war scenario, gets identified as the 'other' in the language of the powerful.

The Pakistani writer, Feryal Ali Gauhar's novel *No Space for Further Burials* (2007) reveals the tragedy of such a clash between the powerful and the 'other'. With reference to Gauhar's novel I propose to claim that the war against terrorism involves crossing of borders at multiple levels other than the geographic. The anti-terrorist camp turns terrorist in its dealings; the fighter for freedom turns oppressor when violence is couched in defense of freedom; and the war to preserve civilizations becomes instrumental in destroying them. The myth of infallibility being shaken by the 9/11 attacks, there is an attempt at reordering the world for imperial motives. The central figure in Gauhar's novel is a US army medical technician who having strayed from his base is captured and incarcerated by warlords in Tarasmun, an abandoned mental asylum. Inside its walls, he finds himself in the midst of the mentally deranged, physically crippled and diseased inmates struggling to survive the lunacy raging outside the asylum compound. Sentenced to indefinite confinement in this 'tomb for the living', the 'victor' now becomes a 'victim' and gets drawn into the lives of his captors (*No Space for Further Burials* 8). The ambivalence of his position becomes a metaphor for the Afghanistan and the US situation. As the war progresses, finding food and finding space for further burials becomes a greater problem than guarding prisoners and the dividing line between prisoners and their captors slowly disintegrates. How, Ali Gauhar demands, do people survive in a world where the boundary between sanity and insanity dissolves, reality blends into nightmare and the difference between friends and foes becomes blurred because brutality comes from within and without?

Although it was claimed that the war against terrorism is different from other wars, it began in a most conventional way with an attack on a hapless country, a country already shredded by a history of earlier wars. The hundred years old, Noor Kaka, in the novel states, 'when I was a very young child there was another war, and then another, and several more throughout the time. I was growing up' (*No Space for Further Burials* 72). The asylum peopled with a cast of misfits, each with a scary story, a missing family member or a missing body part, becomes a metaphor for this country ravaged by poverty, deprivation and violence, and the anti-terrorist agenda further aggravates the humanitarian crisis in Afghanistan. The United States chooses to call it the 'War on Terror', but resorts to making it a war fought with terror. Indiscriminate violence becomes the rule rather than an exception because it is a much cheaper option than selective violence. As Greenwilli Byford puts it, 'a scrupulously honourable struggle is an unaffordable luxury' (qtd. in Koshy 39). The novel through the individual stories and the collective fate of the inmates of the asylum, recounts how helpless civilians are killed, maimed, villages destroyed and girls, boys and women brutalized in defense of freedom and civilization. They suffer for actions and decisions they had no involvement in. 'What nags me' broods the American soldier, 'are the things we were taught before we came to this land, the tenets of war, the rules of engagement .... The virtues of our coming over here, the need to liberate these people, the absolute necessity of "enduring freedom" .... Two words which don't mean anything to me any more' (*No Space for Further Burials* 51).

An attack on innocent people is a terrorist act. Targeting mainly civilians and non-combatants is a terrorist act. The 9/11 attacks which took the lives of some three thousand people certainly were acts of terrorism and deserve to be condemned in the strongest terms. But what do the US and its allies have to say about the pain and agony of thousands of innocent citizens in Afghanistan who died or were incapacitated by their carpet-bombing? In Gauhar's novel the half-crazed inmate Bulbul narrates how his father while working on a field stepped on a landmine which took his legs and one hand: 'There was so much blood that even the thirsty earth did not absorb it. It was like the blood of the sheep the elders of the village slaughter for the Festival of the Sacrifice. But this was my father's blood, my own father' (*No Space for Further Burials* 30). Another inmate Gul Agha's wife and four children were killed and one was maimed in a similar bomb explosion. The ironic part was that the incident got reported as the US warplanes having attacked a party of rebels. The American academic Professor Marc W. Herold established an estimate of about three thousand four hundred people killed only in the first two months of bombing, not to mention the thousands killed ever since. The killings of 9/11 are held up as a justification of the bombing of Afghanistan, a logic we can only agree to if we conclude that the lives of Americans are of greater value than the lives of Afghanis.

The narrative of *No Space for Further Burials* records the tragedy of Afghanistan as being caused by the perversity of international politics in which a nation and its people have been made pawns for petty territorial strategic gains. Gauhar uses the captive narrator's journal – ostensibly kept to fight the loneliness of imprisonment – as a literary device with which to draw in the reader. 'I wanted to reverse the experience of looking at America through my eyes' Gauhar explains, 'I wanted Afghanistan to be seen through an American's eyes' ("Femme Feryal: A Woman of Accomplishment"). The reader is asked to empathize with the narrator as he strives to cope with the ironic situation. For, it is the American 'liberator' who is now in confinement in a land he came to liberate. Within the debris of the asylum, he shares a miserable existence with Bulbul, Sabir, Waris, Noor Jahan and others. Amidst indiscriminate bombing by the US air force and random deaths of people in this make-shift prison, the novel becomes a story of solidarity between an American and his supposed enemies. With winter setting in, hunger drives them into a nightmare of horrors as many of them feed on bones and raw carcasses of maggot infested animals. The gory images shock the reader out of complacency and the novel becomes a severe indictment of the lunacy of war.

The American lives through his incarceration and pens horrifying episodes involving real people. There is the one-legged Sabir Shah who is thrown into prison for blasphemous act, but not before an acid attack causes him to lose an eye and fuses his jaw and neck. Then, there is Bulbul who recounts how the US soldiers had chopped off the trees in their devastated fields for fear of the rebels seeking shelter there, leaving poor farmers without fruit and shade. Their grim stories are balanced by positive images of Noor Jahan, a veritable Florence Nightingale in this waste land and her husband Waris, both of whom are the caretakers of this God-forsaken asylum and its forty inmates. It is through these survivors that the story of war-ravaged Afghanistan is untold. The personal stories provide a reflection of the collective complicity so often present in the perpetuation of violence. More importantly, *No Space for Further Burials* inverts the often hackneyed themes of displacement of war, America's role and the suffering Afghanis, ultimately treating these grim motifs by focusing on the tragedy implicit within personal narrative. The fall of the Taliban and the much publicized need to 'liberate' the Afghanis from burkha oppression and Taliban brutality, artfully exonerates the US aggressor. The global imperative links terror with Islamism. As Raja Rumi points out – 'In the age of the constructed 'Islamic threat', the novel deftly attacks the myth'. 'War, violence and suffering in Afghanistan have little to do with Islam', he claims ("Book Review").

In the novel, the reader is given no hints about the asylum inmates who could be refugees or derelicts, fugitives or just ordinary people declared insane. Their identity becomes immaterial in the face of a common constant state of loss – their personal, civil and political lives having being brutally violated. Even the American narrator is disempowered by the war machine and becomes one of them. The medic once aspired to be writer before he was sent to Afghanistan but in recounting the miseries of war he loses the ability to truly communicate. Instead his language is the language of suffering humanity, a thing that cuts across nationality and culture. The novel's narrative becomes a revelation of an oppressive power equation. The tortured images bring forth the brutal exploitation of the 'weaker' by the highly organized 'mighty' in the name of a democratic ideology.

The claim that the attack on September 11 constitutes the greatest tragedy and that it is an assault on justice, freedom and democracy all over the world, is to ignore historical prospective and sense of proportion in evaluating events. When thousands of people died in Hiroshima and Nagasaki as a result of American atom bombs that was Japan's problem. When thousands of children die every year in Iraq as a result of sanctions that is Iraq's problem. When India is torn by terrorist attacks that is India's problem. Any tragedy in any country is that country's problem. But when some three thousand people are killed in the United States, it is supposed to be the whole world's problem. This universalist claim tends to relativize and trivialize the histories, destinies and tragedies of other nations and people. As Gauhar points out – 'an act of violence carried out by "a person of colour" is an act of terror… [but] carried out by a person of 'no colour' is always to protect the freedom and democracy and the way of life of privileged people who have no idea how the other half lives, or in this case dies' ("The Birds Have Stopped Singing in Afghanistan"). Peace, freedom and democracy are elusive in this part of the world because the guns that are pointed at them are manufactured in lands where freedom and democracy flourish.

A US statutory definition of terrorism, frequently cited defines terrorism as 'premeditated, politically motivated violence against non-combatants by groups or individuals usually intended to influence an audience' (cited in Koshy 39). However, in their attempt to beat terrorism the US and its allies are themselves striking at the vulnerable in order to draw attention to the sins of the invulnerable. They have terrorized the entire populations by the threat of their military might for so long that for these people, as the American narrator observes in the novel, 'as if fear has been beaten our of them, as life itself has taken a beating' (*No Space for Further Burials* 21). 'Because in war', he saw that 'the victims are the poorest, the ones who have no choice, no power, no weapons with which to defend themselves' (*No Space for Further Burials* 52). War in international law means armed conflict between nations but the war against terrorism makes no distinction between the terrorists who committed the act and those who harbour them. By targeting the icons of American military and economic power, the terrorist strikes were intended to convey a message. But like the terrorists, the United States also has a global agenda. The war against terrorism is in reality an imperialist war that seeks to make the world secure for global economic and strategic interests of the United States and military occupation is intrinsic to the expansion of the American empire. The unipolar power structure being threatened, the war against terrorism becomes a project to reorder the world with military might.

The conflict as it emerges becomes a clash between the Muslim and the western world. However states and civilizations are not monolithic. Edward Said in an article titled "The Clash of Ignorance" commented that 'downright ignorance is involved in presuming to speak for a whole religion or civilization'. He further states that the carefully planned horrendous suicide attacks of 9/11 should be seen for what they are, 'the capture of big ideas by a tiny band of crazed fanatics for criminal purposes' (qtd. in Koshy 23). The perpetrators are terrorists that adorn the self-relegated title of 'freedom fighters'. The Bush administration, by declaring the fight against Al Qaeda to be a 'war', reinforces the terrorist narrative that they are warriors, not outlaws and are, therefore, entitled to kill their enemies. But who are the enemies? The war paradigm stretches, distorts and plays with the definition of an enemy, so that often the rebel soldiers end up brutalizing and terrorizing the defenseless people of their own country. The US medic in the novel, while narrating such an incident in his diary, writes: 'the rain came sooner than expected and the soldiers came with it, turning the water in the well red with blood, shooting for sport .... Three men were killed, their bodies dumped in the well. Their crime? They resisted the soldiers who wanted their shoes – broken, mended, scuffed pieces of leather and rubber, which cost them their lives' (*No Space for Further Burials* 42–43).

The war claims to be an intermingling of militarism and moralism. The rhetoric used is that the war on terror is the war against 'the evil of terror' as the cold war was against the 'evil of communism'. It was to free the people of Afghanistan from the oppressive fundamentalist regime of the Taliban rule. But since the Al Qaeda leadership was a baby of the United States, fed and nourished to fight the 'evil of communism', its ideology sabotages the fight against 'the evil of terror'. In Gauhar's novel, the American soldier's inability to escape the asylum depicts the American frustration of having been caught in one's own trap. He was to fight to liberate the Afghanis from the Taliban regime but is himself taken a prisoner by the Afghan rebels. Also victimized by his own country, the American soldier is not sure of who the enemy is any more and the coldness and insensitivity of the perpetrators of war hits him. 'The bombers in their jets' he observes, 'would have been so far in the sky that they would not have seen any living thing except on their radar screens, and they would have released the bombs according to the computations of the latest technology'. 'I don't know who the bombs were targeting' he says, 'all I know is that it cost many lives and none of them was the enemy' (*No Space for Further Burials* 69).

The problem is that the revulsion that the US shows against terrorism is selective. By defining terrorism by the nature of the act and not the motivation behind it is like treating the symptoms and not the disease. Dealing with symptoms can only be an emergency measure. The war against Afghanistan was the immediate anti-terrorist coup, but terror cannot be fought by terror. It is important to look beyond the terrorist acts and specifically address the causes of grievances and frustrations that motivate terrorism. It could be the unusually bitter polarisation between the 'haves' and the 'have-nots'. Or, as Andrew Johnson puts it, 'The danger for America is that its overwhelming power is feeding resentment' (qtd.in Koshy, 24). But fighting terrorism through terror only establishes what is resented. The vicious circle complete, the war goes on. As Gauhar points out, 'unless the dynamics of domination and submission is changed, unless greed and hatred and prejudice are whittled away, the terror will continue to breed in camps of the disenfranchised and the desperate' ("The Birds Have Stopped Singing in Afghanistan"). A credible approach towards combating international terrorism, therefore, must be founded on general ethical principles including those of human rights because however noble or legally justified a cause may be, the end does not always justify the means.

By touching at the colonial great game in Afghanistan *No Space for Further Burials* echoes the continuation of violence that has become a part of Afghanistan's reality. The novel is a severe indictment of the lunacy of war which is undertaken to bring 'liberty and democracy' to Afghanistan, ideals that back fire at the natives of the country for they are incomprehensive to their agents – the US armed forces. The neo-colonial bully uses the 'Savior' act to monitor its borders, exterminate 'tyrants' and thereby build its empire. Gauhar's novel explores the hollowness of democracy and the outrage committed in its name and moves us to interrogate parallel war cultures.

Works Cited

Gauhar, Feryal Ali. *No Space for Further Burials*. New Delhi: Women Unlimited, 2007.

Koshy, Ninan. *The War on Terror: Reordering the World*. New Delhi: Left World, 2003.

Online

Gauhar, Feryal Ali. "The Birds Have Stopped Singing in Afghanistan". http://www.mindfully.org/Reform/2003/Birds_Stopped_Feryal/16 Oct. 03 11 May 2008.

Herold, Marc. W. "A Dossier on Civilian Victims of United States' Aerial Bombing of Afghanistan: A Comprehensive Account". http://www.cursor.org/stories/civilian.deaths.htm 11 May 2008.

Raza, Rumi."Book Review: *No Space for Further Burials*, a Novel on Afghanistan by Feryal Ali Gauhar". http://blogcritics.org/archives/2008/02/18/012250.php. 24 October 2008.

Raza, Rumi. "Femme Feryal: A Woman of Accomplishment". http://pakistaniyat.com/2007/03/20. 24 October 2008.

6

PURABI PANWAR

Violence and Life in a Metro City: A Look at *Maximum City* and *Sacred Games*

Violence has become an integral part of life in a metro city, anywhere in the world. No I am not talking of specific instances of man made aggression that has resulted in large scale violence, starting from the Holocaust down to acts of terrorism that resulted in death and destruction on a large scale all over the world. Two recent cases that come to one's mind are the 9/11 incident the World Trade Centre and the terrorist attacks on the local trains in Mumbai. In this paper I propose to discuss something far more sinister because it goes deeper than the sporadic instances mentioned earlier. I propose to look at the way in which violence has become inseparable from life in big cities. This would be done on a literary level with substantiation from two books – *Maximum City* by Suketu Mehta – a chronicle of life in a metro city, in this case Mumbai and *Sacred Games* by Vikram Chandra – a novel based largely in Mumbai, that traces the nexus between the underworld, police, intelligence agencies that operate under cover, godmen, arms dealers, film stars, politicians and all those who matter.

The question that one is sure to ask at this point is why violence has become a part of life in a big city. As Frantz Fanon, the Marxist ideologist puts it, 'Violence alone, violence committed by the people ... and organized by the leaders makes it possible for the masses to understand social truths and gives the key to them' (*The Wretched of the Earth* 118). To put it very simply, the inequalities of life and living standards in a metro city breed resentment which, in turn, generates violence. Roughly speaking six out of ten people live in slums or similar places whereas the rest live a luxurious life. This is bound to lead to seething discontent on the part of the have-nots who feel that they have every right to lead luxurious lives and feel frustrated at the kind of lives they are forced to lead by circumstances beyond their control.

Suketu Mehta left Bombay (before it was renamed Mumbai) at the age of fourteen in 1977 with his parents to settle in New York. When he came back for a visit twenty-one years later, he wanted to rediscover the city by writing a book on it. He realized while working on the book that a lot had changed about the city. From Bombay it had become Mumbai and along with the name much else had metamorphosed. All the joys of coming back to a familiar place evaporated and he is brutally frank about it: 'Any nostalgia I felt about my childhood has been erased. Given the chance to live again in the territory of childhood, I am coming along to detest it' (33).

However, as one reads the book, one realizes that it is the non-resident Indian, the exile who is a 'citizen of the country of longing' (33) to borrow Mehta's words, who is able to portray the city in a realistic, almost surreal manner, a love-hate relationship that is in keeping with the innate violence that pervades the book. One should keep this in mind as one reads through the three sections in the book: Power, Pleasure and Passage, which deal with the three main obsessions of the city. As Mehta moves through the slums of Mumbai, talking to people there, he is amazed at their vitality. He describes the slum vividly, 'Much of the slum is a garbage dump. The sewers which are open, run right between the houses, and children play and occasionally fall into them. They are full of a blue-black iridescent sludge.' If one were to read between the lines, the open sewers and the 'blue-black iridescent sludge' might be taken as a symbol of the innate resentment that could very well explode into violence.

Sacred Games starts on a note of violence. Fluffy, a white Pomeranian, is thrown out of the fifth floor window of a high rise building by Mr Pandey, who suspects that his wife, an air hostess, is having an affair with another man. As Sartaj Singh, a policeman and one of the central characters of the novel, goes to the flat intending to pull Mr Pandey up, the latter shows welts on his body where his wife had hit him with a stick, as well as scratch marks. Sartaj's reaction, 'Love is a murderous gaandu. Poor Fluffy' (5). Marital violence sets the scene for violence on a larger scale. What about the colourful language used by Sartaj Singh here and elsewhere in the novel, rather literally? Like the 'blue-black iridescent sludge' referred to earlier, this could be another symbol of innate violence that one associates with policemen (as well as gangsters in the novel). In *The Wretched of the Earth* Fanon talks of violence in the colonial situation as the colonized try to rid themselves of the colonial shackles, but I feel that is a limited perception. In any relationship or situation, an assertion of power, to capture or retain power, leads to a manifestation of violence.

This can be manifested in all kinds of ways, some rather subtle and a casual look might not reveal the innate violence. Parulkar, a Deputy Commissioner of Police, is Sartaj's guru in a way, having taught him how to live and work as a policeman in the city, surviving all kinds of odds. Parulkar's achievement as a police officer as perceived by his subordinates needs to be quoted to make one aware of the extent of power wielded by the police, any time, any place. 'he was a grand-master of the subtle art of contact and double-contact and back-channel, of ministers and corporators cultivated and kept happy, business interests allowed room for profits, backslapping and exchanges with commissioners of police, favours finely weighed and dispensed and remembered, deals made and forgotten – he was an aficionado of the subtle sport, he was simply the best' (9). Yet, when the time comes, Sartaj does not hesitate to make use of him to further his own means, something that makes Parulkar commit suicide as he is cornered. Survival at any cost is the name of the game and naturally it involves violence.

A sensitive writer like Amitav Ghosh responds to violence quite differently. He was in Delhi in 1984 during the mob violence that followed Mrs Indira Gandhi's assassination and this had a great influence of *The Shadow Lines*, a novel that he was to start writing within a few months, to the extent he referred to it later as 'a book that led me backwards in time to earlier memories of riots, ones witnessed in childhood. It became a book not about any one event but about the meaning of such events and their effects on individuals who live through them.' ("The Ghosts of Mrs Gandhi", *The Imam and the Indian*). Ghosh generalizes, 'The truth is that the commonest response to violence is one of repugnance and that a significant number of people everywhere try to oppose it in whatever way they can. That these efforts rarely appear in accounts of violence is not surprising: they are too undramatic. For those who participate in them, they are hard to write about for the very reason that so long delayed my own account of 1984' (162).

However response to a similar event would differ from writer to writer. The way Suketu Mehta handles the description of the underworld, is a case in point. Most persons writing about Mumbai would feel uncomfortable being explicit about the underworld for fear of annoying the dons. Not so Suketu Mehta, he is very open about it. To quote him, 'In Bombay, the underworld is an overworld, it is somehow suspended above this world and can come down and strike at any time it chooses' (145). This imminence is frightening but one cannot deny that it exists, nor wish it away. He talks with Satish and Mohsin, Hindu and Muslim gang "shooters" who take their orders from Chhota Rajan and Dawood Ibrahim, who went the polarized way of the underworld of Mumbai, post-1993.

A newspaper interviewer asked Mehta if he ever got into danger while interviewing these people and he admitted that there were at least two such occasions. To quote, 'Once my driver had taken me to meet some hitmen in a hotel. When I did not return for some hours, he called up my wife in panic. But I had not been in any trouble that time. There was another instance when I had been dead scared. A trigger happy gangster pointed his gun at me and said, *"Tumhe maut se dar hai kya?"* Thankfully he decided it was not the right time to kill me.' Mehta's encounters with persons from the underworld are juxtaposed with his meetings with Ajay Lal, Additional Commissioner of Police and taken together, they throw a light on the deteriorating law and order situation in the city where the underworld has become the overworld and extortion has become an almost regular *dhanda*. He manages to talk to Chhota Shakeel who tells him repeatedly that he never gave interviews and this was an exceptional case, 'he has no need of fame, and he is doing this only because I, a man from America, have travelled so far to talk to him' (263). The question that occurs to one at this point is whether Suketu Mehta asserts his superiority as the chronicler of Bombay/Mumbai who has travelled all the way from America to talk to the 'black-collar workers' like him in which case it is an assertion of his first world identity. Or is it that he is trying to show the indispensable role to the underworld hence dwells on characters like Chhota Shakeel who help the parallel economy to run smoothly?

Whatever the case might be, the seamy side of Mumbai appears much more fascinating, even glamorous to an extent, as seen in the writings of Vikram Chandra. Of course one has to take into consideration the difference in the genres of the two books. A chronicler has to operate within a certain framework whereas a novelist can let his or her imagination run riot without worrying too much about consequences.

How is it that Ganesh Gaitonde, the don, appears more attractive than Sartaj Singh? Chandra appears to be exploring the constant, explicit, almost poetic violence which threads itself into the narrative. What does Chandra have to say about this? His words, 'Somebody like Gaitonde, I did want him to have that exultation when you destroy an enemy. Just trying to get that feel down on the page … . If you like watching American football, for instance, it's the same impulse really. No matter how much we try to deny it, all of us have some weird corner which has something like that. The history of the human race is fairly demonstrative of that … . The human propensity for violence. People do it. So I certainly didn't want to flinch away from that aspect of the character, or of the world we live in.'

The key phrase in the passage just quoted is 'the human propensity for violence', something which aggravates in a city because of the physical conditions, the density. One must also remember that it is easier to portray violence and make it more attractive. All the virtues seem to wane when compared to violence or evil. A classical example: Milton's Satan always appears more attractive and real as compared to his God. Of course in *Maximum City* and *Sacred Games* there are very few characters who are absolutely virtuous, except for Sartaj's mother and Mary Mascarenas. Paradoxically, she is the sister of Jojo Mascarenas, Ganesh Gaitonde's close confidante and friend, someone he has never slept with and does not intend to, but trusts completely. The end when it comes, is violent, he is paranoid about staying put in his nuclear shelter while she is desperate to get out of it. So he kills her and then shoots himself. The two sisters are absolutely opposites, possibly indicating polarities of life in a city.

No current study of Mumbai is complete without a reference to the growth of communal hatred in the city, post-1993. Mehta recalls his growing up years in Mumbai, 'In the Bombay I grew up, being Muslim or Hindu or Catholic was merely a personal eccentricity, like a hairstyle.' Not any more. 'Now being a Hindu, Muslim or Christian mattered. Because it mattered to Bal Thackeray' (62). Mehta's study of the Shiv Sena based on his conversations with Sunil as well as other Shiv Sainiks, combined with his visits to the Sena Shakhas, reveal an understanding of the static violence generated by the Sena in its heyday, that was part of life in Mumbai. Chandra does not highlight politics or politicians in his novel but focuses on the underworld with which they have close links.

While analyzing the phenomenon of urban violence in a general way, one cannot overlook some of its basic characteristics and contributory factors. The process of urbanization is much faster in developing countries like India as compared to developed ones. Here the pace is accelerated by a declining rural economy as holdings become smaller and smaller with each generation. This pressure on the economy creates an influx of migrant population from the rural belt to the urban centres. Cities and towns become new found shelters for the unskilled labour force in search of a livelihood. A close look at members of underworld gangs in both the books, reveals that many of the younger ones belong to this category. Unable to find a regular job/means to earn a livelihood, they have joined a gang. It seems an easy way to earn a lot of money in a short time. Some like Aadil join radical political groups. Frustrated with social inequalities, they kill policemen, loot weapons, hoping this would arm them for the greater struggle that would eliminate class altogether, something they innocently believe in, having been indoctrinated. Slowly violence becomes their way of life. As Chandra puts it, 'Aadil planned the operations, the executions in response to massacres, the ambushes of police convoys and kidnappings of engineers and doctors. He discovered an instinctive feeling for feint and counter-blow, for subterfuge and evasions. He delighted in the success of his scheme. He was no longer sickened by the smell of human blood' (861).

Revolutionary philosophers like Marx and Engels justified violence as part of the historical process of class struggle. They believed that social change and development are the products of class struggle and its intensification will lead to a social revolution. Once the dictatorship of the proletariat is established, it will ruthlessly use force to eliminate every vestige of capitalism and also prevent the possibility of counter-revolution. It is not easy to fit the underworld into this scheme of things but one must keep in mind the notion that they too believe in a sort of rough dispensation of justice, settling disputes, looking after the interests of a certain community etc. Violence is glorified, not only by the Marxists but Bollywood as well. So one comes across films like *Shootout at Lokhandwala* based on a real life shootout at the same venue and *Deewar* a film based on the life of Haji Mastan, a Mumbai smuggler and don of the seventies.

Interestingly, in both these films as in the books under discussion, the bad characters appear more interesting than the law enforcing agencies. In *Sacred Games* too, one finds Ganesh Gaitonde more interesting than Sartaj Singh though one is aware from the beginning that the latter would win. Chandra once told a journalist, 'Writing Gaitonde was an interesting exercise in sympathy with a man who is quite unsympathetic.' His story is best told by himself (ironically to Sartaj Singh). A destitute and scarred childhood, a struggle to survive, a shot in the dark and a cache of gold biscuits, Gaitonde's story is recounted by himself as a steady progress from triumph to triumph. That is, till he loses his wife and son in a shootout in which twenty two persons die. The intensity of grief is brought out in a deceptively simple passage. To quote, 'But all my hard-won calm was taken from me by Abhi's laughter which I heard floating in the afternoon sunlight. At night, I went regularly to my pillow because I knew he would come to me in my sleep, but my very waiting chased sleep away' (467). There is nothing to anchor him any more, to bring out the humane side of his nature.

This is the heart of the matter. Most characters in both books are without roots, have nothing to anchor them. This brings out the violence in them. This again is the characteristic of a big city. There are no roots and there is an intense desire to succeed, conditions that contribute to an explosive situation, which in turn is more than likely to erupt into violence – domestic violence, caste violence, communal violence, political violence, in short violence at every level in society. Frantz Fanon observed as I have already pointed out, 'Violence alone, violence committed by people, violence initiated and organized by leaders, makes it possible for the masses to understand social truths and gives the key to them.' This is a debatable point. While one sees that violence is committed by the people and quite often initiated and organized by the leaders, one is not sure how it enables people to understand social truth and access power. Violence at different levels has become part of life in a metro city and is therefore reflected in the writing about urban spaces whether a chronicle or fiction. However, one does not quite see the point of justifying it or even glorifying it as Marxists do. One has to accept it and search for ways in which one can negotiate it.

Work Cited

Chandra, Vikram. *Sacred Games*. New Delhi: Penguin, 2006.

Fanon, Frantz. *The Wretched of the Earth* (1961). Translated by Constance Farrington. Harmondsworth: Penguin, 1967.

Ghosh, Amitav. "The Ghosts of Mrs. Gandhi" in *The Imam and the Indian: Prose Pieces*. Delhi: Ravi Dayal Publisher & Permanent Black, 2002.

Mehta, Suketu. *Maximum City: Bombay Lost and Found*. New Delhi: Penguin (2004), 2006.

Rushdie, Salman. "Interview with Wall Street Journal", http://www.suketu-mehta.com/wsje.html.

7

USHA BANDE

The Politics of Honour/Horror: An Analysis of Mukhtar Mai's *In The Name of Honour*

> Cindrella ...
> Now the time has come,
> Say, which side you have to go?
> But do remember that you were alone inside.
> Alone you are, so shall you always remain.
> But outside ...
> Outside there shall be many Cindrellas ...
>
> Saroop Dhruva.[1]

In analyzing Mukhtar Mai's *In the Name of Honour,* this paper proposes to problematize three seminal points: the cultural practice of honour rape; the efficacy of subaltern voice; and the role of translation, in this particular case. These issues are interlinked and while focusing on one, we cannot disregard the others. The question I wish to address is: what happens when a subaltern speaks? Let us presume that the subaltern *can* speak but then let us ask: 'with what results'? Since the time Gayatri Spivak asked: 'Can a subaltern speak?' this question has raised many a literary debates, so much so that it has become a cliché now; though it still holds and can generate several questions/answers. Mukhtaran Bibi's story is saddening; it evokes our sympathy and anger; but the book requires to be assessed as a translation of translation to understand its basic value as a piece of literature.

In patriarchal discourse, the notion of community's identity rests on the modesty of women and any violation thereof becomes a denominator of the shame of the weaker community and the reaffirmation of the rival community's power. By a curious logic of patriarchy, women have since ages been the upholders of man's – and by implication – community's honour: be it Sita or Draupadi, Amba or Ahilya, and more recently, Gudiya or Mukhtaran Bibi. Women not only have the onus to safeguard it but they are the ones to bear the brunt of the rival community's vengeance; and conversely, they become the symbol of the rape of their community and a constant reminder to the menfolk of the assertion of the aggressor's position of power. This happened during partition rapes, and this has happened in recent times to Mukhtaran Bibi and many like her.

Discussing the specific trends in the communal violence during partition, Kumari Jayawardena and Malathi de Alwis observe in their "Introduction" to *Embodied Violence* that taking revenge on the 'Other' community's men by violating their women is a common practice during communal violence (Jayawardena and Alwis xvii).[2] Further in the same book Kalpana Kannabiran, in her paper "Rape and the Construction of Communal Identity" focuses on the two ways in which community identity is established and asserted: one is rape of the 'Other' community's women; and the second is allegations of rape or aggression levelled by the dominant community against the 'Other' community. Rape signifies the rape of the other community as a whole and the allegations serve to create 'a condition for the total refusal of safeguards – constitutional or otherwise – for women' of the weak community (Kannabiran 33). The former entails direct revenge and the latter gives the stronger community an excuse to take revenge. Either way the weaker community is made to suffer in such a 'culture of power.'[3]

Mukhtaran Bibi's case falls within the same parameters as discussed by Kannabiran – first, allegations against her brother and then rape of Mukhtaran to prove the weak community guilty, and also to assert the strong community's power. Mukhtaran Bibi's book, *In the Name of Honour: A Memoir* is an exposition of how in the patriarchal hegemonic structure the concept of honour and identity rests on women and how through them the community is punished. That is not all; punishment is also a warning to women that no compromise with *izzat* would be tolerated. As Shaila Shah points out, 'Violence, and the right to use it is sanctioned, the so-called crimes of honour being designed to keep a woman in her place: silenced, mutilated or even destroyed' (Shah 284).

However, as we read on, our focus shifts from punishment and pain to the triumph of "voice" that the memoir portrays. This is not, however, to deny the magnitude of Mukhtaran's trauma but to privilege her subject position so as to authenticate the power of "speech" and to affirm that marginality does not require the usual over-valorization which hinders human growth. The process to understand her own voice, to question and assess her role in her own culture has resulted in assigning meaning to her experiences for other women. Mukhtaran Bibi breaks her silence but breaking the silence has its severe repercussions which she has to face; the public/private dichotomy gets blurred and she feels vulnerable being thus exposed. Here we encounter two issues: the effectiveness of subaltern voice and the efficacy of translation. The media helps her get global attention, that is one significant point but then, we as literary critics cannot overlook the fact that what comes to us is a translated version which makes it imperative to evaluate the memoir as translation to assess its authenticity.

In the Name of Honour is a first person narrative of Mukhtaran Bibi's sad but daring story put in words by Marie-Therese Cuny, an activist and writer from France. The publisher's "A Note to the Reader" makes it clear that Mukhtaran Bibi speaks only Saraiki dialect and she 'can read or write no other language.' Mustafa Baloch and Saif Khan helped in translating the conversation between Mukhtaran and Cuny and – 'Marie-Therese Cuny transformed Mukhtaran's thoughts, emotions and impressions into the book, despite the hurdle posed by the great disparity of language'. The book is in French and the French version has been translated in English by Linda Coverdale and published by Philippe Robinet.

At this point, let us study the layers of translation: (i) Mukhtaran speaks in Saikia dialect; (ii) it is translated into French orally; (iii) Cuny, the writer picks up the oral version and writes it down; (iv) she translates Mukhtaran's emotions and sentiments via the two men translators; (v) her writing is then translated into English. In the process how much of Mukhtaran's original thoughts come directly to us? Whose ideas come to us – the readers – Mukhtaran's or the author's or the translator's? It is often accepted that translation requires some measure of "faithfulness". But then who should it be faithful to – to the text or to the author or to the reader? There is another point: translation also calls for a certain amount of creative freedom to make it readable otherwise it addresses only the surface meaning missing out on core or quintessence. In Mukhtaran's book one may sometimes wonder if the sentiments are Mukhtaran's or the author's. But, the text conveys the essence and herein lies its success.

Marie-Therese Cuny and Philippe Robinet are white feminists from the First world; Mukhtaran belongs to a remote tribal village of Pakistan. Can these women pave the difference to appreciate the ethnic view-point? Recently feminists have been contending that differences can be silenced by discussions. By understanding women's positions in their respective cultures, a meaningful and unified feminism would be possible if instead of 'passive immersion' in each other's cultures they strive to understand each other's 'voice'. Only then a mutual dialogue is possible, a dialogue that does not reduce women to abstraction called 'woman'. That Mukhtaran and Cuny have been able to articulate their experiences, they have refused to be silenced, and they have been heard is comparable to the feminist strategies of sharing and bonding. Articulation of experiences, it is contended, is the hallmark of a self-determining community or individual.

There is probably nothing new in Mukhtaran Bibi's rape case; what is new is the boldness of her stand, the courage to speak and the vision for the future of her community's girls. With the compensation money she received, she opened a girls' school in her village which is flourishing and a Women's Crisis Center which is the mainstay for battered and abused women of Pakistan. Mukhtaran Bibi is called Mukhtaran Mai – elder sister – and she has become the fountainhead of courage, opening up new possibilities for women as individuals. Mukhtaran's story is of 'honour rape,' a scourge that is ingrained in the patriarchal psyche in both India and Pakistan. Unfortunately this social evil has since long remained unchallenged. The predicament of women victims of these local village *panchayats* has been brought out by me in an article published in *The Sunday Tribune*, Chandigarh, wherein I question the damaging role played by Khap, Oor and other village *Panchayats* in dealing out punishment to women.[4] *Jigra Panchayats* prevalent in the villages in Pakistan follow similar patterns of punishment. Unfortunately, honour crimes are not taken seriously by the hegemony, be it India or Pakistan, and honour criminals are often acquitted. When her case was in the court, Mukhtaran Bibi was apprehensive about getting justice since things as they stand are not affable to women: 'Until now, no man, not even a criminal, has ever been punished for "a crime of honour", so the accused are confident that in the end, they will leave the court room as free men' (69). But public outcry, international focus and the positive approach of a judge helped her to a great extent. She won the case once and is hoping for a fair deal at the Supreme Court of Pakistan, where her case is lying at present.

Mukhtaran's life prior to the ill-fated day was simple. Born in 1972 in Meerwala, a small tribal village in Jatoi tehsil of Muzaffarabad District of Pakistan, Mukhtaran belongs to the Tatla clan – an impoverished and marginalized Gujar tribe. When pitted against the powerful Mastois, the Gujars have no option but to obey their command. This reality of their situation recoiled on the blameless and hapless Mukhtaran when in June 2002 she was gang-raped in full view her own parents and the entire village, and paraded half-naked. Her crime? Only that she happened to be a marginalized woman – not only because she is the daughter of the poor Gujars but also because she is a divorcee, someone fit to be slighted.

Mukhtaran tells of her marriage and divorce in simple straightforward narration. She is illiterate but she had been teaching the Koran orally to the children of the village free of charge; she supplemented the family income by embroidery work. By the village standard, she was a "respectable" woman and hence chosen to appear before the *Jigra* (village council). Significantly, her vulnerability as a divorcee was camouflaged as her "respectability" and she became the scapegoat on whom the Mastois could wreck vengeance. When asked, 'Why me?' her father and uncle explained to her that the other girls 'are too young to do this. Your husband has granted you a divorce, you have no children, you teach the Koran. You are a respectable woman' (4). Our question here could be 'to *do* what?' Get raped and ravaged? Or to cringe before the beastly Mastois begging pardon for an imaginary crime? We tend to ask, 'did the male members of her family know what was in the offing?' In all probability they were in the know of it. Thrice in the course of her narrative Mukhtaran remarks that in their society women are never told or explained anything. They just follow the diktats of their men. 'Mukhtaran, get ready and follow us,' said her father when they were to leave for the *jigra*. This one sentence is enough to prove the point we are making.

Central to Mukhtaran Bibi's rape was power politics. The simple arithmetic of their hegemonic power structure is 'the Mastois decide and the Gujars obey' (7). The Mastois, 'an influential and aggressive local clan' (3), had suggested earlier that Mukhtaran may be given in marriage to one of the Mostois, towards which her father was not favorably inclined. To avenge this disrespect to their power and social position, they tried to implicate Shakur, Mukhtaran's brother, in a sex scandal accusing him first of having 'spoken' to Salma, the wild and wily daughter of the Mastois; then they charged him of committing *zina-bil-jabar*, 'which in Pakistan means the sin of rape, adultery, or sexual relations without the sanctity of marriage.' The allegations against Shakur were ridiculous and baseless, to say the least. Shakur was a minor, just twelve; Salma was in her twenties and of dubious character. But Salma was a Mastoi and nobody dared speak against her in defense of Shakur; it was, therefore, easy to trap Shakur and cover up Salma's waywardness. *Zina-bil-jabar* is punishable by death. The only course open to save Shakur's life was to appease the Mastois and it could be possible only if Mukhtaran was sacrificed on the altar of 'honour'. Summing up the vulnerable position of her community, Mukhtaran Bibi recounts that the marginalized Gujars – economically, politically and socially – were terrified of Mastois retaliation: 'Their powerful clan leader knows many influential people, and they are violent men, capable of invading anyone's home with their guns to loot, rape, and tear the place apart. The lower-caste Gujars have no right to oppose them, and no one in my family dared to go to their house' (5).

In the hierarchical power structure of their system, women are at the lowest rung and the younger women are the lowest of the lowest. The unquestioned pattern is that men decide and women follow. Mukhtaran puts it thus: 'Women are rarely informed about the decisions of men, and my father and uncle have told me very little ...' (14). As regards the younger women, they are never guided by the elder women but are taught through oblique remarks; the young girls are supposed to pick up their knowledge of the laws of life from the suggestions, evocative remarks and suggestive tittle-tattle circulating around them. This creates a vicious atmosphere in their homes where growing up means stealing from 'the words of others' (91). Mukhtar Mai calls it an 'invisible' existence and an education that taught them 'distrust, obedience, submission, fear, abject respect for men. It teaches us to forget ourselves' (92).

The compelling character of this situation is not unexpected, since its essential postulations about their community's organization and human nature are extensively accepted in their society. Neither the men nor the women understand that hierarchies bring out the worst in individuals, and that while those at the bottom suffer particularly, the entire social structure is disfigured, warped and narrowed by such notions of servility. It is never easy to subvert the myth of the powerful nor is it possible to redefine the place of women in a society where the tension between creating consensus and encouraging critical debate is kept alive by the impoverished understanding of its members and by the political climate of hostility to change.

It would be naïve to believe that Mukhtaran Mai's encounter with the patriarchal power structure, the law and the State was smooth and effortless. On the contrary, it was beset with experiences of acute fear and uncertainty from which neither the media nor the international support could guard her. The Mastois were infuriated as soon as the rape was reported in the media. Initially, Mukhtaran and her family had no role in contacting the media – indeed, they were too poor, ignorant and terror-stricken to think of it. The news probably spread when some men of the Mastoi clan boasted of their exploits on their visit to the town, which some local press journalist happened to hear, he investigated and gave an account of it in a local paper. Bronwyn Curran, a Pakistan-based Australian journalist, was the first to report it in the foreign media.

Mukhtaran's role started only after the rape case became public – she was flooded with reporters and cameramen to tell more and she who had locked herself up and was contemplating suicide, suddenly resolved to punish the wrongdoers. Mukhtaran found her voice, narrated the entire story, telling even the rapists' names. This brought shockwaves in her community as it put the Mastois on an alert. They could never imagine that a woman could open her mouth. This courage, despite the counsel of her relatives, landed her in trouble and psychological stress – it was not easy to counter the enraged Mastois, the now-estranged wellwishers and the villagers. There were threats and the panic of being wiped out and the social stigma (not of the rape but, ironically, of speaking out and generating controversy). Added to this was the distress and disgrace of having to spend days and nights in police protection. It was traumatic for the simple Mukhtaran to realize that her female body had become an emblem of personal and political vendetta. But she resolved to speak out, to make things public because it was now or never.

There is no doubt that her determination to speak, to voice her grievances and to avenge her dishonour was a kind of revolt – an absolutely new terrain for the meek young woman. Mukhtaran calls it 'a springboard for survival, a weapon for my revolt as I seek to avenge my humiliation, a weapon still untested, yet precious to me – because it's the only one I have. I will have justice, or death. Perhaps both' (28).

Usually, oppression requires the silence of the 'other.' Once the 'other' recognizes his/her right to speak, he/she participates in the construction of subject-position. Mukhtar Mai's determination to fight back is strengthened because of her father's support and her own reckless thoughts that nothing worse could happen to her now. In her assertion, 'I have learnt to exist and to respect myself as a woman' (110), there is acceptance of the self which implies re-affirmation of her strength discovered through speech. The woman who was reeling under the cruel 'feeling of guilt for having been raped' (24) and who thought suicide was the only alternative to regain her honour, acquired a changed perception of herself when she stood 'a single woman of inferior caste' against the power of the Mastois. 'My presence in this exceptional tribunal can only mean, however, that fate has chosen to show me the way to justice. And if the verdict is fair, it will be my revenge. Standing before these cringing men in chains, I'm no longer afraid to testify, coldly, and without extraneous details' (71).

In her essay "Small Speeches, Subaltern Gender" Kamala Visweswaran refers to speech as agency and shows how the importance of women's speech is directly relational to the social status of her husband or the male member. Although Visweswaran's paper deals with the nationalist movement and Indian women's political speeches (who were from the elitist, educated classes fighting for India's freedom), some of the points she makes apply to general conditions also. 'Speech as agency,' she says, 'invokes the idea of self-originating presence, so that conversely, lack of speech is seen as absence.' In Mukhtar Mai's case, the breaking of silence and her personal presence in the court made her an autonomous subject, in a way. Again, Visweswaran says, 'since speech was often equated with agency, a second means of containing women's agency was to dismiss the power of their speech by arguing for the influence of male relatives. But again, respectability and social status were key, for if a woman's husband was unimportant, she must also be unimportant, and so, therefore, her speech' (Visweswaran 90–91). Mukhtaran Mai's family was 'unimportant' in the sense that they were subalterns themselves, a low status family as against the Mastois. That is one reason for her to be silenced. Second, she was a divorcee and so 'unimportant' because her husband was 'unimportant' in her life. Either way she was fit to be exploited and silenced. Though her family has been supportive, they too applied tactics to bar her speech or movement like her elder brother stopping her from going abroad.

Mukhtar Mai's memoir is inclusive as she narrates many stories of victim women who come to her Crisis Center with their anguish and a hope to get support. Mukhtaran comprehends that the situation of women in her country is not much different from her own. Slowly it dawns on her that torture, rape, battering and suchlike atrocities are common occurrences in her land. These are as much private as institutionalized and to a large extent are deeply ingrained in the social psyche. A small pretext or a minor lapse is enough to dispose of or mute forever a woman/wife and if she speaks out it is construed as a challenge to male power and becomes an unpardonable crime. Mukhtar Mai says,

> 'Whatever the pretext – divorce, supposed adultery, or a settling of accounts among men – women pay the heaviest price. They may be given as compensation for an offence or raped as a form of reprisal by their husband's enemies. Sometimes all it takes for two men to quarrel about something, and one of them will take revenge on the other's wife. The common practice in our villages is for men to take justice into their own hands, invoking the principle of 'an eye for an eye'. It is always a question of honour, and they may do as they please: cut off a woman's nose, burn a sister, rape a neighbour's wife'. (67)

There no end to *honour revenge/honour killing*; it continues even after the death or arrest of the criminal because then his (criminal's) family instead of dousing the fire tries to settle the score. It becomes a never-ending enmity and the victim has no respite from fear, no peace. Violence and its corollaries – fear, anxiety and trepidation – terrorize Mukhtaran and her people. Such terrorizing tactics accentuate the hegemonic definition of woman's place in the fundamentalist society and subalterns' lowly position in their village.

The mechanism of the systemic intimidation – ridicule, false sympathy, official apathy, and nerve-racking tactics like derogatory remarks, jokes, ogling and obscene suggestions – starts as soon as Mukhtaran is viewed as a threat to the ideology. This is not something new or unusual in the subcontinent when the law enforcing authorities get into their trap women or the subaltern. Let us digress here for a while and refer to two examples from Indian fiction. In Arundhati Roy's *God of Small Things*, Velutha is beaten to death in the police lock-up, later in the police station Ammu is not only derided but also humiliated when the Inspector taps on her breasts with his baton and calls her a *veshya*. Kiran Desai, in her *The Inheritance of Loss* describes how the police implicate an innocent drunkard for the theft he has not committed, beat him mercilessly and almost cripple him. His fault? He has no Godfather to speak for him. Both Roy and Desai are furious at the system though they camouflage their rage under bitter humour.

The police officers are not sympathetic to Mukhtaran either. Taking advantage of her illiteracy they twist the case so miserably that there is no similarity between Mukhatran's 'reality' and the police record. The lower court acquits the criminals who now openly pose a threat to her and her family; the villagers have a ridiculously simple solution for her: she should have committed suicide or buried herself alive instead of speaking and embarrassing the authorities; they, in their righteousness avoid her family; indeed nobody wants to be implicated and incur the wrath of the Mastois; Mukhtaran's elder brother always clamps his orders, not allowing her to travel, thus denying her the opportunity to speak at meetings abroad; and above all, the Government adopts a hostile attitude blaming her for selling her country to the West, playing into their hands and exposing her country by exaggerating her problem. Charges are leveled that she was a CIA agent out to malign Pakistan and brew trouble. Most shocking was the Pakistani President's attitude (General Musharraf was in power then). Unfortunately, he too was not above prejudice. Nicholas D. Kristof recounts in his "Foreword" to the book a disconcerting incident when Amna Butter, the Pakistani-American physician who was helping Mukhtaran, was threatened. 'The Brigadier [Ijaz Shah] warned Amna that she and Mukhtar should be careful and not stir up trouble, and he added that Pakistani intelligence knows about everything they do. Alluding to a planned visit by Mukhtar and Amna to New York, he added, "We can do anything. We can just pay a little money to some black guys in New York and get people killed there" ' (xiii). Nicholas Kristof adds that this blunt threat to kill them sounded racist and iniquitous.

This implied acceptance of violence, intimidating practices, and the justification of crimes like rape or sodomy are not specific to any region or country; these are, as western feminists argue, widespread across boundaries of cultures and countries. In her study of sexual violence, Carole Sheffield records that sexual violence may not always be rooted in sexual urge of men but it is often an assertion of power and dominance. Sheffield calls this 'sexual terrorism' and points out that violence is conveniently labeled as 'male entitlement' conventionally falling into the category of the right of men to control the female body (Sheffield 3–19).

These and many such unhappy factors do not deter Mukhtaran Mai. She has tenacity and firm determination to carry on her fight, and continue her mission to educate the girls of her community. 'I'll make sure girls learn to read, and I'll learn to read too. Never again will I sign a blank sheet of paper with my thumbprint' (77), she declares with a resolve that shows her inner strength. As a girl, she was lively and carefree; as a woman she displays strong character and awareness unusual for women of her tribe. In fact, her firmness situates her in the midst of a long-running clash, a conflict that prefigured notably in the feminist 'sex wars', but Mukhtaran does not subscribe to such theoretical concepts; all she knows is that she will fight them as equals and she will recover her lost honour. 'Something inside me refused defeat,' she asserts and demands, 'How does one survive dishonour? How does one overcome despair?' Her reply is unpretentious:

> With anger, at first, with an instinct for revenge that resists the tempting solution of death, an instinct that allows one to recover, go

forward, act. A stalk of wheat beaten down by a storm can spring up again, or rot where it lies. At first I stood back up alone, and gradually I realized that I am a human being with legitimate rights. I believe in God, I love my village, the Punjab, and my country, and all the victims of rape, and future generations of girls. I wasn't really an ardent feminist, although the media considered me one. I became one through experience, because I am a survivor, a simple woman in a world ruled by men. But despising men is not the way to win respect. (110)

Despite gaining new insights into the communities other than her own, and distressed at the plight of women, she does not direct her ire at men but at the system and its primitive approach that has conditioned them all. Both men and women join her in her struggle. She is overwhelmed by her father's role in encouraging her to carry on the fight. The judge's words, 'Don't give up. Carry on, all of you' (66) infuse them (Mukhtaran and her father) with new life and strength to stand up. The chapter "A Most Remarkable Judge" is, indeed, aptly dedicated to the Judge who refused to buckle under pressure and ensured that Mukhtaran and her people get justice. Posters displaying in bold letters, "COURAGE MUKHTARAN MAI – WE ARE WITH YOU!" come as great morale boosters. Stable and strong support comes from a woman lawyer, Nassem – her constant companion, friend and guide whose friendship brings fresh air and light to Mukhtaran's life. Support also came and continues to come from different agencies – the Human Rights Commission, International Women's Organizations, Pakistan Women's Organizations and Forums, NGOs and many more. Mukhtaran understands the value of breaking the silence, 'The press is paying so much attention to me only because I'm taking my case to the courts. And in a way, I have also become the public face of a story that actually concerns thousands of Pakistani women' (46).

The public/private dichotomy has always existed for women. In coming into the public arena of high politics and getting international attention, Mukhtaran Mai crossed the boundaries of her female existence and put herself at stake. Her story of anguish and success stands at the intersections of the Third and the First worlds. This narrative speaks of the 'real' woman with her 'real' problems and help coming from 'real' people. And though it has all the ingredients of feminism, to read it as a feminist text within the feminist discourse/paradigms would be to restrict it within the bounds of theory. And Mukhtaran's life, her experiences and her works are far beyond theoretical framework. Mukhtaran Mai has learnt a twofold lesson: how to assert without being aggressive and how to transcend cultural boundaries without losing identity. She is trying to control her environ without falling back into the safe but deadly trap of passivity; she is attempting to understand herself as a woman and live *with* her world rather than *against* it; her response to her situation is not aggressive, but neither can it be described as passive. Crucially, her story and the debate it generated, take place within a highly sensationalized honour-rape case; it is therefore of profound interest and deep importance how the story is told and how it gets written because the incident has now transcended the media-report stage and has become literature, though not fiction. The authors and translators have remained intimately involved with Mukharan's life while simultaneously transferring her individual dilemma into a social cause. They have constructed a version of the 'reality' by examining what moulds perceptions of 'truth' and how sexual, cultural and even textual politics influence the process wherein specific accounts of violent episodes develop into an established consensus.

In an internet entry entitled "Horror in the Name of Honor" Rehana Azim, a UK based lawyer laments that administration and those in power connive at crimes against women and children in the name of 'cultural' or 'religious' sensitivity; also the concerned community seeks to sweep the unpleasantness under the carpet which results in continuation of violence on one pretext or the other. What Azim says about abused children can well be said in honour rape cases such as these, 'cultural sensitivities' should not be an excuse for silence about ill-treatment of children/women. Pressure groups from outside the community, mobilization of public opinion and courageous women breaking their silence can effectively help change the attitude. Media also can bring forth such cases with impunity because frank discussions, hard-hitting dramas, publications, all have an impact (internet entry http://www. guardian.co.uk).

The publicity in foreign media and the pressure from western countries angered some people, not only the authorities but also others who saw in it a ploy to disgrace Pakistan. But that is a narrow parochial view. If the internal media fails to stand up adequately and if foreign media does the job or if help comes to a hapless victim from any other source, there is no reason to rue it. If the state is unable to protect its citizens it has to be brought to the notice of the nation. The Pakistan Human Rights Commission took cognizance of other cases after Mukhtaran's case came into light. We learn that hers is not a solitary case. Unfortunately, 176 women were killed in the name of honour in the first seven months of 2004 alone; besides there were 151 gang rape cases. Mukhtar Mai got justice not only because of her courage to speak up abetted by her reckless attitude after she lost her honour, but also because she accepted the help from those willing to help and took the first step to speak.

Helene Cixous paints an interesting picture of woman's dilemma when she tries to speak because it is a new field for her to step into. 'Every woman has known the torture of beginning to speak aloud, heart beating as if to break, occasionally falling into loss of language, ground and language slipping out from under her, because for woman speaking – even just opening her mouth – in public is something rash, a transgression.' There is more to it, says Cixous, when men do not take her seriously. 'A double anguish, for even if she transgresses, her word almost always falls on the deaf, masculine ear, which can only hear language that speaks in the masculine' (Cixous 98). Mukhtaran has taken the initiative – she has opened her mouth – and has succeeded in generating public opinion; she has shaken the apathetic hegemonic structure from its slumber and has crossed the borders and boundaries literally as well as metaphorically.

A totally illiterate woman from a remote village of a fundamentalist society, travelling the world over to share the platform with fiery feminists and activists must take an enormous amount of courage, 'I've become a survivor and an activist. An icon. The symbol of the struggle waged by women of my country' (127). Plays are staged to show the corroding effect of the *Jigra* and such other institutions of 'private justice' system; these plays and demonstrations are questioning 'if it really is a sin in her country to be born poor and a girl' (128).

Mukhtaran's image as a saviour of suffering women of Pakistan has spread beyond the borders of her country, and if assessed objectively and seen impartially, her strength should bring honour for her country for having allowed a woman 'to speak out in protest against an injustice.' But we know, the administration is not so generous; and Mukhtaran has ceased bothering for them. She has a goal, a mission to accomplish; she will stay in her country and fight, there is no running away to the safety of some foreign shore or a big town in her own country. She has made it clear several times that she is satisfied to stay where she was born and brought up. She is not even contemplating settling abroad. She has a vision for her country, a hope and she wants to see it fructified. But before that she would ask her country – Pakistan – to do some serious heart-searching to find out an answer to the riddle that 'if honour of men lies in women, why men want to rape or kill that honour?'[5]

The words of a song popularly sung by the Pakistani Women's Action Forum in the 1980s need to be revived as Mukhtaran crosses the boundaries and borders, the proverbial "threshold" and shows to the world:

> No longer friendless in the world around us
> No longer helpless, no longer weak
> It is only your fancy
> That we sleep, yet unconscious.

Notes

1. Saroop Dhruva is a poet from Gujarat. The lines quoted here are from the translated version of her poem in Gujarati.
2. See *Embodied Violence*. In their "Introduction" Kumari Jayawardena and Malathi de Alwis quote Kamala Visweswaran to substantiate their point that woman's modesty becomes 'the symbol of violence as the shame and subjection of her community is represented in her.' (Kamala Visweswaran, "Family Subjects: An Ethnography of the Women's Question in Indian Nationalism". Ph.D Thesis, Stanford University, 1990, p. 68).
3. Kannabiran points out further that the allegation serves to demonstrate the 'lack of character' of minority men who show scant respect for women. Further, aggression on women can then be legitimatized by proving their lack of community or family status (See "Rape and the Construction of Communal Identity" in *Embodied Violence*, pp. 32–33).
4. See Usha Bande *The Sunday Tribune*, Chandigarh. 26 December 2004.

5. While I was working on the present paper on *In the Name of Honour*, another book *Into the Mirror* written by Bronwyn Curron was in book stores. *Into the Mirror* explores the case through investigation into the ways of the tribes providing a journalistic perspective. While the former, a memoir, seems to dramatise the unfortunate event sometimes during the course of narration, the latter gives an impersonal account. Reading these books together can reveal many more facets that one may miss otherwise.

Note: I would like to thank Jasbir Jain for her suggestions which have been of substantial use to me.

Works Cited

Azim, Rehana. "Horror in the Name of Honor" internet entry http://www.guardian.co.uk.

Bande, Usha. "North or South, Arbitrary Judgments Against Women are Similar", *The Sunday Tribune*. December 2, 2004.

Cixous. Helene. "Sorties: Out and Out: Attacks/Ways Out/Forays." *The Feminist Reader*. Eds. Catherine Belsey and Jane Moore. Houndsmill: Macmillan Press, 1997. 91–103.

Jayawardena, Kumari and Malathi de Alwis. *Embodied Violence*. New Delhi: Kali for Women. 1996.

Kannabiran, Kalpana. "Rape and the Construction of Communal Identity." *Embodied Violence*. New Delhi: Kali for Women. 1996.

Mai, Mukhtar with Marie-Therese Cuny. *In the Name of Honour: A Memoir*. Trans. Linda Coverdale. London: Virago, 2006.

Shah, Shaila. "We Will Not Mourn Their Deaths in Silence." *Charting the Journey: Writings by Black and Third World Women*. Eds. Shabnam Greway and Jackie Kay, et al., London: Sheba, 1988.

Sheffield, Carole J. "Sexual Terrorism". *Women: A Feminist Perspective*. Ed. Jo Freeman. California: Mayfield Publishing Company, 1989. 3–19.

Visweswaran, Kamala. "Small Speeches, Subaltern Gender: Nationalist Ideology and Its Historiography." *Subaltern Studies IX: Writings On South Asian History and Society*. Eds. Shahid Amin and Dipesh Chakrabarty. Delhi: Oxford (1994), 1997.

8

SUDHA SHASTRI

New Arrivals: *The Barn Owl's Wondrous Capers*, Graphic Novel

My paper will look at Sarnath Banerjee's graphic novel *The Barn Owl's Wondrous Capers* (2007), in the context of narrative form and strategy. I shall try to link the theme of this seminar – 'Borders, Border Theories and Crossing Borders' – to the way Banerjee uses the border-straddling possibilities of the graphic novel. The graphic novel crosses more than one border: that between text and image as well as the traditional border between 'high' and pop art. It has been defined in different ways:

> A *graphic* novel is a type of comic book, usually with a lengthy and complex storyline similar to those of novels, and often aimed at mature audiences. The term also encompasses comic short story anthologies, and in some cases bound collections of previously published comic-book series.[1]

And here is Lizzie Best, from the *Literary Encyclopedia*:

> The term 'graphic novel' evolved in the 1980s as a way of distinguishing this genre of graphic narration from the 'comics' or 'cartoons' which were presumed to be childish, vulgar, ephemeral, and of poor quality; a 'graphic novel' is, by implication at least, a serious book which adults need not be ashamed to read. This division between the 'low', popular culture of the comic and the high culture of the novel is of course an artificial and historically amnesiac differentiation since many nineteenth-century novels augmented their sales appeal with

sentimental and lurid illustrations, the fine arts of Dickens and his illustrators being merely the higher end of the market. Nevertheless, the term 'graphic novel' is a useful and frequently-used one in the discussion of 'sequential art': any printed art form that combines pictures with written words in order to tell a story.[2]

An implicit hierarchy is understood to exist between 'comic' and 'graphic novel', with the latter occupying a more 'literary' status (see above: 'mature audiences'). 'Comics' as they are popularly known, have never been a part of the canon, until Art Spiegelman broke with tradition with *Maus*, which won him the Pulitzer Prize in 1992.

Born in 1972, Sarnath Banerjee holds an MA degree in Image and Communication from Goldsmiths College, University of London. His first graphic novel *Corridor* introduced the character Digital Dutta. Banerjee's role in introducing the graphic novel in India is historically momentous. Alaka Sahani in an article in *The Indian Express* (29th August 2007) comments:

> Words were not enough. So images invaded the narrative. With this, graphic novels – encompassing a comic book style with a complex storyline – burst into the world literary scene nearly four decades ago. But India needed a certain Sarnath Banerjee to do the job. Three years after his debut book, *Corridor*, hit the market, novels told with images and balloons have grabbed rightful space in the Indian market. (8)

'Graphic novel' is not a term that endears itself to Banerjee. Here is an excerpt from an interview with him reported in *The Hindu* (19th April 2004) by Bageshree S, "The TANGO between panels":

> It's a publishers' jargon that one learns not to pick a quarrel with after a while. "It's an attempt at giving it the legitimate literature status, given that in the English-speaking world, a comic book is either obliged to be funny or adolescent power fantasies for boy-men," he says, pushing back his hay-like hair, even as the cigarette between the fingers threatens to set it on fire. The nomenclature, I learn, was an accident. Will Eisner, who wrote the first graphic novel in 1978, thought of it just as he was talking to a publisher on the phone for the fear that the man on the other end might hang up if he called it a "comic book".

Banerjee is as irked about the running word always being placed higher in the hierarchy over the visual image. Some have even dismissed a graphic novel as a gimmick. 'But an image can explore the larger realities of life, and quite easily at that ... .' He talks of the 'creative tension between word and image' and how the 'final tango between the reader and the text' is completely unpredictable. 'It's in between the panels that the imagination really works.'[3]

The conventional position that graphics argue a lack of imagination does not hold much weight in the light of the fact that many graphic novels encourage an interactive relationship between text and image, so that the reader is not a passive consumer of the visual art but plays an active and independent role in deciphering it.

Let me give an example from *The Barn Owl's Wondrous Capers* of how the reader is occasionally taxed to understand links in the visual narrative. The three panels at the top of page 42 depict the protagonist relaying the information of his grandfather's demise to his lover; immediately afterwards we have a panel below which is a letter written by the Headmaster of his grandfather's school commenting (largely unfavourably) on some traits of the student. The relevance of this information cannot be inferred in a linear fashion, and its role merits speculation. It may be an explanation for the grandfather's dogged pursuit of what he is determined to get; and coming from a critical observer, it plays the role of authenticating whatever observations the protagonist may make of his grandfather. The dimension of space, therefore, creates a complex reading situation where factors like choice, focus and digression become significant players in the production of meaning.

The Barn Owl's Wondrous Capers has an epigraph that sets a context: 'This book is inspired by history but not limited by it'; and there is also a prologue before the actual story (if there is one) begins. The book is divided into 13 sections, the first being titled "The Armpits of History" and the last, "Abravanel's Last Entry". The storyline loosely follows the search of a grandson for the legacy bequeathed to him by his grandfather in Calcutta. By the time he reaches Calcutta from London, however, he finds that his grandmother has given everything away.

How to Read a Graphic Novel

Let me at this juncture (and in this rather pompously titled section) briefly consider the more significant implications of adding image to word. The more obvious effects (and these are not mutually excusive) include:

(a) Enabling perspective, which in turn involves selection: focalising is a more deliberate and obvious strategy here, since the visual space affords greater freedom to the author to choose what to foreground (and at what expense); as Balleshwar asks the protagonist, 'But when you zoom in, don't you lose out on depth of field?' (65). A page earlier, we have this curious juxtaposition of photo and sketch which periodically trails this book. We have the bereaved grandson focusing on the funeral, where the image he is shooting is presented in the form of photos, while he is himself *sketched* in a corner, holding a camera.

Sometimes setting is given in minute detail, as in the case of a restaurant menu; there are also sections which have no setting, as in the case of the *hilsa* and the motorcycle goondas.

(b) Scattering the attention of the reader from word to picture and thereby causing diversion/digression; one perfect example I have from *The Barn Owl's Wondrous Capers* works to draw us back-and-forth between text and image, each of which seems to follow a different storyline, for the first time since the reader has opened this text.

This is Section 5, describing in a typically circumlocutory fashion the reason why Milk of Magnesia is so popular amongst Bengalis.[4] An elderly gentleman is on his way back from the Fish Market, whistling away, and the panels evolve to show him on his way, and thence to a motorcycle and two young attractive girls in subsequent panels. The scene is all set for eve-teasing. The men on the bike are shown to be annoying the women with their loud-noised vehicle and their gestures, while the narrative text continues blandly with the various culinary approaches to hilsa. 'Non-Bengalis are averse to eating hilsa because of the bones', and 'The technique is to chew the bones into pulp before spitting them out', and 'However, a restaurant in Calcutta has devised a way of preparing boneless hilsa. A revolutionary concept, this boneless hilsa' (73).

All of the next page, the graphics take over, and the narrative text has disappeared. The graphics demonstrate yet another (unarticulated) aspect of the *hilsa* in the way the gentleman unerringly aims the fish he is carrying, so that flying out of *The Statesman* in which it has been rolled, it finds its mark and demolishes the motorcycle goondas.

The graphics are still relating this scene when the narrative text resumes, to comment further: 'But all this ground and squeezed mustard' 'Is not very good for the delicate Bengali constitution', 'The city suffers from endless stomach problems', 'The only solution is Milk of Magnesia, a lifesaver' and 'It has become an integral part of the legendary Bengali cuisine' (75).

What we have here is parallel narration, a technique where the form of the graphic novel gives it an advantage over the regular novel.

(c) Parallel narration is a strategy that enriches, or at least, layers the process of interpretation with more than one sign for the reader to decipher. In instance b) the two narrative threads run on parallel lines. But signs could also mutually conflict, whereby complexity and ambivalence infuse the interpretation. Sometimes the text and the graphics are entirely different, sometimes they intersect subtly. Take for instance, that while describing the book and the inheritance, the pictures show the grandfather's funeral – thus creating a fine ironic-tragic counter-pointing.

(d) Generating distance through two levels of narration, where the narrator's text, usually descriptive, complements the speech bubbles of the characters in the picture. This in turn creates two levels of ontology, with the narrator occupying a privileged position of knowledge, as well as a potentially self-reflexive situation where story and story telling work alongside each other.

The principle of multiplying a narrative voice is applied quite creatively in *The Barn Owl's Wondrous Capers*. Section 2 begins with a new narrative voice – the radio, as it turns out. Not just any radio, but one that has a role to play in the plot of the grandson-protagonist as well. The voice in the radio is describing a scene that is part of a play being played in it, and thereby announcing a scene which is one ontological level down, thus giving an added interpretation to the observation that 'comics are a nested system' (Jessica Abel).

What can a graphic novel do that a regular novel cannot? This is a more difficult question to answer even though it cannot be avoided, and one answer to it is found on page 133, when Mandar and his girlfriend go to a restaurant, and the picture shows a menu board sliced longitudinally, because part of it falls out of the frame. A novel could perhaps indicate such a thing by emphasizing perspective, but not with the ease that is natural to this medium, where not only perspective but also setting (and issues like accommodation/selection) is established through such details as this.

Storytelling

I want to address the question of layout in this section: how do you read a graphic novel, literally? Not necessarily from left to right, or top to bottom.

In other words, one problem encountered by readers in *The Barn Owl's Wondrous Capers* is that of coherence. So for example, before we move to the first section titled "The Dark Armpits of History" there is a prologue-like section with xvi pages, which throws up seemingly random events in history and leaves you to consider what these events might add up to. Such open-endedness in fact reappears through this book, say for instance in the narrator's refusal – for a long time – to tell us the result of the duel between Francis and Hastings. In fact the introduction of these two characters itself happens in a by-the-way manner by establishing, first, the context of the *Khooni Judwa*. Similarly the first two pages of Section 2 do not seem to connect with what follows.

It is in fact difficult to keep track of any 'main' story, since storylines disappear, re-emerge and lose themselves to reflections that abound in the novel. It is possible, if you tried hard, to discover one main underlying story, which takes the shape of a quest. This is the story of the protagonist-narrator's legacy left to him by his grandfather. A quest on part of the grandson for a book, a radio, a motor-cycle and a pair of binoculars. It is perhaps no coincidence that in order to fulfil his quest, the protagonist must return to the land, nay the city of his birth, which is, from one perspective, the real protagonist of this novel: Calcutta, quixotic, idiosyncratic, decadent.

An eclectic mix of themes and storylines, *The Barn Owl's Wondrous Capers* is also about chronicling. Section 6 starts with a description of different kinds of chroniclers (those who travel, those who stay put in one place, those who travel a lot and then strike roots and the fourth kind – 'an elite club of chroniclers who seldom travel in space and almost never in time') before introducing Digital Dutta as a chronicler par excellence, a 'traveller of the mind' (83). Overarching all of these is the Wandering Jew.

Who Am/Is I?

The owner of the narrative voice[5] encasing the book *The Barn Owl's Wondrous Capers* surely shares some privileged space if not identity, with the protagonist searching for what has been bequeathed to him by his grandfather.

As the narrative unfolds we find that there are at least three people calling themselves 'I' in the narrative text (as opposed to the voices within panels): the first narrative voice that lives through centuries, who makes tongue-in-cheek claims as 'I am the impartial timer, truly impartial because I have no fondness for either gentleman. Particularly not Francis' (17), who calls Calcutta 'Home for me' (47), and who says 'The reason I had access to such ridiculous events was that I was part of them – the magician who could supply any object of whim and fancy to the rich' (123); the second, the grandson who speaks in Section 2; and finally Kedar babu who becomes 'I' from '*He*', for a brief while, from page 200 onwards.

The signifier I is thus appropriated by three people in this text, adding to the disorientating effect of the reading experience.

The Barn Owl's Wondrous Capers

The Barn Owl's Wondrous Capers is the name of the book that has been bequeathed to the grandson, and which is in the possession of Digital Dutta, who is persuaded to return it to its rightful owner by the gargoyle. The denouement is reached through the 'map' given by Kedar babu; it has directions as irrational as 'walk till you feel like a smoke' (212) interrupting more 'regular' directions like 'walk down the street', 'On your left you will find the signboard of youth club' (215) etc. The gargoyle that greets the grandson at the end of his journey (217) is the same that has figured earlier on the building in front of which the grandson meets Digital Dutta (84), though its link to Digital is established only at the end.

In a resolution characterized by an imaginative leap, the reader finds that the restoration of this book to its rightful owner leads to a revelation of the mystery earlier withheld to her: the outcome of the duel between Hastings and Francis. Page 235 in fact presents a mis-en-abyme with the reader holding the same book in her hands that is being held in turn by the Babylonian, the 'I' who has lived centuries.

With this I will end my paper, if without the sense of closure that is so inimical to the graphic novel.

Notes

1. http://en.wikipedia.org/wiki/Graphic_novel
2. http://www.litencyc.com/php/stories.php?rec=true@UID=1356
3. http://www.hinduonnet.com/thehindu/mp/2004/04/19/stories/2004041901630300.htm
4. See Appendix for the visual text.
5. There are at least two kinds of narrative texts in graphic novels, as I have elsewhere mentioned: one is the overarching narrative voice, which provides a commentary on the text (usually inside word balloons) inside the panels, thereby creating two levels of ontology, already. I call the outer commenting/commentating text the 'narrative' text.

Works Cited

Abel, Jessica. http://www.artbomb.net/comics/introgn.jsp 24 September 2007.

Bageshree S. "The TANGO between panels" The Hindu Online, 19 April 2004 http://www.hinduonnet.com/thehindu/mp/2004/04/19/stories/2004041901630300.htm 24 September 2007.

Banerjee, Sarnath. *The Barn Owl's Wondrous Capers*. Delhi: Penguin Books India, 2007.

Banerjee, Sarnath. Wikipedia: http://en.wikipedia.org/wiki/Sarnath_Banerjee 24 September 2007.

Best, Lizzie. "Graphic Novel". The Literary Encyclopedia. http://www.litencyc.com/php/stopics.php?rec=true&UID=1356 24 September 2007.

Sahani, Alaka. "Double Deal". Mumbai Newsline. 29 August 2007. http://cities.expressindia.com/local-news/fullstory.php?newsid=253306 24 September 2007.

Appendix

New Arrivals: *The Barn Owl's Wondrous Capers*, Graphic Novel

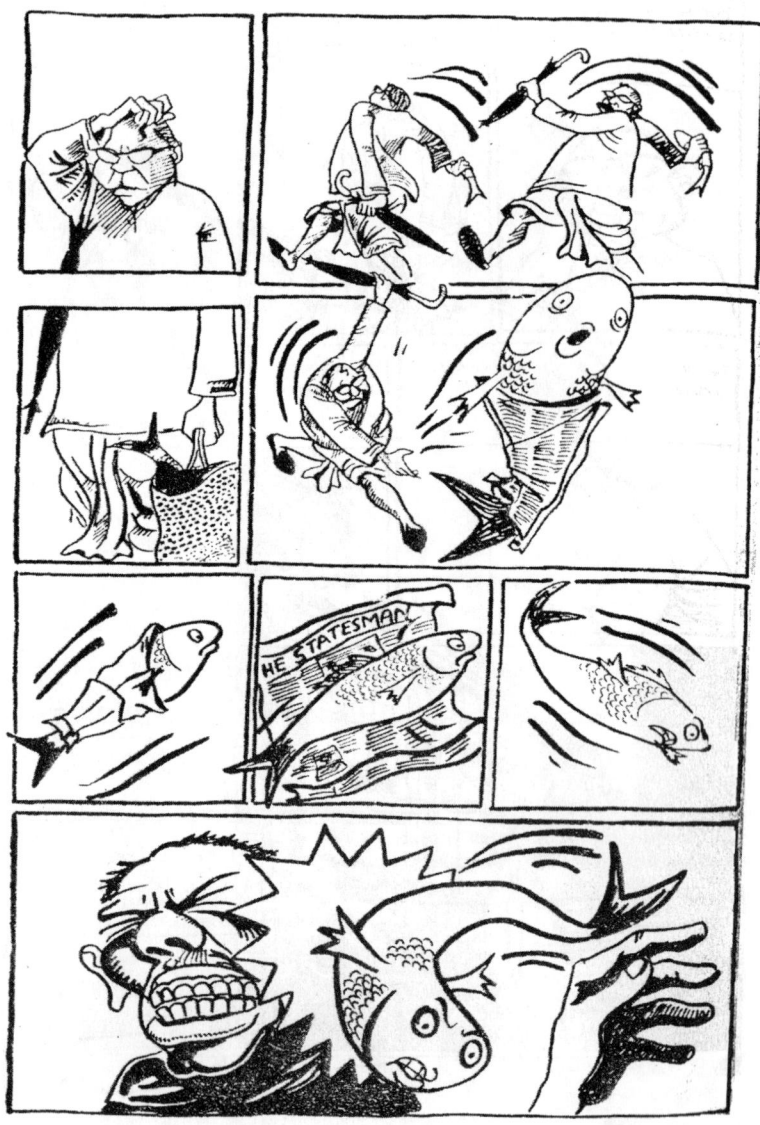

New Arrivals: *The Barn Owl's Wondrous Capers*, Graphic Novel 93

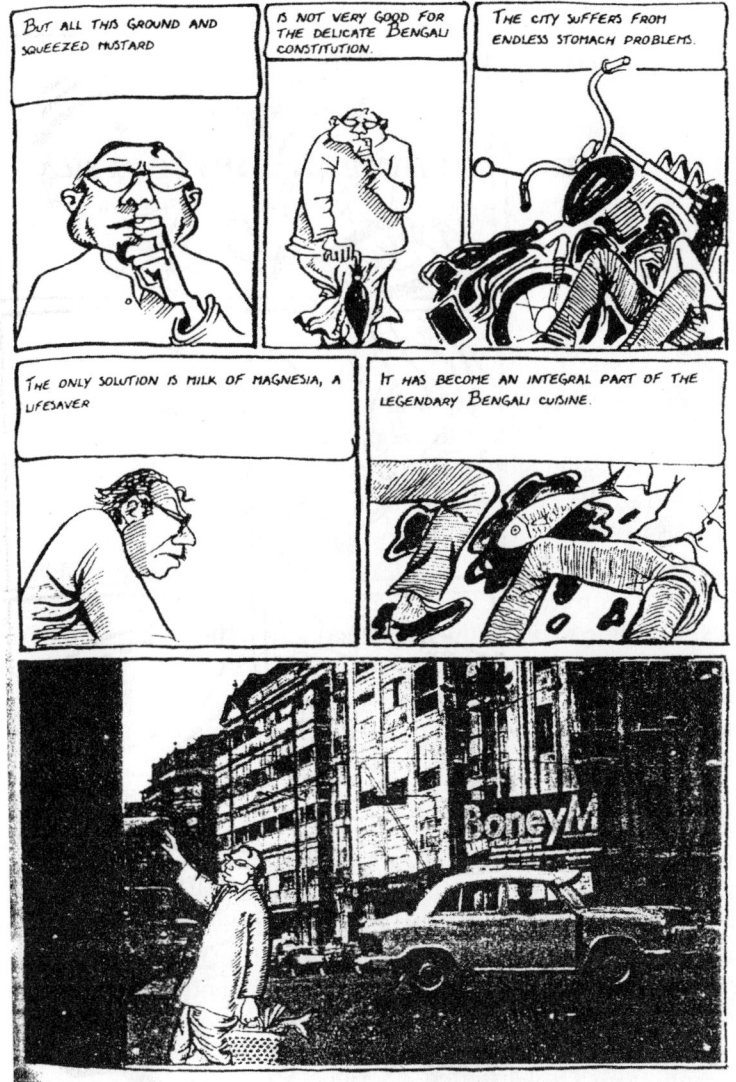

9

SAVYASAACHI JAIN

One Crossing, Many Journeys

Many journeys begin in the Doaba.

Doaba (which, in literal translation, means between two waters) is the name of the region of Punjab lying between the rivers Beas and Sutlej. It comprises the districts of Jalandhar, Nawanshahr, Kapurthala and Hoshiarpur.

In recent decades, the people of Doaba have firmly established themselves as travellers. They migrate across borders at a surprising rate. According to one estimate, 40 per cent of the young men of this area are abroad. It seems everyone wants a passport. In 2007, the passport office in Jalandhar issued 2,15,750 passports, which is about one thousand every working day. This figure has grown rapidly – in 1997 the number of passports issued was only 91,627.

Not only do people from the Doaba travel across borders, many as irregular migrants, each individual journey encompasses many other journeys. Every geographical movement hides within it social, economic and psychological journeys that fundamentally change people, lift them to a different level of worldly existence and earn them the respect of their neighbours, or fill them with resentment against their own families and drive them to emotional breakdowns. Even those journeys that seem to end happily represent a painful transition. When we made a documentary on the journeys of irregular migrants from Doaba in 2006 and 2007, we found that practically nobody in the region – even those who are left behind – is untouched by these journeys.

Shores Far Away (Door Kinare in Punjabi), directed by Savyasaachi Jain and produced by IntegriTV, 2007. For further information or the documentary the writer can be contacted at saachi@integritv.com.

The rush to get out of the Doaba is evident at the Passport Office in Jalandhar. The passport officer calls it a 'passport factory'.

It's commonly heard that there isn't a single household in Doaba that hasn't sent at least one person abroad. This is an exaggeration, but only slightly. If you visit a village gurudwara at a function hosted with the money sent by a migrant to his family, you will notice the absence of young men. You can see women of all ages, elderly men and children, but the young men are not here, they are in Canada or England or Germany or in countries they hadn't even heard of when they set out.

Most of those who emigrate are single men from rural landowning families. They have a level of education that unsettles them – too much education to make them feel comfortable with manual labour on their land and too little to get a decent job. During the making of our 2007 documentary on irregular migration, *Shores Far Away*, the Passport Officer in Jalandhar, Amarjeet Singh, described the typical migrant as one who cannot even fill his own application form. The following is an extract from the script:

> AMARJEET SINGH: Most of the people who seek the passports, they are from the rural background, and they are unfortunately school dropouts. Most of them think that there is no use of studying. So let me go abroad. So they get themselves out of school and are searching for avenues and via media how they can go abroad.

The "via media" that Amarjeet Singh refers to are agents. Travel agents abound in the area, and they often trawl the villages for potential migrants. Many of the agents are active participants in an international chain of human smuggling. Human smuggling – as opposed to trafficking, which entails an element of coercion – is crime organized on a global level by collaborating networks of mafias and criminals in many countries. It is believed to be one of the most lucrative forms of organized crime and it generates revenues comparable to those from drug smuggling.

For agents that feed human smuggling networks, the Doaba region is fertile hunting ground because local tradition and a host of social and economic factors have combined to provide a great psychological push for migration. Among the most powerful of these factors is the eye-catching presence in the countryside of those who have emigrated in decades past. Locals call them foreigners because many of them are now citizens of other countries. They are immediately distinguishable from those left behind by the way they dress and speak, their confidence and even their houses.

The Doaba landscape is littered with grand but kitschy mansions incongruously set in large tracts of agricultural land or standing out among a cluster of modest and run down village dwellings. They look very different from the houses around them and typically sport ceramic tiles on the exterior or a large distinguishing water tank on the terrace made up to look like a football, a flying bird or even an aeroplane that says Alitalia.

Many potential and failed migrants from the area told us they had been spurred on in their efforts to travel across borders by these very visible 'foreigners' and their houses. In these extracts from the script of *Shores Far Away*, Hardeep Singh is a village photographer from Lahdra village near Jalandhar and Sukhdev Singh is a village preacher:

> HARDEEP SINGH: We meet those who return from abroad. We ask them what your life is like. They only say they make a lot of money. They come here and lead a lavish life, wear gold, take friends for rides in fast cars, spend a lot of money. That is when we also get tempted to go abroad.
>
> SUKHDEV SINGH: Life here is not natural, it's about showing off. If you buy a car, I will also want one, if my neighbour builds a big house, I will also want a huge house. This jealousy is the push that sends a person out.

Tarsem Kaur's husband, Kashmir Singh, disappeared on his dream journey to 'vilayat'. He made a phone call, saying he had reached Mali in Africa, but hasn't been heard from since.

Both of them tried to emigrate but failed, but not because they were lesser men than those that succeed. All those who try are, in one sense, the pick of the crop because they are the enterprising ones. They are also brave, for many of them are aware that their journeys will be uncertain. The risk of failure (this often means deportation) is high, and there is a small but significant number who literally disappear and are never heard from again. Sometimes their fates can be guessed at, as with the infamous 'Malta boat tragedy' when about 170 irregular migrants from Punjab drowned off the coast of Greece on Christmas day in 1996. However, in many other cases, the families have no way of finding out where they went and what happened to them.

When migrants disappear, it is a double blow to the family. The loss of a family member is serious in itself, but it is compounded by a financial loss represented by the investment made in the hope that the migrant will be successfully smuggled across borders. Smuggling does not come cheap, and the rates demanded by agents, depending on the destination country and the ability of the family to pay, range from Rs 4,00,000 to Rs 25,00,000 (which converts to US$ 8,000-US$ 50,000 in November 2008). Those who cannot afford to pay these fees can sometimes pay them partly in kind, by recruiting other potential migrants for the agent.

Often families sell a plot of land to make this payment to agents, and this is an investment made by the family in their future. The intention is for the migrant to travel abroad, settle there and send money back to the family that will enable it to both keep up with the Joneses and buy back the land sold to finance the journey. Families and their desire for social mobility are instrumental in the push for migration.

Agents undertake to transport the irregular migrant to the country of their choice safely. The destination is usually one where the migrant expects to find social support from relatives or acquaintances who have migrated successfully, such as England or Germany, or one that has emerged as a hot destination because of the constantly shifting patterns of migration and migration law. An example of the latter in the first decade of this millennium is Italy. Most of the time, the geographical knowledge of the potential migrant and his family is limited to the name of the country, and agents take advantage of this to make promises they have no intention of keeping. A standard promise is that the migrant will travel by air directly to the destination, but this promise is seldom kept.

After pocketing the hefty fee, agents might try and obtain a legitimate visitor's visa for the potential migrant. The idea is to enter the destination country on a legitimate visa, then disappear and join the ranks of those working there illegally. Legitimate visas can be difficult to obtain, because embassies and high commissions in India have become wise to the methods used by agents. It is also a gamble because a refusal stamp from one embassy acts as a signal to other embassies. Sukhbir Singh, who now lives in the UK, had a tough time obtaining a visa:

> SUKHBIR SINGH: It was only on my fifth passport that I could get a visa to come abroad. On my first passport, I got a refusal from Malaysia. I got a second made. I changed my date of birth and name. The photograph was mine. On that I got a refusal from Germany. For the third passport, I again changed my date of birth and name. On that I got refused by Holland. On the fourth I applied for a British visa. On that I again got a refusal. My first four passports were issued in Jalandhar. I got the fifth from Chandigarh. I showed my year of birth as 1972, though it is actually 1978. Long beard, moustache, glasses. I gave myself a mature look and presented myself as a businessman. All the papers were fraudulent. My income tax returns, everything – all fraudulent. Nothing was authentic. That's how I got a visa.

To make a stronger case, agents often send migrants on short visits to Asian countries that are not so stringent about granting visas to Indians. Several visas and exit and entry stamps on a passport can be used to make a case that the holder is fond of travelling, and that could be useful when applying for a British, US, Canadian or Schengen visa. It's the best case scenario, but not easily attainable any longer.

The next best bet is to transit through the airport of a desired destination country while ostensibly travelling to a third country, and either seek asylum at the airport or somehow slip out of the airport. Rajinder Singh 'Rinku', a young man from Anandpur Sahib, travelled the world before he reached Vienna:

> RAJINDER SINGH 'RINKU': We came via Paris, via Paris sometimes to Bangkok, sometimes to Madagascar in Africa or to Denpasar in Indonesia. I came to Austria also. I took 15 flights.

This method is probably the reason that most of the western world now requires even transit passengers to obtain a transit visa. In the constantly evolving cat and mouse game that immigration authorities play with human smugglers, each tries to stay one step ahead of the other. For instance, several countries treat with great suspicion those who approach immigration counters in the host countries saying they would like to seek asylum but have no passport. This is because human smugglers routinely take away the passport of the would-be migrant, both to keep them in their control and also so that the migrant's origin is not easily identifiable. A migrant without documentation is not easily deported back home without a lengthy process of 'redocumentation' and verification to satisfy the government of the country of origin.

While this process is undertaken, many countries release migrants into their societies instead of housing and guarding them in expensive facilities. The migrant may be asked to report back to the immigration authorities in a few weeks, but more often than not, he doesn't turn up again. Indians have often been beneficiaries of this unintended largesse because many western governments implicitly recognize them as hardworking and honest in comparison with migrants from many other countries. For the migrant, of course, this is an ideal opportunity to disappear.

In recent years, airlines have also been alerted to look out for passengers who might fit the profile of an irregular migrant and are travelling only with hand baggage. If the plan is to approach an immigration counter without a passport, smugglers advise potential migrants not to check in any baggage because an unclaimed bag going round and round on a baggage carousel can provide enough information to identify the passenger.

The method that is most difficult to check is the one that is popularly known to travellers from the Doaba as *donki*. It means to cross international borders on foot, but its etymology is difficult to determine. Some think it is a bastardisation of the word donkey, and others claim it has origins in the Russian language. Most of those who use it have passed through the hands of Russian or Eastern European mafias involved in human smuggling. It is commonly used in phrases that would translate as doing a *donki* or performing a *donki*.

Naggi, jailed for human smuggling in Austria, studied engineering in Ludhiana before emigrating. He says human smuggling was an easy way of making money.

The *donki* route that has become most popular in recent years begins with a flight to Moscow, from where the overland journey begins. At the Traiskirchen refugee camp in Austria, we met a young man from the Doaba, fresh out of school, who claimed to have begun his journey by emerging from Moscow airport and telling a taxi driver of subcontinental origin that he wanted to go to Europe.

The typical *donki* journey takes the irregular migrant from Moscow to Kiev in Ukraine, Minsk in Belarus and Bratislava in Slovakia as he journeys into the European Union from the east. As immigration authorities take note of one route, the smugglers change the route. A lot obviously depends on the geographical base and links of particular groups of smugglers. The story of Balbir Chand, who now lives in Vienna while he waits to hear whether he will be deported, is about capture, confusion and some hard walking:

> BALBIR CHAND: I first came to Moscow. I was caught three times. The first time was in Minsk. I was told that from Minsk I must go to Poland. They told me I'd go comfortably in a taxi. They sent me on. I was caught again.
>
> In jail, for 50 days we didn't bathe or brush our teeth. They gave us nothing and kept us indoors all the time. We were in bad shape. We missed India a lot. But we couldn't do anything. We didn't have any documents. Our passports had been taken away (by the smugglers).
>
> I decided to return to India. But another agent said what will you achieve by going home. He said stay here and we will send you further. You'll be alright. But I was adamant on returning. But they convinced me. I also thought what I will do if I go back. How will I face my family? I had taken a big loan and the interest on that had mounted. So for the fourth time, I set out on a *donki*.

Donki journeys can entail long delays as each gang of smugglers waits for the right opportunity to slip migrants across the border, or as they wait for the group to build up. Many of the irregular migrants we met in Europe talked of travelling in groups of 25-50 with people from China, Pakistan, Afghanistan or Sri Lanka. While they wait, the groups are confined to cramped, unhygienic accommodation. A lice infestation forced Sukhdev Singh, the Sikh preacher, to set aside his religious beliefs and cut off his hair. Sometimes they waited while a deal was struck to send them on. They were sold on in subcontracted deals:

> SUKHDEV SINGH: The agents in Moscow sold us to Ukraine. The Ukrainians were to sell us to Czechoslovakia and they were to send us on. This is how the chain works.

Smugglers subdue the migrants with physical threats and bullying while they extract their price for their transport sub-contract. The migrants enter a terrifying world where they are held at ransom while a price is negotiated with their families. Smart smugglers who confine them give them barely anything to eat, partly to minimise pressure on toilets:

HARDEEP SINGH: I reached Moscow in December 2003. They kept me there for 3-4 months till March-April. There was nothing there, no telephone, nothing to eat. We got one ladle of porridge at 5 o'clock everyday. They gave us beef soup. Cow meat, horse meat, buffalo meat, I don't know what. We were hungry, so we ate it.

They took us in cars to a jungle. There was snow all around. We had to walk. Then they shut us in a room and asked us to call up our families and ask them to pay more. We refused. A Pakistani human smuggler used to beat us. They tortured us using irons. We finally gave in to the torture. They would beat us and lay us on ice. We told our families to pay them, saying we've reached Europe. After we paid, they left us alone. The Pakistani used to tell us: 'I'll torture you so much that even your unborn generations will shudder'.

(Showing photographs) These are the marks of cigarette burns. This is what I looked like on my return. Even my family was unable to recognize me. Most people couldn't recognize me.

Undertaking a *donki* is not for the faint of heart. Rajinder Singh 'Rinku' talks of trudging for days through snowy terrain. Stragglers or those who broke a leg were likely to have their throats slashed and left in the snow, he said, so as not to slow the group:

RAJINDER SINGH 'RINKU': I saw many dead bodies along the way. One boy was sitting under a tree, frozen to death. In another case, one boy with us wore out his shoes. He saw a pair of boots sticking out of

Rajinder Singh 'Rinku' in his lodgings in Vienna. "Someone who's undergone a donki can never forget it," he says, "It will always stay in his head."

the snow. He ran and pulled out the boot. Attached to it, came a leg. A man was lying dead in the snow.

Those days of the *donki* were the worst days of my life. We were treated worse than animals, just for the sake of coming here. I pray to God that no one should undergo this. Someone who's undergone a *donki* can never forget it in his lifetime. It will always stay in his head.

This physical breaking down of the migrants and its psychological accompaniment are defining journeys for the migrant, marking many of them for life.

Irregular migrants collect at dawn to offer their services as casual labour: "We get up at 5 or 6 am, cook our lunch and stuff it along with our work clothes and shoes in our bags."

Another journey is down the road of bitterness. Irregular migrants work in labour markets, usually in the neighbourhood of settled Indians, because that is where the fresh migrant heads. More likely than not, he has been told the name of someone from the Doaba who he can 'contact when he reaches there'. They cannot move out of relatively safe areas and, because of their irregular status, are vulnerable to exploitation by their employers, who may be Indian settlers of a generation ago. There is a difference of economic interest and thus a level of friction relationship between the settled community and the fresh migrant. He expects to be included but is not successful in integrating.

Life as a migrant is tough, and the increased focus on immigration since 9/11 places clear bounds on the migrant's access to employment, information and services. It keeps them on the fringes of society. This exclusion drives the migrant's journey into bitterness.

Parallel to the distancing from the host society, there is a distancing from the family. One factor is that the irregular migrant is geographically removed from his family, and his immigration status precludes travel across borders for births or deaths. Another factor is psychological. He lives in squalid conditions to maximise savings and send money home, and values every penny he earns. But he sees his family as demanding or grasping when they ask for and ostentatiously spend his money. Some migrants openly speak of feeling exploited by their families.

RAJINDER SINGH 'RINKU': Money is the prime thing. The world is a slave to he who has money. Where there's no money, even parents will take a step or two back, if not remove themselves entirely. Ask any of us in Austria what they talk about to their parents back home. If not the first or second, the third thing they say is, 'Son, send some money'. That's how it is. There are no real relationships today. Nobody is yours. It's all about money.

There's an intense loneliness, almost a feeling of abandonment, in some irregular migrants.

Shaukat, who sleeps in a plastic sack in the alleys of London, complains of exploitation by other Indians. "They want us to die working rather than ask for our wages," he says.

For those who fail to come good – sometimes this means being deported without being able to even recover the huge investment made by their families – the sense of failure can also be a heavy burden.

Indian labourers at work in the Southall area of Greater London. Not only are they prone to injuries, they have no access to medical or social services because of their immigration status.

However, most migrants manage to make some kind of a living. Even if it is a very basic living by the standards of the host country, the migrant squeezes savings out of it by living very frugally indeed. It is not unknown for men who deliver newspapers in Vienna or clear construction debris in Southall in Greater London to send home Rs 20,000 every month, and for the vast majority of rural families that is a stupendous sum.

Even though the migrant scrimps and saves, he has a lifestyle that is envied by those back home. He has seen the world and, when he returns, will do so with some money in his pockets. At the same time, he cannot tell people in the Doaba what he does for a living. Many in India secretly sneer at the settled migrant who cleans toilets at Heathrow airport, but the jobs available to the fresh arrival are far more demeaning, hazardous or exploitative. Mixed emotions is how Gulzar Singh might describe it. He works with builders, and to get work he has to run faster than others when building contractors draw up in their vans at a makeshift labour market in a parking lot in Southall.

GULZAR SINGH: When we go to India, we get off the flight walking tall. Our families receive us very well because we've returned from England. Why do they do that? Just for money. We can't tell them that in reality we clean toilets here.

The migrant and his family all undertake journeys. Different narratives play out in their lives, but conditions have become tougher with increased focus on security and immigration, and the narrative of irregular migrants is taking on increasingly exploitative tones. Almost all the irregular migrants we met during the production of our documentary were very clear that the irregular route is not one they would advise their 'brothers back home' to undertake. So, why didn't they tell their brothers back home the truth, we asked? We can't tell them, they said, because they'll think we are trying to deny them this 'good fortune'. There's no way they'll believe us, they said.

10 KEKI N. DARUWALLA

Love Across the Salt Desert

The drought in Kutch had lasted for three successive years. Even when clouds were sighted they passed by, ignoring the stricken country. The monsoons had, so to speak, forgotten to land. The Rann lay like a paralysed monster, its back covered with scab and scar-tissue and dried blister-skin. The earth had cracked and it looked as if chunks of it had been baked in a kiln and then embedded in the soil-crust. The cattle became thin and emaciated. The oxen died. The camel alone survived comfortably, feeding on the *bawal*, camel-thorn. Then one day the clouds rolled in like wineskins and the lightning crackled and the wineskins burst. Though two years have passed since the drought ended, everyone remembers that it first rained on the day when Fatimah entered the village. This is how she came.

What would he not do for her, the daughter of the spice-seller, she who smelt of cloves and cinnamon, whose laughter had the timbre of ankle-bells, whose eyebrows were like black wisps of the night and whose hair was the night itself? For her he would have crossed swords with the devil! For her he would have become a heathen in case she had decided in a moment of perversity to only take a Kafir in her arms! For her he would cross the salt desert!

He had stayed the day at Kala Doongar, a black hill capped with basalt, the highest in Kutch. He had set his camel, Allahrakha free to crop on the *bawal* trees. At dusk he paid homage to the footprints of the Panchmai Pir on the hilltop. He left some food there and started beating on his thali, according to the custom here. In a few minutes jackals materialized and gobbled up the food. This was auspicious. If they had not turned up he would have considered the ill-effects of the omen serious enough to have cancelled the journey. A lamp was lighted in the Pir's honour every night on the hilltop and the flame could be seen all the way from Khavda. Over a hundred years earlier the Panchmai Pir had trudged these salt wastes serving the people, accompanied, as legend had it, by a jackal. Reclusive by habit he used to retire to thorn jungles, where apart from his vulpine companions none else dared to disturb his nocturnal trysts. The custom of feeding the jackals lingered since then.

Najab bowed before the flame and set out. He left behind the camel-thorn shrubs and the area once famous for its savannahs of stunted grass, but now sere and brown as the desert. He had left behind all human habitation, Kuran being the last village. For the next three days he would not be seeing any *bhumgas,* those one-room mud-houses, circular at the base, but tapering into conical thatch-roofs at the top. Now only the sandscapes stretched out before him, mile upon mile. Water splashed in the *chagals.* With the name of the Pir on his lips Najab Hussain set forth.

Najab's diffidence was notorious among his friends. He was known to have blushed at the mere mention of a girl. A smutty remark made in his presence almost gave him a touch of eczema. A strangely introverted lad with dreamy eyes, no one had ever associated him with any act of bravado. His father, Aftab, would say, 'All that my ancestors and I have acquired during a hundred years, this lad will squander away, not because he is a spendthrift but because he will be too shy to charge money for what he sells!'

He had crossed the Rann on four occasions earlier, though he had turned twenty only a month ago. But each time he had either accompanied his father or that wily old smuggler, Zaman, the veteran of a hundred illegal trips into Sind. Each time they had taken *tendu* leaf worth about five hundred and sold it across the border for twelve hundred. But between the pay-off to officials and to the intermediaries who arranged the sale of the *biri* leaf, to the man who took the camel out to graze and to the friend or relative who harboured them, there was precious little left. It was just enough to buy some used terylene garments or cloves and then it was time to make the long trek back across the desert. It was during one of these trips that they had stayed with Kaley Shah, the clove-seller. 'He is a distant relative of your mother,' his father had told Najab. Kaley Shah was tall and well-fleshed and his thick-jowled faced had a purple tinge about it as if somewhere along the way it had got stuck with a discolored patch. He always wore a *tahmat* of black and white checks. Within a day Najab discovered that the fellow was an absolute rouge who drove such a cussed bargain that for the first time in his hearing his father started mouthing obscenities.

But his daughter Fatimah was a *hoor,* with eyes so bright that they would have lit up the darkness of the underworld. She was taken by this quiet, pleasant young man so ready with his smiles. But she could hardly elicit a word out of him. Fatimah had been under pressure to get engaged to someone in the village known for his slurred speech and grotesque stammer. 'Just my luck to run into mutes,' she thought. But then, as she caught him staring at her, she laughed back. And in the evening when Fatimah repeated the performance and her face flooded with excitement as if she dared him to take the next step, he had flung his arms around her in a reckless, dizzy moment. Yes, he would come again, he told her, and saw her start with disbelief for he seemed to have answered her inarticulated question, would he come again? This time he would come alone with no father or uncle to cramp his style. And as he left he looked behind to find her gaze following him, her eyes like a pair of storm lanterns in the dark.

Ever since his return to Khavda, Najab had been straining to get away. What was there about the Rann that he did not know? He could cross the Rann in the daylight, leave alone starlight, a thing none of his elders had dared to do ! 'You can't keep a randy buck on the leash,' his father Aftab had philosophised to his mother. And the next day he had gone and bought himself two maunds of *tendu* leaf used for *biri* wrapping, and hence highly priced in Sind. And one morning Aftab was woken up by a shout from Zaman. What does the old rogue want, he muttered, rubbing his sleepy eyes. Zaman asked about Najab's whereabouts.

'The boy has been sulking of late but he should be around. Anyway, what business is it of yours?' The old man could not hide his irritation.

'Whom are you trying to fool, Aftab Mian?' asked the smuggler. 'Don't you know that Allahrakha is also missing?'

In these border villages the pattern of life was such that if a man was absent along with his camel, it was taken for granted that he had made a foray across the desert into Pakistan.

Aftab went into the mud enclosure where his camel was kept and found it empty. His heart sank. He ran into the house to see if the bundles of *tendu* leaf he had bought had been taken by the boy. 'Oh the fool! That son of a fool!' exclaimed Aftab, almost shaking with fury, 'he has forgotten to take the leaf with him!'

'Whom are you trying to fool with all this drama?' called out Zaman who was still standing at the door. 'That son of yours is not as innocent as the world believes. He is a pig and the son of a pig.'

There was no limit to his chagrin. Zaman was the 'chief', the man who kept the Rangers across happy. Anyone crossing the Rann without his support was running the gauntlet with the law. And here this fledgling had blundered in without as much as a word to him, or a salaam or a hundred rupee note?

'May Allah bring him safely out of this!' said the old rogue piously. He means just the opposite, thought Aftab. Nothing would please him more than to see Najab turned into carrion with vultures hovering around.

'Don't worry Zaman, Allah will see him through!' he said testily and banged the door in the smuggler's face.

As Zaman stalked off, Aftab went in to break the news of their son's escapade to his wife. She would faint, he thought. He found her crouching with her back against the mud wall. She did not even blink in surprise, once. She just sat there cowering as if he had just slapped her and was about to do so again. Allah! She knew it! She knew it all the time! She was waist-deep in this conspiracy along with her son and never even breathed a word about it! His eye fell on her bare arm.

'Where is that gold bangle my father gave you, woman?'
'You need not worry. Najab will return with cloves.'

The long-striding Allahrakha kept a brisk pace. A strong south wind drove the tang of the Kori creek back into Najab's nostrils. He followed the stars, the milky way flaked with mica, the great bear shambling towards the north. Before dawn he had reached his destination, for a sandy elevation palisaded with the bones of dead animals told him that he had arrived at Sarbela, over twenty miles from Kala Doongar. He was already beyond the international boundary. Here he rested. During daylight movement was impossible. The Indus Rangers would be looking from their bamboo watch-towers. And in the heat everything became a mirage. A depression in the sand looked like a splash of water, a freak, stunted cactus gave the appearance of a grove and a camel looked like a huge prehistoric animal on the move. Any movement was sure to be noticed through binoculars. Otherwise too, the day was no time to venture out. For the hard flat surface of the Rann, littered with shingle and salt, turned loose and soft under the sun and the wind whipped it into the eyes.

When the sun came up Najab took his first drink of water from his *chagal*. At noon he had his first meal – dry, stale bread with onion. By now thoughts about Fatimah took a vice-like grip over him. An entire night lay between them, he thought. And the distance was less than ten miles! The thought of it made him writhe even as the sun started beating its hammer on the anvil of the desert. A whiff of the tangy south wind caught his nostrils again. But this time it brought with it a thin, dappled veil of cloud, patches of which lay overlapping like fish scales. Within an hour this corrugated cloud had covered a substantial portion of the sky, looking for all the world like a stretch of wind rippled sand. Yes, this was the time! He got up and shook the sand from his turban. Even as he harnessed his camel he thought that Allahrakha was looking at him quizzically as if asking what the hell he was up to. At one level of consciousness he knew that this was madness. He knew of overworked camels dying of fatigue, of the patrolling parties of the B.S.F. and the Indus Rangers and the mirage-chequered, trackless wastes of the desert. But he succumbed to a rush of blood and the face of Fatimah beckoned him like a mirage.

Najab crossed the International Boundary Pillar No. 1066. He knew the track he had to take, bisecting the two posts of the Indus Rangers at Jagtarai and Vingoor. But he strayed ever so slightly, and from their watch-tower they saw through their binoculars this sleek camel, warped and distorted by the heart-shimmer into a lumbering leviathan. An Indian slipping into their territory with *tendu* leaf right under their noses, and that too without paying any hush money! They were not going to stand for it. Najab was in a trance now, events flashing past him like figures on a screen. The mile-long chase, the firing from behind, the spent bullets flopping in the sand and then rose between the hunter and the hunted. When the dust settled half an hour later he was alone in the Rann.

The next few hours passed in a daze. He was mortally scared that Allahrakha may die of fatigue. To ease him of his burden he now started walking beside him. Within an hour the salt had scraped the callus from his feet and scarred them with agonizing cracks. Under a hot tin sky, the Rann was blazing now, throwing up white needles which hurt the eyes. And as the Rann palpitated, it haunted him with its mirages, pools of shadow, scooped half-moons of water. Hours of wandering as if in a trance, attempting to lick the receding edges of the mirage. Then light thinning away, and an hour or two later, dusk, and a thin plume of smoke rising from a dung-fire. Allah be praised! He was now within range.

He waited for night to descend and then struck out hobbling on his toes, for this desert odyssey had cost him his heels. Within an hour he was at the clove-seller's door.

Fatimah rose from her bed like a panic-stricken doe as he called out her name softly through the window bars. It took some anxious moments for it to sink in that it was Najab. Her lustrous eyes lit up the dark of the room as she opened the door. Thank God she has a room to herself, he thought. And later, thank God her bed doesn't creak!

After the gall, the honey, after the cactus-sting, the feel of rose petals, after the scorching day, the waters of the night.

Two hours before dawn, Kaley Shah was woken up by the beat constable banging on the door. 'A smuggler has come across the Rann, Kaley Shah. You wouldn't know anything about him, would you?'

'*Kasam tumhari* not a sparrow has entered the house, or the village. Even the dogs have not been barking tonight.' Then he added with a knowing wink, 'Why should a smuggler come to me? What can I give him except some red chilli powder to carry in his backside!'

But the law was not amused. 'Kaley Shah,' he said sardonically, 'your belly is stuffed full with silver. It would outweigh even the dirt in your heart!'

The constable's words rattled like a sack of empty cans in his head and prevented him from sleeping.

'You have a guest,' said Fatimah as she brought him his tumbler of hot, steaming milk next morning. 'It is Najab. He stayed the night in the cattle-shed.' For a moment he was terrified. A smuggler in the house, the police prowling all around and he did not even know of it! One would think he had been on ganja! His meeting with Najab had been brief. The wretched fellow had brought no *tendu* leaf.

'First you come unannounced, dragging the police behind you, and then I find you have come with nothing! Trading with you is going to be a dead loss, son, with the cops on your back and your hands empty.'

Najab thought that Kaley Shah's waistcloth, with its black and white checks looked like a chessboard. He would have to make his moves carefully. He showed the gold bracelet. 'I have come for cloves, *chacha jan*. And I shall pay in gold.'

The next two days Kaley Shah was busy buying cloves and arranging to get Allahrakha grazed a few miles away, by a cowherd. Otherwise the presence of a strange camel would have let loose a babble of tongues. Najab slept in the cattle-shed in the evening and slipped into Fatimah's room late at night.

'They want me to marry Mahfuz Ali,' she told him. 'He is related to us from my mother's family. The way he stammers! You should hear him! His tongue just gets stuck on certain sounds, as if gum had been applied to half the letters of the alphabet. Urchins start mimicking him the moment they set eyes on him. It is just a step removed from being hounded like a madman and pelted with stones.'

'Has it never occurred to you to take a ride on Allahrakha across the Rann?' She had kept silent and silence was assent. It was as simple as that.

The first lurch of the camel next evening and they were off. He had waited with his camel at the outskirts of the village and she had slipped out after her father had started snoring. The moment was too big for them and they did not speak. It was only in passing that she thought of the village she was leaving for good. As for quitting one country and entering another she never gave it a thought. Where did one have the time for Pakistan and Hindustan when one was eloping with one's love and crossing the desert which divided, both physically and symbolically, the two countries? For her it meant just a shift in dialect, a smear of Kutchi added and a little of Sindhi sandpapered away.

And the camel lurched and bumped onwards and Najab drove him hard. By the time they reached Sarbela she was exhausted and fell asleep.

She woke up in the afternoon to find the sky overcast. It turned ominous in the evening with depth upon depth of dark-edged nimbus gathering at the summons of a storm-god. Another night they journeyed facing the wind which hurled the sand in their faces. As they neared Khavda, the thunder started rolling and reverberating across the skies.

Three times during the night Aftab had opened the door, thinking his son had come. But it was only the wind knocking against the door. This time the banging was persistent. When he unlatched the door he found Allahrakha shying away from a streak of lightning. Huge, isolated drops of rain were falling, kicking up the dust. Aftab steeled himself. He would not allow any relief, any expression of joy to show on his face.

'Son, have you brought anything?' he asked, an edge of iron deliberately introduced into his voice.

'Yes,' replied Najab, as he ushered Fatimah in.

The rain stormed down and swept away three years of drought.

11 JEAN ARASANAYAGAM

The Journey

> Oneself is one's own protector (refuge); what other protector (refuge) can there be? With oneself fully controlled, one obtains a protection (refuge) which is hard to gain.
>
> **The Dhammapada**

Two ... three ... five ... eight ... twelve ... sixteen ... Always the counting. Numbers. Under the breath. In soft, sibilant whispers. There must be no slip in their precise numbering. But we had names. Must we forget them now? Names that were known among friends. Parents. Loved ones. In which country? One that seems so distant now. The one we have left behind. Home: hills, fields, valleys; rivers, jungles, habitations; trees, flowers and fruit. They pass through my mind like those Jataka tales unfolding in the temple murals of my country. Tales of the several lives of the Bodhisattvas. The striving of The One to reach Enlightenment, become a Buddha. But first to reach the highest state of perfection. Until then he is on the road to Enlightenment and on that road which he travels through successive births, he will live and speak with all beings – animals, birds, humans. That journey of his, that Road to Perfection ... And ours? We are travelling on many unknown roads. Taking unfamiliar routes through alien terrain, crossing frontiers and borders. On and on we travel. To reach what destination and why?

The guide knows where we are being taken. We must trust him absolutely. We are walking through a forest. There are no tracks. The trees are silent and watchful sentinels. Yet they offer us protection too. Oak. Birch. Beech. Pines. The snow piles up silently. Our boots sink deep as we step cautiously through it. We cannot afford to flounder.

Or delay. In the darkness we have to keep together. By instinct. Animal instinct. If we veer off the track we will be lost. Losing our way will mean that we can never make it to our destination. There's a woman among us, with her young son. That makes sixteen of us altogether (asylum seekers, refugees call us what you like). Seventeen with the guide. The guides change from time to time and place to place. No names. Just gestures to follow them. Trust. Absolute trust.

The woman doesn't ask to be treated in any special way. Bears everything silently. But she is always watchful and alert where the boy is concerned. She's prepared for any hardship. Tough woman. Only tender towards the child, but doesn't cosset him too much. I'm the only Sinhala male in the group. The others are Tamils, from the North of the country which we have left. And the guides? Who knows? They change. German? Russian? Swiss? Jewish? No one questions. No one asks with easy and casual familiarity, 'Hey, what's your name? Where are you from? A family? Children? Have you ever travelled before? Visited my country?' No, no. No time for questions, for entry through the slightest aperture into any life other than one's own. Danger lies in too much knowledge. We do not share information about each others lives. We have learned to store away all facts that are useful to us. When the time comes we will unearth that store. Moreover, identity isn't important here, at this juncture. Identity is still the burning question of the day in our part of the world; identity that separates and divides. But here we are one, because we share this journey and all its travails. We eat the same food. Bread, cheese, apples. We quench our thirst from the same flask of water. No one makes me feel that I am not of them. It would have been easy for them to have done so.

We maintain silence most of the time. I have no one to talk to in my own language at any rate. Nor can we speak in each other's language. We use signs to communicate with each other when the necessity arises. What keeps us together, keeps us going in a landscape that has no recognizable signpost or landmark is just one purpose and that is to reach Berlin. To disappear there or to seek, through legal means, political asylum. The question of maintaining an individual identity will come later.

Two routes lead to Berlin. One through France, the other through Russia. We have taken the route through Russia.

We continue to move stealthily. Fear. It is perpetually with us. We need physical and mental stamina too. We must be strong in body, mind and will. No sign of weakness must be shown, or we might be left behind. We must not impede the rest of the group. We must move together. I am reminded of the stories about the plantation workers who were brought to our island two hundred years or more ago. Brought from south India in their hundreds in ships. Disembarking at Talaimannar, they made the long trek from the north, through thick, animal infested jungles, to the central highlands to work on the tea estates. So many died on the way of cholera, dysentery, malaria. Many were left behind to be attacked by wild bear and leopards or to grow weaker and weaker and die, leaving their skeletons as new landmarks on that terrifying journey. And of those who reached the central highlands, many hundreds died of fever, chills, pneumonia in those mist-veiled mountains. Always the weak have had to succumb .... No, we must keep up our strength. There is no letting go even for a moment. And always to remember that we are a group. Numbers. Each of us is a number. The numerals reverberate in our minds: sixteen of us, seventeen with the guide. No one should go missing.

Our dependence on the guide is total. This is unknown country to us. We are not human beings to them. With names. Personal lives. Habits. Feelings or emotions. When we are handed over at the border for the next stage of the journey to the next guide or agent, we are 'dollars'. We bear with the irony. We're not people, we're money to them. We provide employment to them. They take risks too. We understand that. Dollars. Money. What do they care about the politics of our individual countries? About war and violence. Conflict. Ethnicity. Massacres and assassinations. Revolutions. Human rights violations. Disappearances, torture, death. Though it's nothing new to anyone, really. The soldier justifies his rape of women in war. He asserts the triumph of the victor. He has to let off the tensions and the horrors of the battlefield, has to have his booty. The map of Europe has been changed often enough and is still changing. People are reclaiming the territory that once belonged to them before the invasions and conquests of historical eras and epochs. The changing of borders and frontiers leads to extensions of power. And now, ethnic cleansing, so that the reclaimed territory rests on a foundation of skeletal remains: bones that branch out like a subterranean forest, the flesh nourishing the soil yet its poisons creeping through the still veins to create a monstrous foliage. We know the histories of all these worlds. They haven't had time to learn ours. Our wars, our revolutions, our conflicts, our displacements, are important only to ourselves. We become refugees, asylum seekers. Their laws restrict our entry into their countries. Yet there are people who help us to bend these laws. They've got to eat too, haven't they? We serve their purpose. They serve ours. When we reach a destination, the desired one, we can't expect a friendly welcome. Although looking back on our own history, didn't we open our doors to the invader? Didn't we even adopt the colonizers' way of life? Change our language, our religion, our culture? Didn't Kuveni herself take Vijaya for a lover?

To reach Europe we had to pay thousands of dollars. Somehow we made it. To Russia. We reached there by Aeroflot. Not as tourists, of course! No one questioned our identities. We had passports and visas we had purchased at a price. And hard currency in our pockets. That would help us through part of the journey. In Moscow we were all put in one room. It was winter. There was no heating. We were grateful for the warmth of each other's bodies. The comfort of each others breath. Our being together. We had glimpsed streets white with snow piled high, snow crisp like mounds of freshly laundered linen. We still did not have the freedom to treat those streets.

The woman and child were cold. I saw her remove her fur-lined jerkin and wrap it about his shoulders. I had a warm woollen muffler. I unwound it from my neck and held it out to her. For him, I gestured wordlessly. She looked at me, uncertainly, almost unbelievingly, took it, gave me a tentative smile. Why had I done this? I was thinking of my *malli*, my youngest brother, I suppose … . It wasn't gratitude I wanted, or even friendship. Just a little human feeling. We weren't divided in this country according to our racial or ethnic groups. We hadn't brought our weapons, our arms to this country. We didn't bear labels here – terrorists, militants, subversives, misguided youths … . Those identities had been left behind. We had a different mission here. The journey. The pilgrimage. We weren't a warring people here.

The other talk to each other. In whispers. But in very few words, and in their own language. I wish I could join in. I feel lonely sometimes but most of the time I am not. I think of the next stage of the journey. I've reached so far, but then, what happens next? I count the dollars in my wallet, open my travelling bag, touch my warm clothes. I have my passport with me and a photograph or two of my family. No letters; I have no address as yet. it is best this way. I don't want to reveal my whereabouts to anyone. We travel incognito. No longer in touch with the outer world.

I wonder what's happening at home. When I was there I sometimes felt I would like to join the Security Forces. Ideas of courage, of patriotism spurred me on but I had seen too many young friends missing in action, or blinded or crippled for life ... when they had hardly begun their journey. Landmines. Ambushes. Dying in action. Dying for the Motherland. Too few people caring anyway. Each in his own way dividing the country further. And would any of us want to return? But this is no place to talk politics. Though why should I, who has not suffered in any way through displacement, loss, bereavement want to leave my comfortable home? Why should I be with this group that I would have had nothing to do with in my own country, with whom I have nothing in common, neither language nor culture nor tradition?

I have my own reasons for making this decision to leave home. I'm not like these people. They have other reasons; so many things to escape from. The long and protracted war that has been going on for ten years and more. Armies of occupation on their soil. Their sons, and daughters too, martial women who have their own regiments, have gone against all the traditions of their society, joining the militant movements. Fighting for a cause. Families broken up. For them, seeking political asylum is often a matter of life and death. Am I, belonging to another ethnic group, the majority group in the country, am I too responsible for making them refugees? No. I'm not guilty. I'm really a peaceful kind of person. I have been more or less privileged all my life. I've had a good life. My father is a businessman, he has wealth. So I've always had what I've wanted. I was educated in a good private school too. Maybe life was too easy for me. I didn't join the revolution like many of my friends did. I had no interest in destabilizing the State. I was not one of those who were socially deprived by caste, a feudal power structure, or lack of wealth. I had no social conscience either. I didn't rave and rant against the exploitation of my own people by multinational and vested interests. I had no purpose in life. So many of my friends had disappeared, died or been detained in camps during the revolution that my father was only too happy to give his consent for me to go abroad. He had enough money to give my sisters in marriage. Besides, I didn't have a profession or a career. I wanted a change, some adventure. I wanted to make a journey that would change my life. I wanted to venture into an unknown country; make my own predictions and decisions, question the revelations that would confront me at the end of this long saga.

I was as yet unenlightened in many ways. For one thing, in my own land would I ever have undertaken a journey with people who were not of my own kind? We had looked upon each other as strangers, even enemies, dangerous to the unity of our motherland. To me they were people who were trying to divide the country, claim territory for themselves. We too had moved into their traditional homelands, changed the demographic map. Each ethnic group had accused the other of untold crimes. Was I joining a band of pilgrims disguised as asylum seekers? Was I innocent enough to think that in the new country I would find enlightenment which would release me from all suffering, *dukkha*? I ...? Taking the path of the Bodhisattva, is it also the route of the asylum seeker, the refugee? Is the shedding of an identity also the path to enlightenment, if that identity is part of an existence that entails hatred, enmity, violence? With these people that I am travelling with, there are no such feelings. We do not look upon each other as brothers, nor do we look upon each other as enemies. We can learn a lot about survival from each other. Even without a shared language. The guide knows the route, that's all we need to know.

And yet sometimes I feel unsure and afraid. Who will meet me at the end of this journey? One thing, however, we are well fed here. They bring us plenty of food. Pans of steaming hot, boiled vegetables and soup. Cabbage. Cauliflower. Rye bread. Black bread. Borscht. Nothing spicy, but the food fills that pit in the stomach. We eat, then sit on our haunches, stand around, smoke cigarettes, wait. Wait until it is time to get the OK to move on. To leave this temporary shelter, take the lorry or truck or container to the next assignment.

In Moscow too we had waited. We could see nothing of the city. We were not there for sightseeing anyway. No strolling along the streets or sitting in restaurants drinking vodka. I would have liked to see the Kremlin or shop in their markets. Taste caviar perhaps. All we heard was news of the White House being under siege, of the deaths, the surrender, the trials and imprisonment of the leaders. The epochs we moved through were historical. We were part of it all, caught up in that turbulent stream of events.

Yes, we continued to wait. On the way we had learned yet another lesson: Patience. Nothing would move until the right time approached. I knew there were risks. We had always to be hidden. Once, a man's body had been found wedged into the compartment of an air-conditioning unit in a container. Suffocated. Chilled to death. What a slow, long drawn out and agonizing end. And those three men, my own kind, who were flung out of the truck they had been loaded into on a journey similar to ours in some part of Germany. It was winter. They had smuggled themselves into a truck among crates and packages and when they were discovered they were scarcely breathing. They were hardly thought to be human, to have breath. No one investigated closely. They were left in the frozen ice and snow, still half alive, crushed by the weight of the crates, to die by the wayside. Slaughtered animals. All they needed was to be suspended from meat hooks.

When the call finally came we were asked to get into the back of a huge container truck. It was already packed with heavy wooden crates. We could neither sit nor stand upright. We had to lie one on top of the other the way firewood is loaded in our country. The journey lasted for so many hours. We travelled hundreds of kilometres. We were conscious of the bodies beneath ours, their breathing almost imperceptible, trying to be as still as possible so as not to cause the other discomfort. Layers of bodies. Orders were tersely barked at us:

'Head down! Lie down. Flat! No moving. Still! You can die'.

The container moved swiftly on a silent empty highway. Suddenly it lurched. Came to a halt. The doors of vehicles slammed shut. Footsteps sounded on the hard asphalt. Our bodies tensed. Grew chill. Petrified. Flashlights bathed the container in harsh white-green flares. Voices, many voices, high-pitched, interrogative, assailed the man at the wheel and the guide. Their voices had already warned us: 'Polizei! Polizei!'

My heart thudded against my breast. Fear. Fear of being discovered. Arrested. Put in police cells. Deported.

'What are you carrying?'

The voices of the driver and the guide answered calmly and matter-of-factly, 'Wine. Here, have cigarettes.'

'Cold. Cold tonight. Well below zero. Not good for asylum seekers ... contraband goods. This is the route they always take.'

'Not us. We don't carry them. Flooding into Berlin from everywhere ... creating problems'.

'How many kilometres to go yet?'

'We travel tonight and tomorrow. Then we deliver our beer and wine. Everybody's thirst quenched!'

We heard them walk around the container truck. Boots clicked on the asphalt. How long since we had ceased to breathe? I stifled a cough. The order was finally given for the vehicle to proceed.

'OK. Go'.

We drove fast, it seemed for several hours. The vehicle stopped. The guide came round to the back. There was a slight gap among the crates for us to move out.

'Get off. Quick!'

We stopped at the edge of a vast forest filled with fir trees. It was freezing outside. Our sweat chilled in no time. The trees stood still. So silent. Great giant crosses. Black. The snow glittered on branches with touches of silvery frost. Our blood was an icy current in the veins. The guide led us into the heart of the forest. He would remain with us. The container would proceed on its journey.

There are no discernible pathways here. Only white blankets of snow. And silence. We are at the mercy of this stranger, this unknown man. We have learned to trust these guides. It's better that they are impersonal. Then there are no loves, no hates. Once more the counting begins. One ... three ... six ... seven ... ten ... twelve ... fifteen ... sixteen ...

'Go. Go,' He urges. 'Quickly. No delays. Understand? Quick. No delay. Before light comes.'

We feel dwarfed by the trees. So small. So human. So puny and insignificant. We look at our guide. What do we do next? We know he must have a new set of plans.

'Take only what you need.'

Some begin to unzip their travelling bags and rapidly dress themselves in as many suits as they can. Three pairs of trousers. Shirts. Coats. Socks. But of course only one pair of boots.

'No more bags. No more carrying anything with you.' Discard all the things we had thought so necessary for survival? Passports. Cameras. Clothes. Personal possessions. Now the time has come for us to assess their importance.

'Throw away your documents. Tear them into little pieces. Your passports, letters, diaries, photographs, everything.'

Those passports and visas had cost us thousands, no, lakhs and lakhs of rupees. Well, they seem to have served their purpose. We don't need them anymore. I begin to tear up everything meticulously. It's my past life I'm tearing up. I am aware of that.

'From now on, no identity. No identity. You understand that? From now on, no names. Nothing.'

No names. No identities. On no man's land. In a sense the load grows lighter. I begin to experience a new kind of freedom. Heady. Yes, its heady as if I've drunk a lot – champagne, now that I'm in Europe – for celebration. Celebration of some kind of victory. I look at the woman, the child. It's so cold. Freezing. She keeps the boy close to her all the time. There is a deep, wordless communion between them. A bonding that no one can share. She smooths the thickly knitted pullover on his chest. It's grey in colour. Drab. The clothes we wear are all drab and anonymous. His eyes look trustingly into his mother's. She will protect him with her life. She is strong. Asks for no special treatment at any time. Eats what is given her. Drinks what is given her. But first sees that her son is fed and his thirst quenched. She walks the long distances without complaint. The boy too. His body still trembles, perhaps more with the tension and exhaustion than with the cold. I have one jerkin too many. I hold it out to him.

'*Malli*,' I say hesitantly. 'Take. *Méka gandé*. For you.'
He looks at me. Points to my shoulders, my chest.
'No, no. It's OK. I'm fine. Not cold. Not cold.'

He reminds me so much of my *malli*. *Malli* must be playing cricket with his friends at this moment. Waiting for a letter from his *loku aiya*. From me. Waiting to show off the stamps and boast about me.

'*Loku aiya* is in Germany. He'll send me a new video camera soon.'

The boy's thin shoulders are covered with my jerkin. They stop shaking. He looks at me as if at an elder brother. What is there to divide us at this moment? Nothing. Even lack of a shared language is no barrier to our communication.

'Now we go. To border.'

Very little is spoken. We conserve our energy. Our voices will give us away if there are any guards searching the forest for people like us. The *polizei* are on the alert constantly. All of us begin walking together, shambling along. Our names, our identities relinquished. I can take on any name now. Gerhard. Or Pieter. Or Samson. No, no; Dollar – that's my new name. Dollar. The agents never have names. The guides never have names. And we are thought of only in terms of dollars. The counting begins again – one ... five ... eight ... ten ... fourteen ... sixteen ...

Each one is concerned about himself but is aware of the others too. We will not abandon the weak. There is an unspoken bond between us now. I'm not one of them but it no longer matters. It will never matter again.

Our dangers have been mutual. When it's a matter of survival the politics of a country left so far behind do not get first priority. If there's no food, we all go hungry. If there is food, we eat. We share out equally. I keep the apple I am given in my pocket for the boy. I silently hand it over to him as we walk. My *malli* loves apples, the red ones. I'll see plenty of apple orchards, I'm sure, laden with fruit of bright colours – russet, yellowy-pink, green – when winter is past, when I'm settled somewhere in Germany. If I reach my destination safely, that is. The boy takes a bite and offers the fruit to his mother. She smiles. Shakes her head.

'You eat,' she tells him in their language. They smile at each other. At home, the militants, the 'Boys', bite on cyanide tablets when they're arrested. I'm glad he won't have to do that here. I've grown too fond of him. He's become my *malli*.

We come out of the forest. The timing is perfect. There's a truck waiting on the side of the road. We get in. 'Quick. Quick,' the guide orders.

We begin our journey again. To the border. The German border.

At the border the truck stops. It's instantly surrounded by border guards with their loaded weapons. Our hearts are quaking. We're hiding behind the crates with their frozen carcasses of sheep and cattle.

'What are you carrying?'
'Frozen meat.'
'OK, proceed.'

We scarcely breathe. The boy shows no fear. Even at a tender age the young ones know how to handle firearms, set off landmines. They're not weak by any means. I'm not sentimental or homesick or anything. It's just that *malli* keeps coming into my mind. He knows where I'm going. To Europe. To Germany. To become rich. Get a job, gain wealth. I know he looks forward to letters, photographs, gifts from a foreign city. He's likely to boast and I'm sure he does, about me, to his friends.

'*Loku aiya* is abroad. In Germany. Look, he has sent me this shirt and this watch and money, too, German Marks to buy a new cricket bat … . He's promised to send me lots of things …'

He will never know the realities we have to face. The fear, tension, terror. The humiliation. But we can't complain. We asked for it, didn't we? This journey. And at the end of it … what kind of enlightenment? Will we find it in a cell when we're arrested and locked up? And even if we manage to find safe passage, what about the attacks of the neo-Nazis we'll have to face? There was the case of two youths, neo-Nazis, who were responsible for killing a Turkish woman and two of her granddaughters by fire bombing their house in Mölln. Yes, we'll have to face the neo-Nazis too. They are the same although they have other names. Skinheads and Rightists. Everywhere the minorities will face such dangers. Ironically enough, I'll become the minority here, in this country. Not only will I have to relinquish my identity but also the power attached to it in my own country. We are newcomers here; the Turkish woman Bahide Arslan and her granddaughters Geliz and Ayse, two little girls, were long established residents – yet their houses had been torched. Reminds me of what happened in our island in '83. The torching of the houses and the business places, the killings. History will always question these facts. My parents gave shelter to Tamil families during that time. I understood their fear. Is that the fear I must now feel?

Once more we get off the truck. We have to cross a field. We crawl through mud and slush. We're caked with it. Our clothes stiffen and grate against the skin. When was the last time we had a good wash? A hot bath? I. seems like ages and ages ago. We reach a township. Turkish music comes from the cafés. We see people drinking foaming beer, eating off steaming platters of food. A cooked meal. Cups of hot coffee.

Where to wash off the mud and slush? There's a fountain in the heart of the city. We wash ourselves thoroughly in it. The water is icy but fresh.

The guide leaves us.
'Another guide will come to lead you,' he says and disappears.

We're alone. Abandoned. He never turns up. We move out of the city, walk endlessly along a gravel road. No one to be seen. No dwellings. No habitations. Walking into the countryside, only the woods on either side. Silent trees. No birdsong. Scrunch of gravel underfoot.

Suddenly patrol cars drive up.
'Police, police,' someone calls out.
No escape for us.
'Aliens. Aliens. Asylum seekers.' We understand what they are saying.
'Passports. Show. Where passports?'
We have no identities any longer.
'Inside. Inside. Get in.'

Car doors open and we're bundled in. Doors slam shut. We're driven off. Taken into the city. Berlin – we're here at last.

We reach the Police Station. They take us in and lock us up in cells. I can see the police officers seated round their desks laughing, talking, smoking. Have to think fast. Really fast. I remember the telephone number of the original agent. It's in my mind, flashes across my memory. I make signs to the police officers. I somehow get the message across to them.

'Embassy: Sri Lanka. Embassy. We go ... there. Country embassy. Go back ... country ... home. Home. Get taxi. Here, hundred dollars I have. I pay ... for all. All of us. Others have money also. We pay taxi.'

It is my plan of escape. They are convinced, only too happy to get rid of the burden.

I first go to a phone booth. I repeat the number which I've carried in my head. Establish contact with the original agent.

Instructions are given.

'Wait at the railway station. I will send someone else.'

Another guide arrives and we prepare for the next lap. The last lap of our journey. We look at him silently. We have got to trust him.

We pile into the taxi the policemen have arranged. Halfway, we tell the driver, 'Look. Money. Dollars. Dollars. Free us. Let us go free. Free.'

The driver accepts the money. We are several kilometres away from the city. He counts the notes before tucking them away in his wallet. Then he opens the doors of the taxi. We get off. We stand in the middle of nowhere. We have to make a split second decision. From this point onwards we will walk back with the guide, to the city. Past the wood. Oak. Birch. Fir trees. Ancient woods. Fugitives can hide here but for how long? And food? From where? We have nothing. Better walk on. A motley group of us. Hope no police patrol cars come upon us again. We reach Berlin and enter through the Brandenburg Gate.

We enter the Unter de Linde. We see parts of the old city which still remain left over from the bombings of the Second World War. There's no East, no West any longer. No Wall. We see trams. Cars. Innumerable cars. Volkswagens. They remind me of home. The trams belong to East Germany. Police cars stop at the pedestrian crossing. There are little green men with hats in them. That again is part of East Germany. The green men without hats belong to the West. Berlin has known defeat. The defeat of two World Wars. It's a city that seems to be seeking a new identity, one made up of many nationalities and races, not just pure Aryan alone. For us too it will provide a new identity. We see bulldozers flattening out the past; cranes, cement mixers. We also see the new synagogues like monuments to change. Do the Jews still face persecution, I wonder? No, they are strong now. No longer the victims of the holocaust. It is a past they will carry with them, but the new breed of Jews will be different. I am told that the survivors used to visit clinics in Israel to have the tattoos of the concentration camps removed. The numbers. They did not want that identity any longer. It was unacceptable to the new race of Jews who wanted to be identified with their blond, blue-eyed Aryan counterparts.

We pass huge apartment blocks with murals in brilliant colours on the walls. Graffiti too. I am reminded of the graffiti on facades of buildings and on walls in my own country during the revolution of 1989 and the 1990s. The bold, eye-stabbing red and black announcements, messages, statements of the subversives. The country was in flames. What graffiti will we discover about ourselves here in time to come? When will we be free to go undetected on these cobbled streets where no one will ask to see our identity cards? Can we find employment here? It will be difficult, I know. There's an influx of East Berliners here and asylum seekers of all races. Not safe either, at anytime, with the neo-Nazis. Apartment houses, refugee centres set on fire; the exiles beaten up, killed.

Plenty of people like us on the streets. Africans, Turks, Sri Lankans, Indians, East Europeans. But we don't talk. As soon as we spot a telephone booth, the Tamils go directly towards it. They have all their phone numbers in memory. Before long, taxis and cars arrive and one by one they are whisked away. Only the woman, the boy and myself are left behind. I have nowhere to go. No contacts either. She gestures to me, points to the two of them, as if to say, 'Join us, be with us. You can come where we go.'

Why this invitation? Because of the occasional kindness I showed her along the way? No one thought either of us traitors for talking to or helping each other. No suspicious looks or fear of me being an informer. We will never know each other's names, yet I've got to trust myself to her. The last guide we were to have has left us. His responsibility to us is over. We are now on our own. I am fortunate that this woman has decided to befriend me. Does she see me as a brother or as her young son grown up? Does she think me another political asylum seeker, one who has escaped the detention camps after the revolution? What about her husband? Probably here already in Germany. Must have arrived earlier, prepared the way for her, sent her money to get across. What a reunion they will all have. But what about me? I know the realities. Just as much as the others do. The safe houses. Old dilapidated buildings. Bullet holes still pock mark some of the walls. Peeling plaster. Endless spiral stairways. Bunks. Blankets hanging as room dividers. Rooms full of immigrants. Refugees. See them passing by. Some of them look as if they've assimilated the new culture. We're not wanted here. We'll have to be illegal workers and merge among the others. Don't want to be noticed.

The woman, the boy and I get into a taxi. The woman speaks one word:

'Saarbrucken'

We travel a thousand kilometres away from Berlin. We arrive at the address she gave. On her arrival she and her son are greeted and welcomed by their own people. As soon as they see me they decided that I should be among my own. How can they be responsible for me?

Again, numbers. They make calls. My people arrive in a taxi. The first question they ask, is, '*Machan*, how did you get here?' They sound incredulous.

I am handed over to them. I feel at home in their presence. They give me a cup of tea, some food. I have a hot bath and change my clothes. They are generous. My beard has grown and I look different. My eyes have a more worldly look, my recent experiences, the risks, tensions and dangers, mirrored in them. My journey has been no ordinary one. It is not a mere adventure story. I have made my pilgrimage on this road. But this pilgrimage, this journey has not yet ended.

The red tape involved in granting asylum must now begin. I am taken to the place where I have to register myself. Official matters. I have to give all the details about myself. Then the trial will begin. I want to stay here. I don't want to be deported. But I am not a political asylum seeker. What legitimate reason then do I have to remain here?

What can I say?

The truth?

12 SUNITI NAMJOSHI

Summer Days

There are, as everyone know, winners and losers, workers and shirkers, those who can and those who couldn't, those who must and those who mustn't. That is how, after all, life goes on in the global village. And so, when a grasshopper sang all day long all through the summer and did no work, and when an ant laboured and stored away a great deal of food, this surprised no one.

Winter came and the grasshopper was hungry. The ant gave her food (about half as much as she actually needed), a short lecture and a bit of advice. The following summer the grasshopper sang, the ant worked, and when winter came, as is the way in such matters, the grasshopper was starving. The ant gave her exactly half of what she had given her last time, a long lecture and more advice. The grasshopper survived and when summer came she sang all day long. The ant worked. Winter came and the grasshopper was starving again and the ant, as is the way in such matters, was impatient again. The ant shrugged and gave the grasshopper a quarter of what she had originally given her. It wasn't enough. The lakes froze over and the snow fell. The grasshopper got thinner and thinner, until one day a bitter wind lifted her up to carry her away to a still colder country. On the way the grasshopper died.

The moral of the story? There isn't one. It's an immoral tale.

25 March 2007

E.V. RAMAKRISHNAN

Terms of Seeing: Four Poems

Terms of Seeing

On our way home from school
we often spent hours in that abandoned
orchard of mango, cashewnut
and tamarind trees, where each season
had its fruit and each fruit tasted different.

There we raided the make-shift hideouts
of bootleggers, and broke their buried mud pots.
The crematorium in the corner
revealed an occasional roasted vertebra.

Once we went further and discovered
a disused well, and peeped into its vaporous depths:
the water smelt like freshly distilled alcohol.
Through clotted branches
of close-knit shadows floated white
turtles with glazed, metallic shells.

Moving with a monastic grace, they looked
knowledgeable, like much-traveled witch doctors.
If they cast a spell it was unintentional.
As we bent down, their
shaven heads rose and met a shaft of sudden
sunlight at an angle, tilting the sun into the sea.
Still the light lingered over the hill
like an intimate whisper of something forbidden.

By this time, the terms of seeing
were reset: the well was watching us now.

Its riveted gaze pierced us and even went beyond us.
In the dark cornea of the well
the white turtles moved like exposed optic nerves.
And as if a word was spoken, we stepped
back into the world of gravity, in silence.

On the Way Back from Petra★

The past of another country.
You can't take it home nor can you leave it behind.
It is for viewing from a safe distance.

Then a wedding song begins.
Everything becomes familiar. Homely.
Like the rain in the hills, it is full of kindness.

The cliffs close in on you.
Tombs or Temples.
The Nabataens and the Romans.
Archways and colonnaded streets.

When all the dancers breathe to the same beat,
There is only a single woman. Dancing.
The song marches out of time.
A river begins.

A narrow gorge of Assyrian carvings.
This is rain's footwork on stones.
An evening melody in pink rocks.
For those who missed history.
Stones cascading. Like women dancing.
They are conducting a bride.
They rejoice in some secret knowledge.
They know how to keep the night away.
The past is another country.
Uninhabited. Till dancing women invade the streets.

★ Petra in Southern Jordan houses the remains of the once lost Nabataen city. It has temples, Roman theatres, monasteries and houses carved in pink stone.

In Transit

A Ghazal for Agha Shahid Ali

I hold on to your words like a child lost in transit.
The gestures of bodies invisibly marked "lost in transit".

You claim the land with the lens of your lines.
Give no name to it when memories defrost in transit.

Echoes fill the frozen lake in the valley.
The snowman moves up the mountains, like a ghost in transit.

In the big, bad wolf's tale retold, you speak of perfect timing: every
secret agent has to pay the cost in transit.

The vigil has turned into a wake.
Are birds killed in civil war martyrs?
Why should they roast in transit?

A new script unwinds backstage as an actor breaks out
of his own last words: hell disowns this Faust in transit.

You moved houses but we still track you down to your dwellings.
It is to home that we travelers toast in transit.

We are stranded. Bring us news, Shahid.
Please stand guard as we cross these war zones' wild outpost
in transit.

Letter to an Afghan Friend

Frontiers shift like rivers
changing courses.
Which side of the uprooting tree do you
stand, Farooqui?
The sheep spread on the mountain's waist,
like a rash. the script of the shrubbery
stands out in bold red.
My son articulates his body in the new-found
language of walk.
Have you taught your son the songs of *Pakeezah?*
We keep indoors during an eclipse.

The sheep have come further down,
infecting the private parts of valleys.
Soon we shall celebrate the new year.
We shall pray under high tension wires.
Where are you these days, Farooqui?

To pass for a sane man, most of the time,
I have to choose my words and cast my vote.
The sheep are lost in the smallpox of shadows.
Tonight, I shall read a book of fiction
in which men live and die, like men, in peace.

14   JEAN ARASANAYAGAM

Crossing Borders

Telephone conversations in my quiet room at the
Mayflower, my daughter's voice with its tone of
soft persuasion reaches me from another country
wanting me to move my displaced self from
danger zones to safety, talks of the complex intricacies
in her instructions, of the number of points required
to get 'landed', how many dollars for a house, down
payment, claiming legal status, crossing borders
reaching for all time, safety and freedom from fear.

I, coward, retreat, retreat from the history of my life
already vanquished, clinging to a past I can't let
go of to seek safe haven, stumble in my tracks
think of home and of return to the accustomed,
to the familiar however corrosive the memory
of those terror filled days, of being hunted out,
the human quarry pursued in that breathless fox hunt.

Is it this identity-branding that marks me out as being
alien not here alone but also in the country of my
birth, now that I have assumed this suspect
alliance with the 'other?' Changed a name to one
that evokes hostility?

Once baptized from a brimming font with strange
sounding names the markers of a different rule,
a different order, I find myself although my
lineaments have not changed, treading a penance
path uncertain where to go, where to settle in.

Crossing Borders

I wait my turn to be scrutinized
in a mid-west airport in Iowa preparing to take
off on a flight from which I must return.
I stand, filled with uncertainty and suspense
jostled by thoughts of whether I can embark
on this journey to see my daughter, alive but
safe in that country of her choice
where she has made a choice to live?

I have my bag with me, a few sparse garments
tossed in, place it on the ramp where it's x-rayed
for bombs, my visa closely scrutinized, suspect that
I'm insidious, an infiltrator, a terrorist, a danger to
the innocent traveler or that I'll seek illegal status,
become an unwelcome guest, an asylum seeker.

A homeless refugee.

My throat clogs up suffocating me, choking
me with unspoken syllables of protest.

My voice summons back its strength.
I break my silence with fresh vehemence
I must make this desperate journey
but will they keep me back?

If I defect it will be from my traitor self.
Watch myself crawl beneath the barbed wire
fence, crossing boundaries, surprised to find
that no one sees, that no one notices
my minute insect life, so insignificant
and yet one that conquers space to reach
the territory of that no man's land between
the here and now, where I must become
invisible and anonymous.

A few seconds more for the plane to take off.
Dawoo stands at the barrier, eyes intent,
watching me, tense with fear.

Will I make it?
I am yet to know.

They hustle me through the entrance gate.
I run with Athena's winged feet, but still remain
a mortal.
Reach just in time,
feel myself a fugitive,
an escapee from the minotaurs
that confronted me.

. . . .

Years later after several journeys, several returns
to the country of my birth, I halt at repeated
checkpoints. Go through.
For me there is no scrutiny but for some
there's no friendly banter, no temporary pause.

The bombs go off, the thoroughfares are
mined, the twisted metal of blasted vehicles
swamped with sodden blood-soaked garments
decapitated, mutilated flesh, the guernicas of
our times.

Safe havens, an illusion,
no one records the memories of the anonymous
traveler, the innocent bystander.

The witnesses are speechless,
numb with shock, the suicide bombers
roam the streets, landmarks and maps
engraved upon the mind before they're
blown to extinction.

I recall the suspicion generated by
my alien looks in different worlds.

Question how innocuous I have been,
Interrogate my innocence.

Iowa 1991
Sri Lanka 2008

15 SOMDATTA MANDAL

History and/or a Sense of Place: Reading Amitav Ghosh's *The Hungry Tide*

Like all serious academics, let me begin in a theoretical way. In his seminal essay entitled "Forms of Time and of the Chronotope in the Novel: Notes toward a Historical Poetics," Mikhael Bakhtin analyzes the nature of the artistic chronotope thus:

> In the literary artistic chronotope, spatial and temporal indicators are fused into one carefully thought-out, concrete whole. Time, as it were, thickens, takes on flesh, becomes artistically visible; likewise, space becomes charged and responsive to the movements of time, plot, and history. This intersection of axes and fusion of indicators characterizes the artistic chronotope. (1981: 84)

As in most of his earlier novels, in *The Hungry Tide* (2004), Amitav Ghosh exemplifies the Bakhtinian model of interweaving time, plot and history in a deft manner. He interweaves his narrative by bringing in the history of Nilima and Nirmal's arrival at Lusibari, which, historically speaking, was part of the estate of Sir Daniel Hamilton. But more significantly, through Nirmal's diary (who himself died in the brutal assault), Ghosh describes in graphic details Nirmal's subsequent involvement in the activities of Morichjhapi. Roughly translated as the 'pepper island,' this refers to a particular island in the Sunderbans where long ago (1979 to be exact) some homeless people died of hunger and bullet wounds while resisting the policies of the then West Bengal Government. Many people of Bengal still recollect the actual facts and the political machinations when a group of East Bengal refugees left Dandakaranya and tried to settle in Morichjhapi but were once again forced to abandon that island. Discussing the relevance of presenting historical facts in a work of fiction, this paper will highlight how Ghosh embeds the real history of the Sunderbans with the make-believe world of his novel so skillfully that one cannot ultimately identify how much of it is fact and how much fiction.

Before delving into the manner in which Ghosh has used history in this novel, it would be useful to reiterate the definition of the historical novel. Speaking about Mahasweta Devi's historical discourse, Gayatri Chakravarty Spivak defines 'historical fiction' as history imagined into fiction. The division between fact (historical event) and fiction (literary event) she states, is operative in all Mahasweta's moves:

> Indeed, her repeated claim to legitimacy is that she researches thoroughly everything she represents in fiction. Fiction of this sort relies for its effect on its 'effect of the real.' The plausibility of [her characters] is that they could have existed as subalterns in a specific historical moment imagined and tested by orthodox assumptions ... . Those who read or write literature can claim as little of subaltern status as those who read or write history. The difference is that the subaltern as object is supposed to be imagined in one case and real in another. I am suggesting that it is a bit of both in both cases. The writer acknowledges this by claiming to do research (my fiction is also historical). The historian might acknowledge this by looking at the mechanics of representation (my history is also fictive). (77-78)

In *The Hungry Tide* Ghosh, like Mahasweta Devi, blurs the boundary between both these categories. He frees himself from the obligation to create the ostensible mood of objectivity sought by most factual reporting. Take the case of Sir Daniel Hamilton. A Scotsman by birth, this high level British official served in Bengal for a long time and somehow fell in love with the region. He could feel the tragedy in the lives of the people that arose primarily due to poverty. So after his retirement, instead of going back to Scotland with all his savings, he took lease of three islands in the Sunderbans from the then government. These islands of Gosaba, Satjelia and Rangabelia then gradually came to be known as 'Hamilton's laat.' [Hamilton's Estate]. Hamilton decided that he would turn this snake, tiger and crocodile infested region into a land where civilized people could reside, a land where all people would be treated as equals. It would be a place devoid of hunger, illiteracy, and unemployment. With all his life savings he built up a free school, charitable hospital, cooperative bank, rice mill etc. The aims and achievements of his rural development project was later recorded in his book, *New India and How to Get There*. It was of course unfortunate that his utopian settlement could never really succeed because he had ignored the historical realities of class and his knowledge of the land and its people was insufficient. In the novel, Ghosh incorporates this information thus: 'When the Scotsman looked upon the crab-covered shores of the tide country, he saw not mud, but something that shone brighter than gold' (49). While showing the young Kanai around the house at Lusibari, Nirmal tells him the history of "Hamilton House" built by Lucy's uncle Sir Daniel MacKinnon Hamilton.

> 'And who was he?'
> 'You really want to know?'
> 'Yes.'
> 'All right, then. Listen ... Now that you have asked you'll have to listen. And pay attention, *for all of this is true*'. (40, emphasis mine)

The first question that comes to our mind is do we really need historical truth in a work of fiction? In other words, is veracity a prerequisite for fiction? In the "Author's Note" at the end of the novel, Ghosh states:

> The characters of this novel are fictitious as are its two principal settings, Lusibari and Garjontola. However, the secondary locations such as Canning, Gosaba, Satjelia, Morichjhapi and Emilybari do indeed exist and were indeed founded or settled in the manner alluded to here. (401)

Ghosh also bases the character of Nirmal partly on his own uncle who was headmaster of Rural Reconstruction Institute, the high school founded by Sir Daniel Hamilton in Gosaba and for some years before his untimely death, in 1967, he was also the Manager of the Hamilton Estate. In an interview given to Ramya Ramamurthy, Ghosh narrates how the novel originated in his mind. Among the 'two factors that triggered the novel' the first one was that 'an uncle of mine went to live in the Sunderbans in 1948 and he inspired me to start thinking about the place' (2004). In a chapter narrating how Nirmal and Nilima arrived in the Sunderbans in 1950, fearing persecution by the police in Calcutta, Ghosh reminds his readers that 'in the tide country, where life was lived on the margins of greater events, it was useful also to be reminded that no place was so remote as to escape the flood of history' (77). The Hamilton estate that Nirmal and Nilima came to had fallen into decrepitude and was crippled by lawsuits. As a schoolmaster, Nirmal's sympathies had always remained with the leftists and the diary that he had left behind also elucidates his socialist beliefs.

As Banibrata Mahanta rightly points out, at a complex level, Kanai serves as a conduit to the history of the Sunderbans as the reader and interpreter of Nirmal's diary, which calls for a reassessment of history. Hamilton's failure, his ignorance of history and nature is replicated in the case of Nirmal. Nirmal aligns himself with the dispossessed refugees of Morichjhapi in order to realize his dream of changing the world through revolution. He fails because like Hamilton, he too functions on ideologies that ignore local history, society and nature. His revolution ignores the larger historical reality of the Partition which has produced the refugees at Morichjhapi. Nirmal also forgets that he is in a land where people exhaust themselves in their struggle to exist. Taking neither historical reality nor natural factors into account and functioning on the dictum 'revolution or nothing,' Nirmal looks like a misfit. Like Hamilton, Nirmal too dreamt of a society where 'men and women could be farmers in the morning, poets in the afternoon and carpenters in the evening' (53). He attempted to achieve all this through a 'revolution.' Both men ignored the historical circumstances of the people and natural terrain thus ending in failure (100–01).

Through Nirmal's diary again, Ghosh subtly narrates historical facts through his account of Henry Piddington, Lord Canning and the port town on the Matla River. Kanai narrates this to Piya with a focus on the shortsighted idea of development carried on by governments, scientists and surveyors with scant attention to the natural demands of the terrain. The failure of Port Canning in 1867 as predicted by Henry Piddington proves that man's idea of development when divorced from an understanding of nature paves the way for destruction of human life and poverty.

Apart from this factual documentation, Ghosh significantly blends fact with fiction through the narration of the Morichjhapi incident. Part One of the novel has a chapter entitled "Morichjhapi" (116–127) and it is a name not many are familiar with. As a part of the post-Partition refugee influx, many poor and homeless people had been hounded out from a similar terrain in Bangladesh and repatriated to the parched lands of Dandakaranya in central India. These people decided to travel all the way to the forested marshlands of the Gangetic delta, especially to this particular island called Morichjhapi, in search of land and livelihood, but were evicted all over again in spite of the fact that the then Left Front Government of West Bengal had given them assurances that they would be given land and shelter in the Sunderbans. In *The Hungry Tide* Amitav Ghosh interweaves his narrative by involving Nirmal in the activities of Morichjhapi, the form of whose diary encompasses the objectivity of journalism and the intimacy of a memoir. When Kanai starts reading Nirmal's diary, he sees that there was a date in the top left-hand corner, written in English: May 15, 1979, 5.30 a.m. The first few lines read thus:

> I am writing these words in a place that you will probably never have heard of: an island on the southern edge of the tide country, a place called Morichjhapi .... (67)

As Nilima explains to Kanai:

> Morichjhapi ... was a tide-country island .... In 1978, it happened that a great number of people suddenly appeared in Morichjhapi .... Within a matter of weeks they had cleared the mangroves, built bundhs and put up huts. It happened so quickly that in the beginning no one even knew who these people were. But in time it came to be learnt that they were refugees from Bangladesh. Some had come to India after Partition, while others had trickled over later. In Bangladesh they had been among the poorest of rural people, oppressed both by Muslim communalists and by Hindus of the upper castes. (118)

However since the government was strongly opposed to any settlement at Morichjhapi, Nilima clarified that 'the government [was] going to take measures. Very strong measures' (252). In the "Author's Note" section at the end of the novel, Ghosh refers to an article by Ross Mallick as the only published historical treatment available in English on the Morichjhapi incident. Highlighting the conflict between environment preservation and development, Mallick states that the investigation into the massacre of the refugees 'led in a political direction' and 'raised questions of secular institutional failures and how Untouchables and other marginalized peoples were being presented in Indian studies by those claiming to represent them' (104).

Probing a little deeper into the historical context of this event, we are made aware that the events leading up to the massacre actually revealed a trail of communal and class conflict that had its roots many centuries earlier. After the Partition, the Untouchables became politically marginalized minorities in both countries. The failure of the Congress government to grant them squatters' ownership and its attempts at eviction provided the Communist opposition with a ready following among the refugees, who gradually came to be organized by Communist front organizations. Since these refugees came from lower classes, they lacked the means to survive on their own and became dependent on government relief. They had to accept the government policy of dispersing them to other states on the claim that there was insufficient vacant land available in West Bengal. In this period the left-dominated opposition took up the case of the refugees and demanded the government settle them within their native Bengal rather than scatter them across India on the lands of other peoples. The Communist Party leader, Jyoti Basu, in prophetic words stated that it would not be 'an easy administrative affair to get rid of the refugees from their colonies' in West Bengal, and a 'united movement would make it impossible for the government to carry out the bill's [eviction] provisions.' In 1977 when the Dandakaranya refugees decided to come and settle in the Sunderbans, the Left Front government was already in power and they reversed the erstwhile declared policies. Many of the refugees were arrested and returned to the resettlement camps. The remaining refugees managed to slip through the police cordons, reaching their objective of Morichjhapi island where settlement began. By their own efforts they established a viable fishing industry, salt pans, a health centre, and schools over the following year. Though they did not ask for any money from the government, the state government was not disposed to tolerate such settlement, stating that the refugees were 'in unauthorized occupation of Morichjhapi which is a part of the Sunderbans Government Reserve Forest violating thereby the Forest Acts' (Refugee Relief and Rehabilitation Department 1979).

The rest of the history as described by Ross Mallick and other historians is rather pathetic. With no national party to take up their cause, the Untouchable Namashudras were indeed without powerful allies. On January 27, 1979, the government prohibited all movement into and out of Morichjhapi under the Forest Preservation Act and also promulgated Section 144 of the Criminal Penal Code, making it illegal for five or more persons to come together at any given time. When police action failed to persuade the refugees to leave, the State Government ordered the forcible evacuation of the refugees, which took place from May 14 to May 16, 1979. Muslim gangs were hired to assist the police as it was thought Muslims would be less sympathetic to refugees from Muslim-ruled Bangladesh. At least several hundred men, women, and children were said to have been killed in the operation and their bodies dumped in the river. The CPM congratulated its participant members on their successful operation at Morichjhapi and made their refugee policy reversal explicit stating that 'there was no possibility of giving shelter to these large number of refugees under any circumstance in the State' (CPM West Bengal State Committee, 1982). In a final twist to the episode, the CPM settled its own supporters in Morichjhapi, occupying and utilizing the facilities left by the evicted refugees. Prafulla K. Chakrabarti in his seminal book *The Marginal Men* gives us further details and socio-political repercussions:

> Even if it is admitted that the refugees should not have left Dandakaranya in so sudden a manner after selling out everything they had, the Left Front Government should have shown some more consideration for those whose total participation in the Left's struggle against the Establishment and whose kith and kin in West Bengal voting correctly for the Left Front enabled it to hit the Writers' Building [take state power] ... the Marxist Government had no compunction in driving out precisely those refugees who, according to their own statistical evaluation of the amount of surplus land available in West Bengal, could have been absorbed in West Bengal. (434)

In *The Hungry Tide,* Nilima makes us aware, as Ross Mallick did, that these people were more unfortunate as they belonged to the

Scheduled Castes – they were Dalits or what was earlier known as the Harijans. These 'Untouchables refugees were very different from the upper-caste, middle-class urban refugees of the immediate post-independence period, who were educated, well-connected, and politically influential' (108). Ghosh gives us a graphic description of the resistance that the refugees tried to put up. Many were killed trying to resist the police forces, and the women raped. After the gunshot was fired into the air, Nirmal like many others felt that the settlers would turn their backs:

> *In our heart of hearts we prayed they would. But what happened instead was something unforeseen: the people in the boat joined together their voices and began to shout, in unison, 'Amra kara? Bastuhara. Who are we? We are the dispossessed.' .... Then we heard the settlers shouting a refrain, answering the questions they had themselves posed: 'Morichjhapi chharbona. We'll not leave Morichjhapi, do what you may.'* (254)

With his own strong socialist leanings, Nirmal feels that his home is among the refugees and that it is impossible to abandon them. With Rilke's verse showing him the way, he internalizes the struggle of the refugees whose exodus never stops in history:

> *Standing on the deck of the bhotbhoti, I was struck by the beauty of this. Where else could you belong, except in the place you refused to leave. I joined my feeble voice to theirs: 'Morichjhapi chharbona!.'* (254)

One of the steps that the Left Front Government of West Bengal adopted during the Morichjhapi operation was to hush up the whole thing as much as possible. Thus nothing concrete was ever known about the brutal assault on the settlers. Morichjhapi was declared out of bounds for everyone including the journalists and reporters. In the novel, while reading Nirmal's diary, Kanai asks Horen, the local boatman, about the incidents in Morichjhapi. Initially Horen in an indifferent way replies, 'I know no more than anyone else knows. It was all just rumour' (278). A little later, Horen recalls, '... they burnt the settlers' huts, they sank their boats, they laid waste to their fields. Women were used and then thrown into the rivers, so that they would be washed away by the tides' (279). Eventually, a whole bustling settlement was razed to the ground within a few weeks. Thus we find that apart from depicting the remarkable acts of courage and resistance by people who were poor, helpless, deprived and dispossessed, Ghosh has managed to retrieve a forgotten chapter of partition history. Like historians of subaltern studies, he has shown openness, factual authenticity and compassion that instigate us to look into certain facets of post-partition politics. As in his earlier novels, displacement becomes a leitmotif in *The Hungry Tide* as well. When an interviewer, Amulya Gopalakrishnan, asked Ghosh about the Morichjhapi story and whether it can change minds more effectively than flag-waving activism can, he replied:

> Oh, I'm very aware of the limits of being a writer. But your critique of the world is reflected in everything you do. For me, Morichjhapi was inescapable. I'm concerned with the dilemma of how to balance human needs with nature. In India, the state seems to be so rigid, throwing people out, working under the assumption that they are wicked people with some perverse criminal instinct. But they are so terribly poor, braving the forest for nothing more than some honey. These are some of the poorest people in the world. (75)

Thus it becomes clear that the form of *The Hungry Tide* is both journalistic and novelistic. At the same time, though the novel is history, the facts are not always recounted in simple chronological order and Ghosh presents each incident at the point of the narrative where it is most relevant and dramatically effective.

Before concluding, I want to digress a little on the significance of the Morichjhapi incident via-à-vis Indian political history. It is true that as an anthropologist Ghosh found special interest and retrieved this long-forgotten or rather lesser-known history of subaltern resistance and embedded its facts in his fiction. Though there isn't much research material available on this subject in English [apart from the in-depth study by Ross Mallick and an unpublished 1992 dissertation by Nilanjana Chatterjee, both acknowledged as sources at the end of the novel], Morichjhapi has been referred to off and on in several Bengali publications, and in often different contexts. For example, in a forty-page pamphlet called *Roktakto Morichjhapi: Udbastu Gonohotyar Abhishapta Kahini* ["Bloody Morichjhapi: A Haunted Story of Refugee Genocide"] published on 6th September 1996 to celebrate the '19th Morichjhapi Day" by the North 24 Paraganas District unit of West Bengal Bahujan Samaj Party, Morichjhapi becomes an iconic example of Indian caste politics. Apart from painstakingly recording several journalistic and historical documents related to the incident, the author, who calls himself Bhimraj [journalist], primarily blames the upper-class political leaders for the tragedy. According to him Morichjhapi 'is still filled with the bloodshed and sighs of the Shudras' (5; translation mine). Requesting the future generation not to forget the atrocities inflicted upon the Untouchables, the writer also eulogizes the sacrifices made by the undaunted leaders of the Refugee Rehabilitation Committee. Interestingly, he then turns the whole issue into present day political activism, asking all downtrodden and untouchable men and women to rise up on the occasion:

> That good time has arrived for all the Shudras, Dalits and members of the Bahujan Samaj in India to rise up and create an intense public opinion against these Stalinists who killed innocent Shudra refugees at random, threw innocent children into the river and raped young mothers and sisters. Today we have a king, a leader and a political party. Can't the Bahujan Samaj all unite now, shout the 'Jai Bheem' slogan, clutch the blue flag in our hands and call in unison, 'Come let us visit Morichjhapi?' (6; translation mine)

Coming to even more contemporary times, Morichjhapi has once again been retrieved from the long-forgotten pages of history vis-à-vis the governmental policies in West Bengal related to the forcible acquisition of land from farmers and selling it to multinationals and industrialists to set up factories. Since February 2007 the Left Front Government's actions in Singur and Nandigram under the leadership of the present Chief Minister Buddhadeb Bhattacharya has led to a deluge of protests by people from all walks of life. Local newspapers are flooded with comments, criticism, opinions for, as well as against, such moves. What is interesting is the fact that in a large number of these articles and reports, there are comparative analyses of the present event with that of Morichjhapi. One example will elucidate the matter further. In a front-page column entitled *"Erporh?"* ["What Next?"] published on 10th February 2007 in the Bengali newspaper *Dainik Statesman*, Mahasweta Devi, in her unstinted criticism of governmental action states:

> What I am writing now is exactly how I have understood the situation. Along with Singur, the task of uprooting man from the soil is going on

everywhere. A tree uprooted from its roots dies, so does the farmer ... Buddha is a liar. Today there was a journalist from Maharashtra. He has read the statements of Buddha in English where I have been accused of agitating against industrialization. On hearing this, I told him that in this state lies were being cultivated in the name of industry ... . He asked me whether Jyoti Basu was different from this man.

How do I make people understand? So I had to narrate the incidents of Morichjhapi. I do not know whether this generation has heard the name of Morichjhapi. If I analyze the source of this name, this is how it stands.

In order to support her point of view, Mahasweta then quotes from a book called *Morichjhapir Kanna* [The Tears of Morichjhapi] by Shibnath Chowdhuri that lucidly explains the entire history of that subaltern resistance:

> 'After the Partition, the uprooted refugees were sent outside Bengal to Dandyakaranya. During that time many eminent people including members of the undivided Communist Party and other leftist parties had opposed the move. After the partition fifty lakh refugees came to West Bengal. Out of that forty-seven lakh people arranged for rehabilitation on their own. About three lakh refugees needed to be resettled.'

She goes on to comment on this:

> But three lakh refugees remained in Dandyakaranya. I have further read in this book that in 1975. Jyoti Basu had gone to address a meeting at Bhilai ... . On 17.12.1977 Jyoti Basu stated: 'If the refugees want to live without any help from the government, they can do so.' He also informed that if they came to West Bengal, the police would not act in the manner that they did during the Congress regime. The refugees from Dandyakaranya started coming to West Bengal from March 1978 onwards. They advanced up to Hasnabad when the state police and party cadres started inflicting unspeakable torture upon them. It was then that with the help of a particular reckless minister these people landed at Morichjhapi in the Sunderbans. They built a eight-to-ten feet high and thirty-mile long embankment. They built houses, primary and secondary schools, markets, hospitals and roads. They sank tubewells, developed bidi factories and bakeries, and even wood and handloom industries. If Morichjhapi remained as it was then, it would be a worth visiting place.

After this, Jyoti Basu's police force tortured these people, killed them, sank their launches and forced them to return to Dandyakaranya. Narrating that story will leave this article incomplete. I am writing all these things today because if Jyoti Basu did it very crudely, Buddha is doing the same thing now in a more cunning way. So Buddha is behaving in such an uncivilized manner today and the word 'man/human being' has no value for him. (translation mine)

The purpose of including such a long extract from Mahasweta Devi's article here (which is reiterated in many such indictments by Sunanda Sanyal and other intellectuals) is to come back once again to Amitav Ghosh and his treatment of subaltern history in *The Hungry Tide*. When the novel was published in 2005, the Morichjhapi incident seemed to most readers a unique piece of a micro-event in Bengal's long political history. But somehow, by blending fact and fiction in his own signature fashion, the author has unknowingly stoked the embers of post-partition politics in the subcontinent. Morichjhapi is raising new issues, thoughts and ideas for us today.

Works Cited

Bakhtin, M.M. "Forms of Time and of the Chronotope in the Novel: Notes toward a Historical Poetics" in *The Dialogic Imagination: Four Essays*. Ed. Michael Holquist. Austin: University of Texas Press, 1981.

Bhimraj, (Sangbadik). *Roktakto Morichjhapi: Udbastu Gonohatyar Abhishapto Kahini*. Panchpota, South 24 Paraganas: Bahujan Sahitya Prakashani, 1996.

Chakrabarti, Prafulla K. *The Marginal Men: The Refugees and the Left Political Syndrome in West Bengal*. Kalyani, W.B.: Lumiere Books, 1990.

Chatterjee, Nilanjana. "Midnight's Unwanted Children: East Bengal Refugees and the Politics of Rehabilitation." Ph.D dissertation. Brown University, 1992.

Devi, Mahasweta. "Erporh?" ["What Next?"]. Kolkata: *Dainik Statesman*, 10 February, 2007: 1 & 5.

Ghosh, Amitav. *The Hungry Tide*. Delhi: Harper Collins India, 2005.

—. "I think in images." Interview given to Ramya Ramamurthy, *MidDay*. August 4, 2004. http://www.mid-day.com/entertainment/news/2004/august/89207.htm

—. "A praise book of the tides." Interview with Amulya Gopalakrishnan. *Frontline,* September 10, 2004: 75.

Mallick, Ross. "Refugee Settlement in Forest Reserves: West Bengal Policy Reversal and the Morichjhapi Massacre." *The Journal of Asia Studies* 58. No. 1 (February 1999).

Mahanta, Banibrata. "Foregrounding the Local: Nature, Language and Human Enterprise in Amitav Ghosh's *The Hungry Tide.*" *The Indian Journal of English Studies* XLIV, 2007.

Sanyal, Sunanda. *"Sarah Poschim Bongo Ekhon Poshu Khamar, Manusher Upasthiti Sekhane Ashojya"* ["The Whole of West benga; is now an Animal Farm, the presence of Man there is Intolerable"]. Kolkata: *Dainik Statesman,* 8 April, 2007.

Spivak, Gayatri Chakravorty. " 'breast-giver': for author, reader, teacher, subaltern, historian …" in *Breast Stories: Mahasweta Devi.* Kolkata: Seagull, 1997.

16
KINSHUK MAJUMDAR

Crossing Cultural Boundaries: A Study of Amitav Ghosh's *The Hungry Tide*

Amitav Ghosh in all his novels talks about intermingling of different cultures and the interaction of people of different regions and culture. Cross-cultural encounters are, therefore, an important feature of all his novels and travelogues. In his earlier novels like *In An Antique Land*, *The Circle of Reason*, and *The Shadow Lines* this theme has been dealt with in detail. In *The Shadow Lines*, Tridib, the narrator's uncle, is a regular visitor to places like London and Calcutta as well as Dhaka, and the Tridib-May relationship is a direct outcome of these visits and meetings. In his work *In An Antique Land* the author himself is a visitor to Egypt and he stays in a village where he talks of the intermingling of people of various cultures and civilizations of both past and present. The constant reference to Ben Yiju, the medieval traveller, and references to the past glories of Egypt make us realize that Egypt has a long history and its present day situation is a direct outcome of that history. Ancient Indian civilization is also a part of this novel. *The Glass Palace* provides an account of the imperial encounters in three countries, India, Burma and Malaya. The cross-cultural encounters are an essential part of his writings as his characters mostly travel from one place to another gaining new experiences of life.

The Hungry Tide presents an intricate situation where three people – namely Kanai, a businessman running a translation bureau, Piya, a cetologist and Fokir, an illiterate fisherman-meet in Sunderbans. They actually belong to different cultural backgrounds and for the first time in any of Ghosh's novels does a man living in the lap of nature occupy a position of importance. Fokir is described by Ghosh in the chapter "The Fall" for the first time as observed by Piya. Piya notices that he has a:

> grizzled look of an experienced hand: around his chin and mouth was a dusting of white that suggested stubble or a beard. There was some kind of turban wrapped around his head but his body was bare except for a single twist of cloth, wound between his legs and around his waist. His frame was skeletal, almost wasted, in the way of a man who'd grown old on the water, slowly yielding his flesh to the wind and the sun. (42–43)

This young man is representative of the abject poverty and exploitation of the refugees and offers a contrast to the middle class, urbane, polished Kanai and Piya, and is symbolic of the economic disparity of different socio-cultural background brought about by the political structure in the present day West Bengal. Despite being poor, he is a man of honesty and integrity whose main role is to act as Piya's guide through the dangerous waters.

The Hungry Tide is divided into two parts entitled "Jowar" and "Bhata", synonymous with the ebb and the tide of the sea. The novel talks of the Sunderbans; Kanai wants to visit the place because he has to meet his aunt whose deceased husband's notebook he has inherited. He meets Piyali Roy at the railway station. Piyali is visiting the Sunderbans as she is doing research on marine species. As Piya begins her research she is harassed by local guides and is saved from drowning by Fokir, a boatman. They become friends and Fokir helps her to achieve her goals. Her journey across the river is a success and the story moves back and forth with time, to deal with the historical realities of time. The colonialist Scot Hamilton started a rehabilitation project in Lusibari for the upliftment of the downtrodden which was carried on by the idealist, Nirmal many years later. Scot Hamilton purchased ten thousand acres of land from the British and employed people of all castes and religions. The area was known as Hamilton-abad. He wanted to build a new society run by co-operatives. As Nirmal points out, 'It was a dream, Kanai, ... What he wanted was no different from what dreamers have always wanted. He wanted to build a place where no one would exploit anyone and people would live together without petty social distinctions and differences. He dreamed of a place where men and women could be farmers in the morning, poets in the afternoon and carpenters in the evening' (*The Hungry Tide* 53). In both the generations, the desire to discover the secrets of nature and also rehabilitate the downtrodden, is met with disaster. The journey in the boat unites the two generations and the novel ends with the death of Fokir while saving Piya and she continuing her research work and looking after the welfare of the people with the help of Badabon Trust.

Fokir is not the only man who has been victimized by the inequalities of society. Ghosh makes an attack on the political system of West Bengal by presenting a pathetic picture of the refugees in contemporary West Bengal who had settled in Morichjhapi. The political system in contemporary West Bengal does not allow the refugees to settle in the Sunderbans. The government whether of India or of Bangladesh has no sympathy for these poor people. Says Ghosh, in the voice of Nilima, Kanai's aunt:

> In 1978 a great number of people suddenly appeared in Morichjhapi. In this place where there had been no inhabitants before there were now thousands, almost overnight. Within a matter of weeks they had cleared the mangroves, built *badhs* and put up huts. It happened so quickly that in the beginning nobody knew who these people were. But in time it came to be learnt that they were refugees, originally from Bangladesh. Some had come to India after Partition, while others had trickled over later. In Bangladesh they had been among the poorest of rural people, oppressed and exploited both by Muslim communalists and by Hindus of the upper castes ... . But it was not from Bangladesh that these refugees were fleeing when they came to Morichjhapi; it was from a government resettlement camp in central India. In the years after Partition the authorities had removed the refugees to a place called Dandakaranya, deep in the forests of Madhya Pradesh, hundreds of kilometres from Bengal. (118)

The position of the migrants, as mentioned in the diary of Nirmal, Kanai's uncle who is now no more, is extremely pitiable. The story moves backwards and forwards as in all of Amitav Ghosh's novels. It portrays the evils existing in the national political system. The investigation taken up by Piya in the Sunderban delta regarding its marine ecosystem becomes a potent tool in the hands of a skillful writer like

Ghosh, to expose the corruption in the existing political system where young fishermen like Fokir were exploited. The politicians are merciless in their attitude to the refugees and also to the poor whom they do not even recognize as human beings. To quote from the novel:

> Earlier that year a Left Front ministry had taken power in West Bengal and the refugees may have assumed that they would not face much opposition from the state government. But this was a miscalculation: the authorities had declared that Morichjhapi was a protected forest reserve and they proved unbending in their determination to evict the settlers. Over a period of about a year there had been a series of confrontations between the settlers and government forces. (119)

Amitav Ghosh deftly exposes the mask of a communist worn by the government of West Bengal which runs the state and controls the machinery in capitalistic or feudalistic style. The state is quite indifferent to the sufferings of the people. Morichjhapi is a small area in the Sunderban delta which has been ignored for generations together and it is here that Ghosh voices the need of the subaltern and Fokir becomes their representative. According to Rollason:

> The idea of utopia, as conceived by the visionary Hamilton and hankered after by Nirmal, always runs the risk of eliding the concrete historical realities of class. The vexed issue of social class barriers appears in Ghosh's novel twice over, across two generations – in the refugees' revolt of which Kusum is a part, and the friendship (if that is the word) that develops across class lines between Fokir, her illiterate son, and the cosmopolitan outsider Piya.

Utopia is what even Piya, another idealist, thought the Sunderbans to be. She mistook the area to be nature's gift and believed that the delta region far away from the hum and bustle of city life should be one of calm and peace, where her research on marine species would blossom. However, the complexities of human life are too subtle. Her fateful meeting with Fokir quite early in the novel points not only to the complexities of human relationships but also to the socio-political aspects of the Sunderban delta which would deeply impinge on the action in the novel. But on the optimistic side, it must be observed that the quest for moral order is eternal and will always be hankered after by some. They might be crushed but will not be stifled down for ever.

It is here that the cross-cultural encounter in the novel gathers importance. The goal for achieving peace and harmony in a world of chaos will always continue.

Fokir, despite being illiterate, has a helpful, co-operative nature; he is an intelligent young man whose folk wisdom and knowledge of the local area regarding dolphins, becomes instrumental in Piya's success in discovering the secrets of the sea. The relationship between the two transgresses all barriers – social, cultural, and political. The action as presented in the novel is to be seen as a journey by Piya and Fokir through which Piya makes her research on marine life. This happens because Piya the cetologist rightly realizes that Fokir being a fisherman who is an integral part of the rural culture of the Sunderbans will be responsible for the success in her campaign about marine life there. She tells Kanai in clear terms that Fokir was of great help in the boat ride and the journey was a success. To quote from the text: 'Fokir's abilities as an observer are really extraordinary. I wish I could tell you what it was like to be with him these last few days – it was one of the most exciting experiences of my life' (268). This is an unpalatable truth for Kanai. His intellectual arrogance makes him jealous of Fokir and makes him feel small. He is not able to digest it and retorts sharply with words that are loaded with jealousy and reveal his deep-rooted inferiority complex. He says:

> Piya, there's nothing in common between you then and there isn't now. Nothing. He's a fisherman and you're a scientist. What you see as fauna he sees as food. He's never sat in a chair, for heaven's sake. Can you imagine what he'd do if he was taken on to a plane? (268)

Kanai cannot appreciate the necessity of having a guide like Fokir as he cannot cross the class barriers. He is rooted at this point of time in the mentality of a typical upper class, educated businessman stereotyping people and measuring their value with intellect. This makes him insensitive towards Fokir at times. This intellectual arrogance of Kanai is further revealed in his conversation with Fokir where he asks the latter about his parentage. While Fokir confesses that he hardly remembers his father whom he did not see after his mother's death. When Kanai asks whether he remembers his mother, the conversation becomes extremely interesting:

And your mother? Do you remember her?
How could I forget her? Her face is everywhere. He said this in such a plain, matter-of-fact way that Kanai was puzzled. What are you saying, Fokir? Where do you see her face? He smiled and began to point in every direction, to the ends of the compass as well to his head and feet: Here, here, here, here. Everywhere. (319)

The answer is puzzling to Kanai as he is no longer in touch with natural life. He cannot measure the importance of Fokir because he has lost touch with the spontaneous life of strong emotional bonds. For him emotions are not of much importance as compared to concrete material achievements. It is essentially the presence of Fokir which makes the novel different from Ghosh's other novels. The omnipresent maternal figure, loving and affectionately looking after the child, caressing him lovingly even after her death through his memory depicts a strong tie of love between Fokir and his dead mother. As Suresh Menon says: 'It is a world apart from Kanai's expertise in many languages which ultimately weighs him down, and keeps him from soaring towards an unsaid, unexpressed but felt affinity for Piyali.' Fokir's eternal bond with his mother lends depth to the novel. The topographical details provided by the author in the novel regarding the mangroves, the rivers, the Gangetic delta and the socio-political realities of contemporary West Bengal become the vast backdrop before which the drama of human relationships is played out. And Fokir becomes a poignant figure, almost a tragic hero. In the above conversation with Kanai, he asserts the importance of the bond of love which for him puts things in proper perspective for the whole humanity and is the main reason for his living.

In the course of time the proximity to Fokir has its positive influence on Kanai. He becomes a more sensitive person and does not tend to look at matters from the crude intellectual point of view. He learns the lessons of humility from a rustic, whose goodness he cannot help but acknowledge. This is evident when he becomes somewhat apologetic when Fokir's wife, Moyna charges him with being indifferent to Fokir and leaving Piya and Fokir in Gorjontola on that fateful night. To quote the relevant lines from the conversation between Kanai and Moyna:

You left them behind? Her eyes flared in angry indignation. With the cyclone coming – you left them behind in the jungle?

It wasn't my decision, Moyna, Kanai said. It was Horen who decided. He said there was nothing else to be done.

Oh? The mention of Horen seemed to calm her a little. But what they will they do out there, with no shelter, nothing?

They'll be all right, Moyna, Kanai said. Fokir will know what to do, don't worry. Others have survived storms on that island, his grandfather included. (380)

The usual brutal and indifferent attitude towards a rustic is no longer to be seen. Instead a tone of concern and a sense of fellow-feeling does develop in the mind of Kanai. For Kanai the illiterate fisherman has become a dependable expert on nature who will act as a saviour for Piya. It dawns on Kanai that a simple, uneducated man is of greater help to Piya than him. He accepts the view that supremacy of one man over another is not always to be measured through intellectual capabilities or formal education. Kanai realizes that here is a simple, innocent rustic boatman who despite his illiteracy, is dependable and loyal to their cause. This reminds one of Rousseau who laid stress on the goodness of the natural man. Fokir reviving the cult of the noble savage, becomes the hero in unravelling the mysteries of the sea without whom the journey would have been incomplete.

The most moving incident in the novel is Fokir's death because he becomes the sacrificial scapegoat in the name of humanity. He dies by getting drowned in the river. He dies while protecting Piya. Kanai, Moyna and Horen come to look for them when the storm abates. Moyna faints when she realizes that Fokir is missing. Piya explains:

Her voice was almost inaudible: 'He didn't make it.'

It had happened in the last hour of the storm, she said. He'd been hit by something very big and very heavy, an uprooted stump; it had hit him so hard that she too had been crushed against the trunk of the tree they were sitting on. The sari had kept them attached to the trunk even as he was dying. His mouth was close enough to her ear so that she'd been able to hear him. He'd said Moyna's name and Tultul's before the breath faded on his lips. She'd left his body on the tree, tied to the trunk with Moyna's sari, to keep it safe from animals. They would have to go back to Garjontola to cut it down. (392)

The consequence of natural disaster can be horrifying. The storm proves too strong to break the relationship between Fokir and Piya. Fokir remains till the last moment of his life loyal to Moyna and their daughter, Tultul. The principles which form the basis of all human relationships remain clear in the mind of Fokir, asserting his strong moral values in a rather morally convoluted society.

The death of Fokir leaves Piya shattered. Despite the gap between the two, at the cultural and educational level, they had become good friends and were jointly responsible for the success of Piya's venture There is a deep sense of guilt in her:

> Piya's face was stonily expressionless, as if to suggest that she had retreated deep within herself.
>
> Piya's in shock Kanai had said to Nilima one day, shortly before his own departure. It's hardly surprising. Can you imagine what it was like for her to sit through her last hours of the storm, sheltered by Fokir's lifeless body? Leave aside the horror of the memory – imagine the guilt, the responsibility. (395)

Ghosh has clearly shown how much Piya has felt the impact of Fokir's violent end. She has been portrayed as a humanist whose feeling for her fellow human beings is praiseworthy. She decides to continue her work for the people of Sunderbans, and keeps her word as his true friend. She gives a report about her dolphin sightings of the area and gets several offers for funding from various environmentalist groups. Piya's decision to continue her affiliation with Badabon Trust involving the local fisherman shows how much concern she has for the local people. Her interest in their welfare has now turned into her mission.

Fokir, though dead, becomes a legend who has created an indelible impression on the readers who have realized that they cannot ignore the man of nature who is a key to the understanding of the complexities in the Sunderban delta which is varied in its flora and fauna. The boatman represents the subaltern who has been given a voice through Fokir and although he himself is a reticent, simple person he represents the cult of the 'noble savage' propounded by Rousseau in *The Social Contract: Discourses* (1762) which begins, 'Man is born free; and everywhere he is in chains. One thinks himself to be the master of others, and still remain a greater slave than they. How did this change come about? I do not know. What can make it legitimate?' (3) Fokir represents the 'general will' of doing well which lurks in the primitive man. This is what has made Fokir different from Kanai and many others. His simple life has helped him to maintain his goodness and helpful nature. He becomes a means to tell people that simplicity and goodness is not dependant on man's cultural or educational background. Kanai, on the contrary, tries to master others and behaves as the lord and master of the situation he is in. He continuously tries to prove that he is indispensable for Piya's success and, throughout the novel, Ghosh is constantly at pains to show that his claims are only hollow. The exhibition of such a strong will and arrogant assertion of his intellect at the initial stages is changed towards the end into a profound realization through Fokir that one must be humble.

The cross-cultural encounter between two educated upper class persons and their relationship with the illiterate but proud, honest and upright boatman makes *The Hungry Tide* a very different novel from Ghosh's other works. It is much more significant in terms of characterisation as a layman emerges as a hero in the novel. Probably, the only character who comes close to Fokir is Khalil, a rickshaw-puller, in *The Shadow Lines* looking after the demented old man Jethamoshai and getting butchered in the 1964 riots along with him and Tridib. He is introduced very late in the novel when Tridib, May and the narrator's grandmother go to meet the grandmother's uncle in Dhaka. He is seen to be in charge of this old man and is described by Saifuddin, a mechanic, as follows:

> Khalil and his family look after Ukil-babu, Saifuddin explained to her. He's a nice fellow. He came over from India too; from Murshidabad, in Bengal. He's a bit stupid, but he's got a good heart. That's what I always say to people – I say, he may be foolish, but he's got a good heart, otherwise why would he bother to look after that old man, a Hindu too, when he could have easily thrown him out and kept both rooms for his family? (*The Shadow Lines* 209)

Like Fokir, Khalil too is a simple illiterate man with a large heart who in this political world of turmoil and the communal frenzy prevailing in Dhaka and Calcutta, maintains his sense of humanity and despite his poverty reaches out to look after Jethamoshai, the bedridden old man. He does not bother about religious considerations. He is poor and it must have been difficult for him to maintain Jethamoshai. Rather, he, like Tridib, sacrifices his life for Jethamoshai. As May Price tells the narrator at the end of the novel: 'When I got there, I saw three bodies. They were all dead. They'd cut Khalil's stomach open. The old man's head had been hacked off. And they'd cut Tridib's throat, from ear to ear' *(The Shadow Lines* 251).

Since Khalil is a minor character his death does not draw as much attention as the death of Tridib who is the driving force of *The Shadow Lines* or of Fokir who becomes the centre of attention in *The Hungry Tide*. The reasons for the death of these characters are different. But they both give up their lives in an attempt to save others. Fokir dies in trying to save Piya and Khalil is killed, for the sake of Jethamoshai. Khalil comes at the end of the novel and we know little about his emotions and feelings. He has no independent role but is a means to show how political violence leads to the butchering of innocents. Fokir on the other hand is more clearly etched in the novel becoming an independent and important character with a personality of his own. But, in the final analysis they both represent the essential goodness of the human heart which is necessary for sustenance of humanity in a chaotic world.

The cross-cultural encounter and the interaction of Fokir, Kanai and Piya stresses the need for translation and the need for knowing a number of languages to understand the people of different backgrounds and culture not only between India and the west but also within different parts of India. Kanai is the means by which Piya gets in touch with the wider world. A number of people come close to one another and the language in which they communicate becomes important. Supriya Choudhuri lays stress on the importance of language:

> Most remarkable is Ghosh's treatment of Kanai, a self-important, sometimes cocksure individual who ultimately becomes the locus of some the novel's central reflections on language and on translation. It is through Kanai's translation, his mediating sensibility, that Nirmal's

personal record, the Rilke that he reads in Buddhadeb Bose's Bangla translation, and the folk narrative of Bon Bibi that he writes down from Fokir's recitation, reach us, so the novel seems to claim, in English prose and verse. Some Bengali reviewers of *The Hungry Tide* have already asserted that their experience of reading a novel was like reading a novel in Bangla. This claim seems to me mistaken. Rather the novel seem to push everything in the novel is translated, in that it seeks to represent, in English, a life, a culture, that is experienced principally through the medium of Bangla and its local variants.

The English language becomes a tool in which Raja Rao says, 'One has to convey in a language that is not one's own the spirit that is one's own. It is the language of our intellectual make-up – like Sanskrit or Persian was before – but not our emotional make-up. We are all instinctively bilingual, many of us writing in our own language and in English ... . Our method of expression therefore has to be a dialect ...' (v). Ghosh uses the English language mixing it with Bangla, something which an illiterate man like Fokir would use more frequently to add verisimilitude to the novel. That is why, the character of Kanai is deliberately introduced to act as a communicator between Fokir and Piya and he has to mediate between the sophisticated city-bred woman and the illiterate boatman. The cross-cultural encounter automatically lays stress on plurality of languages and an educated translator has to bridge the gap between Fokir and Piya. As Rollason says, 'The need for translation arises from the phenomenon of multilingualism in an interrelated world. Multilingualism has always been a part of the Indian context, Ghosh himself is multilingual and his earlier novels contain episodes reflecting a keen awareness of the complexities and difficulties of language interaction, both among Indians and between the Indians and the wider world.' The language gap between Piya and Fokir, pushes one to realize that given the socio-political realities of our country we cannot communicate with one another effectively in one language only. We have to bridge the gap between the two diverse cultures but only by using two different languages, mediated by a translator. It is here that Kanai becomes important, because he is instrumental in bridging the gap between Piya and Fokir. Even in the case of Nirmal and Kusum, Fokir's mother, the gap between education and social class arose as they have different intellectual wavelengths and cannot communicate in the same language, though both speak Bangla. One has to learn to inhabit both the language and the world of the other. Piya makes this effort and this is manifested in the transformation that takes place in her after Fokir's death. *The Hungry Tide* is a work about blurred boundaries, false divisions and the courage to go across.

Works Cited

Choudhuri, Supriya. "A Sense of Place." *Biblio*. 10.04.07. http://amitavghosh.com/review_books_htm/.

Eakambaram, N. "Theme of Violence in *The Shadow Lines*." *The Novels of Amitav Ghosh*. Ed. R.K. Dhawan. New Delhi: Prestige, 1999.

Ghosh, Amitav. *The Shadow Lines*. Delhi: Ravi Dayal, 1988.

—. *The Hungry Tide*. London: Harper Collins, 2004.

Menon, Suresh. "Love in The Hungry Tide." *Deccan Herald*. Sunday, August 29, 2004.<http://www.deccanherald.com/deccanherald/aug292004/artic5.asp>27.1.06.

Rao, Raja. *Kanthapura*. 1938. Delhi: Oxford University Press, 1974.

Rollason, Christopher. "In Our Translated World: Transcultural Communication In Amitav Ghosh's *The Hungry Tide*." 21.11.06. <http://www.seikilos.com.ar/ghosh.pdf/>.

Rousseau, Jean Jacques. *The Social Contract: Discourse*. (1762). Trans. G.D.H. Cole. London: Dent, 1913.

Spivak, Chakravorty Gayatri. "Can the Subaltern Speak?" *The Post-Colonial Studies Reader*. Eds. Ashcroft et al. London: Routledge, 1995.

17 MADHURI CHATTERJEE

Home and the Travelling Self: Amitav Ghosh's *The Hungry Tide* and Vikram Seth's *From Heaven Lake*

Travel and rootedness cruise endlessly on the fluidity of our conditions and are shaped and enhanced by the radical geopolitics of the new age. The two texts I have chosen are Amitav Ghosh's *The Hungry Tide* (2004) and Vikram Seth's *From Heaven's Lake* (1983). Both are border texts – one fictional and the other a travelogue – and explore cultural and disciplinary border crossings and identities formed through acts of dislocation, voluntary as well as involuntary. Borders can be defined in different ways. They become self created when an individual creates or crosses them, also often borders are circumstantial or socially created as in most of Ghosh's writing. Despite being members of a dominant culture, the characters face marginalization. In theory, and effectively in practice, borders are neither inside nor outside the territory they define but simply designate the difference between the two. They are not really spaces at all but act as the sites of difference between interiority and exteriority; and as Jan Mohamed has observed are 'points of infinite regression' (103). Both texts are articulated from the neutrality of the border. Similarly the subjectivity of the experience depends/coincides with response from home which again can be associated with culture, environment and the process of growth. Travel thus becomes a kind of displacement akin to multiple border crossings: cultural, geographical and ideological. In the process travel sets a series of transformation both within outside. Bartkowski defines travel as 'not only leaving home for some place else, but also the capacity for movement, a lack of fixity, a knowledge of shifting grounds' (159). Travel becomes a trope for passing through space or time into situations outside oneself and one's social place and national identity, dispensing with all borderlines. It also involves an encounter with the 'other' resulting in self-exploration. It may be linear for Seth but cyclical and enriched with repetition for Ghosh – and a shift in experience, almost in sense of going away and coming home.

In *The Hungry Tide*, the author has made way for those who prefer isolation and bohemias of their own instead of falling into the trappings of settled fixities. Also the fact that in a 'secular and contingent world, homes are always provisional. Borders and barriers which enclose us within the safety of familiar territory, can also become prisons, and are often deferred beyond reason or necessity' (*Mind of Winter* 54). Ghosh reveals his anthropological fascination with Sunderbans, a maze of floating islands covered with mangroves (known as Sundari trees in Bangla after which the region takes its name) and weaves a narrative around it. Between the sea and the plains of Bengal, on the easternmost coast of India, lies an immense archipelago of islands. Some are vast and some no larger than sandbars. Some have lasted through recorded history while the others have just been washed into being. It is also a place where there are no borders to divide fresh water from salt, river from sea, even land from water and for hundred of years, only the truly dispossessed braved the man-eating tigers and crocodiles to rule here, to eke out a precarious existence from the mud and where at the beginning of the last century, a visionary Scotsman (Daniel Hamilton) founded a utopian settlement where people of all races, classes and religion could live together, thus eliminating borders completely. The novel is about two travellers who venture into Sunderbans – Piyali Roy, an American cetologist of Bengali origin who is researching the endangered Irrawaddy dolphin said to inhabit the tidal waters of Sunderbans and Kanai Dutt, a suave worldly-wise New Delhi translator and businessman, who is visiting his aunt to receive an old notebook written by his uncle before he died mysteriously in a local uprising. It is the travels of this dead man which form a third journey and the notebook becomes a fixity containing the explorations of a restless soul. Kanai's uncle's notebook reveals the shocking story of the Morichjhapi incident, where tens of thousands of displaced refugees, who had tried to settle on one of the uninhabited islands, but were violently evicted by the government in the name of conservation. Piya hires an illiterate boatman Fokir, to guide her through the backwaters in her search for the dolphins and Kanai comes along to translate. The tension between the three grows as they are thrown against each other and are drawn unawares into the hidden undercurrents of this isolated world and the tide begins to turn for them. In the defining movement, everything else collapses and the mind is a swamped by pure sensation. 'The tide flows between events, perspectives and impeccably drawn moments' (376) in the lives of the characters. His characters cross borders, break barriers of thought and expression in a strange way.

Kanai lives in a translated world and is not at ease while journeying through the socio-cultural hinterlands. He rushes into this place of perpetual change and transformation but his return to the lingocentric world is an indirect comment on those who prefer cozy spaces of habitat at home for Kanai is in a temporarily 'adopted' place and resides in the culture being studied or as Clifford says 'the field is a home away from home, a place of dwelling ...' (99). However Piya is a homebody abroad, it is journey that regulates most of her life she says, 'Home is where the orcellas are'. Piya thus redefines home as a shifting domain, a place that can be created anywhere in this world. For Kanai's aunt Nilima 'home is wherever I can brew a pot of good tea'. These two expressions dissolve borderlines because while Nilima is rooted in Lusibari and is completely dedicated to this re-invented space, a place she had moved to in 1950 first from Dhaka to Calcutta and then to this place. Piya is a free spirit and the law of transgression doesn't hold her, as her 'self' is at home where she can pursue her desire and re-discover her own imagined space. Home for Nilima also means commitment not merely the contours of a geographical location, but for Piyali Roy it means absence of an anchorage. Moving or travelling for them may not mean homelessness but it would be finding a new place for sheltering their desires. For Moyna, home means deprivation. To move across specific locales may mean betrayal for some. The dichotomy between home and homelessness is reflected in Nirmal's character who displays a duality that propels him to fight for Bangladeshi refugees by forsaking the comfort of his home. Fokir's love for life across the frontiers towards which the river flows, sustains him. Thus home becomes a site of conflict as well as a metaphor of unity and harmony. Ironically home and travel also become synonymous – an unending quest or as Neil Bissoondath sums it up, 'For many, the journey is inevitable ... cast the new land in a sharper and more compelling light ... but they must make it before they can truly move on with their lives' (Bissoondath 26). The river journey in open space which Piya and Fokir undertake together may offer them a metaphor of home that never was and never can be. Piya chases dolphins that carry her across fixed boundaries and Fokir remains trapped in the river, caught between its ebb and tide.

However, secular criticism places home and homelessness in a binary opposition. While 'home' comes to be associated with 'culture' as an environment process and hegemony that determine individuals through complicated mechanism, homelessness cannot be achieved without multiple border crossings, indeed without a constant, keen awareness of the 'politics of borders' (110–112). The idea of home is sustained through fixity and ceaseless negotiation in space. A specific location can be called 'home' as long as one lives there but when the location is made to cast its shadow on its inhabitants, dogging their steps and compelling them to return to its fold, it becomes a tyranny endorsed by those who see locations as inalienable and integrated wholes of their consciousness from which escape proves futile. Nirmal, Nilima's husband, discovers in the island people a space for his dormant activism and self-expression in working for a cause. The consciousness of home as a fixed destination and homelessness as state of uprootedness makes Ghosh explore the plight of displaced people, the Bangladeshis, who found themselves in a confrontation with the Indian state in 1979. The ruthless suppression and massacre in East Pakistan had made the refugees run away from Dandkaranya refugee camps to Morichjhampi as they felt that the later regions would provide them with familiar environs and therefore a better life. The theme of immigration, sometimes voluntarily sometimes forced, runs through his work. Ghosh fits in a different category as he 'is neither an exile nor an immigrant' and able to develop, out of his border status, a theory of exile as an ascetic code of willed homelessness' (Said,

"Secular Criticism" 7) and debates in his writings how ideas and theories are transformed when borders are crossed.

Borders are constructed in a variety of ways in Ghosh's text – personal, methodological (anthropological), cultural and linguistic – and his persistent theme is of the ephemerality of concepts of national and ethnic identity. The multilayered structure of the novel reveals the multiplicity of names and Sunderbans is a metaphor for that ephemerality. In keeping with the theme and mood, the novel is divided into two parts: the ebb – bhatta, the flood – jowar. For the inhabitant of this island – this land is known as bhatisdesh – the tide country – except that bhatta is not just the tide but one tide in particular, the ebb tide, it is only through receding that the water gives birth to the forest. The idea of home in the river country is nothing short of the gift of the river, for what the hungry tide does not devour is home and what remains like silt under the raging waters is Bonbibi's mythical kingdom – who is the reigning deity of the tide country and the power of rivers, tides, winds, storms and all the elements that transcend kingdom. The elemental factor is very powerful and overwhelms all the characters but nature is not always malevolent, for though Fokir dies, the storm brings Piya and Fokir very close, something that man-made society never had. Even Kanai, who seems a little frivolous, is changed after this experience. Fokir's death can be taken also as the catalytic agent that changes perceptions considerably. In Ghosh's vision – a plural syncretic local cult presides over this flood – a goddess of hope and vengeance is the chief protagonist in the book and she is not a person, but the ocean tide. It is also the tide of history, emotions and rediscovering.

However the idea of home and the travelling self still contain each other. The two binaries can be both worked and erased simultaneously as the 'return' is always there. For home is where one lives and this can be anywhere in the world and the self in a state of travel – is a state of enlightenment, as homelessness contains all suppressed desires of home, a route into dialectics that feeds on the realization that it is necessary to have a home first in order to move out of it. For Vikram Seth this kind of unhousedness is not new and as Rushdie has said in an interview, 'the loss of home happens all the time we are all unhoused in this world. The second house we make is over our home. You carry the other place in your heart' (1999). Vikram Seth thrives on the pleasure of having experienced a multiplicity of homes and he doesn't disagree with his status of cultural traveller. Seth's subject is therefore migratory and this travelogue *From Heaven Lake* is a record of a personal, cross-cultural interaction between a member of one Asian giant, travelling through another, particularly places like Sinkiang and Tibet. One can schematically identify four different modes of border crossing – those used by the exile, the immigrant, the colonialist and the scholar, the last typified by the anthropologist studying other cultures. Here Vikram Seth as a tourist traveller comes in the subcategory of scholar anthropologist. Seth draws attention to the lack of exchange between Indians and Chinese in recent times, despite geographical proximity and observes, 'Neither strong economic interest nor the natural affinities of a common culture tie India and China together ... the fact that they are both part of the same landmass means next to nothing. There is no such thing as an Asian ethos or mode of thinking' (178) or as he says, 'If India and China were amicable towards each, almost half the world would be at peace yet friendship rests on understanding ... . In Tibet and South East Asia, we find a fusion of the two cultures, but the heartland of the two great culture zones have been almost untouched by each other. The only important exception to this is the spread of Buddhism' (178).

There are number of such interesting discourses in the book of nineteen chapters. Apart from travel, the text also includes autobiography – Seth's childhood years and discussions of economics, art and philosophy. As narrator Seth is a travel writer, as protagonist he is the traveller and, as travel writer he is an economist and cultural theorist. He argues that while the Chinese administration may have evolved a better system of social care and better administrative hierarchy, it is not answerable to the people.

The travelogue commences with Seth at Turfan, an oasis town in the depression in Xinjiang, the extreme north-west province of China bordering on the Soviet Union. Interestingly the name Xinjiang means *New Borderland*. A dispute between the two imperial powers had left the boundary in dispute and the settlers or the nomadic people scattered on both sides of the border negotiated or controlled by other, have no allegiance to the Russians or the Hans who are in a majority in China. They are Muslim in culture and religion and their script Arabic and therefore Seth communicates with them in Urdu. Vikram Seth is part of a three-week tour organized by Nanjiang University for a mixed group of foreign students an arrangement with which he is unhappy but to break loose he has to overcome restrictions peculiar to travel in China. Due to sheer luck, he is able to get a pass to Tibet because of two unlikely events. At an evening programme, Seth sings a theme song from a 1950s film, Raj Kapoor's *Awara*, which cuts across languages and cultures and is popular with the Chinese. He is then lucky enough to meet Akbar (an officer in the police station), who has keen interest in Indian movies.

From Turfan, Seth reaches *Heaven Lake* which lies part of the way up the range of Mount Bogda, near Urmugi, about 2,000 metres above sea level, at the foot of higher snow peaks. Seth excels in the poetic description of natural splendours as in his work pictures the spectacular region of Tian chi or Heaven Lake 'an area so large that one can wander for days and not exhaust its limits' (22). Seth as a travelling observer has an access to 'sanctioned' regression that may 'carry the phantasm of unmediated bliss, wonder, solitude and wordless communication' (Bartokoskwi 160) while for Ghosh there is an intersection of the lives of 'travelling' subjects with those of the ethnic.

Seth faces many border problems because as an Indian citizen he is unlikely to get permission to cross over from the area which is the disputed border between India and China. The border with Nepal provides him a possible exit route, the prospect of crossing the Himalayas motivates him to journey all the way back to Nanjing Beijing and travel almost a week to return to the same point to continue onwards with his journey. He actually hitchhikes the entire part of the journey in four weeks. His companions happen to be Sui and Gyanseng, a Tibetan, and they together undergo severe discomfort, cold, altitude sickness. Seth writes:

> Here we three, cooped alone
> Tibetan, Indian, Han
> Against a common dawn
> Catch what poor sleep we can
> And sleeping drag the same sparse air into our lungs
> And dreaming each of home, sleeptalk in different tongues. (98)

On this journey to Tibet, Seth faces waterlogging and floods but the maximum discomfort is because of the border restrictions. When he reaches Lhasa foreign office, Seth learns to his dismay that his exit visa with no specified port of exit does not apply to Tibet and that he needs specific permission in order to go via Tibet. He is advised that the only possible way he can avoid the circular route of returning back to India via Hong Kong, is to head for Nilamu and walk for four days on foot through the hills, cross the border into Nepal, take a bus to Kathmandu and finally catch a flight to Delhi. At Zhangamu, Seth leaves the Chinese checkpost and begins to walk through the forest infested with leeches, mites and midges. He doesn't realize just exactly when he crossed the actual 'border' until he is suddenly stopped by a Nepalese custom officer who in excellent Hindi informs him sternly 'that stream there, that's the border. You've just crossed it' and Seth remarks 'this is the first time a custom officer has stepped out from behind a tree to announce himself' (170). He draws attention to the irony of political borders by commenting on the woman wringing her clothes in the very stream that makes the border and Seth observes, 'She couldn't care less which country she is in' (170).

Once again, when Seth moves along the red soiled valleys towards Kathmandu, he becomes nostalgic about Dehradun and home and writes 'these things affect me more powerfully than I would ever have imagined ... that I can be affected by a few phrases of the bansuri or by a piece of indigo paper surprises me at first, for on the previous occasions that I have returned home after a long absence abroad, I have certainly not invested them with the significance I now do' (173). Seth attributes these sentiments to the gradual progress of his journey. The return home is more poignant for him, as the family, parents, brother and sister get together after seven years and the country, the climate all strike with simultaneous impact after the air travel. Finally in Delhi, when the custom officer inquires if he has 'anything to declare' he raises the question of travelling self – for how does or can a traveller declare what he or she carries back each time within the self?

Vikram Seth marvels at those who travel through unfamiliar environments for years but as he says, 'My desire to arrive is too strong'. Or as Chambers puts it 'travel implies a movement between fixed position, a site of departure, a point of arrival, the knowledge of an itinerary' (Chambers 5). The book received the Thomas Travel Book award, Britain's most prestigious travel writing prize in 1983 and it celebrates Seth's wanderlust and spirit of humanity – as he focuses a great deal on the unexpected kindness that he encountered in the course of the journey – friendly policemen, amicable officials, store managers, tailors and citizens who helped him. In the "Foreword" to the 1990 edition, Seth protects against the brutality of the Chinese authorities against non-violent Tibetan demonstrators and the massacre of June 4, 1989.

Travelling in a way prepares the person for his future role by facilitating the cultivation of his historic consciousness and artistic tastes. He acquires works of art and surrounds himself with objective confirmations of his self worth. The process of travel helps to enrich the mind with knowledge, to rectify judgements to remove the prejudices of education, to compose the outward manners and in a way form the gentleman (Nugget xi). However as Mildred Mortiner observes, the traveller in strange surroundings often posits 'another binary opposition the crucial distinction between self and other' (169). In the first category 'Slamming' the traveller criticizes the other and focuses on his own sensibility and in the second category a questioning takes place and there is a desire or commitment to expand horizons. The author however offers more possibilities of understanding a different socio-cultural environment and bridge the gap between self and other and referring to incidents (Sino-India conflict), a border soldier says 'You couldn't tell where the border was one day it was here, another day it was there' (something which is echoed in Ghosh's *The Shadow Lines)*.

Vikram Seth subscribes to the idea of *Vasudev Kutumbam* – the idea of one home. Like Amitav Ghosh in *The Hungry Tide,* Seth reflects on the pan-universality of natural elements that prevail over political boundaries, when he is overwhelmed by the waterfalls of Nilamu. For Seth, true cross-cultural human understanding and bending can come by transcending the political. Also knowledge of ourselves and not others is therefore the real discovery that is made through travel.

Interestingly, both Amitav Ghosh and Vikram Seth have formulated their diasporic experiences and projected the subcontinental reality against western perspectives and given metaphorical interpretation to the idea of home and travelling self blurring the borderlines in the process. Once the gaze of the traveller reflected the singularity of a dominant culture, today the gaze is more multifocal, reflecting the demise of a world view that separated us from them. I conclude with Seth's poetic lines from his anthology *Mappings*:

I know that the whole world
Means exile for one breed
Who are not home at home
And are abroad abroad. (41)

Work Cited

Bartkowski, Fran. "Travelers v Ethnics; Discourses of Displacement", *Discourse* 15; 3, 1993.

Bissoondath, Neil. *Selling Illusions: The Cult of Multiculturalism in Canada.* Penguin, 1994.

Clifford, James. "Traveling Cultures", *Cultural Studies.* Eds. Lawrence Grossberg, Cary Nelson and Paula Treichler. New York: Routledge, 1992.

Ghosh, Amitav. *The Hungry Tide*, New Delhi: Harper Collins Publishers, (2004), 2005.

Jan Mohamed, Abdul R. "Worldliness-without World, Homelessness-As-Home: Towards a definition of the Specular Border Intellectual," *Edward Said. A Critical Reader.* Ed. Michael Sprinker. Oxford: Blackwell, 1992.

Mortimer, Mildred. "African Journeys", *Researches in African Literature.* Vol. 22, No. 2, 1991.

Nugget, Thomas. *The Grand Tour.* London, 1778.

Said, Edward W. "The Mind of Winter: Reflections of Life in Exile", *Harper* No. 269, September 1984.

Said, Edward. "Secular Criticism", *The World, The Text and the Critic.* Cambridge. M.A. Harvard University Press, 1983.

Seth, Vikram. *From Heaven Lake.* New Delhi: Penguin, 1983.

Seth, Vikram. *Mappings: Poems.* Calcutta: Writer's Workshop, 1981.

Sharma, L.K. "We wake up everyday and it is a different planet", Interview with Salman Rushdie, *The Sunday Times of India,* 7 April, 1999.

18 NIDHI SINGH

Identity Under the Shadow of Violence: *The Shadow Lines*

'Every one lives in a story ... they all lived in stories because stories are all there are to live in, it is just a question of which one you chose ...', (182) holds Tridib, the character whose absence is an overarching presence in *The Shadow Lines*. Amitav Ghosh chose to write a story of post-partition India, of divided Bengal, to interrogate identity construction in relation to geopolitical location in an increasingly violent society. Published in 1988, this novel rose from the writer's memory of, and anguished response to the apocalyptic happenings in 1984 (demand for Khalistan, operation Blue Star at Golden Temple, Indira Gandhi's assassination and the riots that followed). Ghosh tries to discover the meaning of such events and their effect on the individuals who live through them. In the process, remembering and reconstituting the past through selective and fragmentary memory, becomes central to the work.

The Shadow Lines emerges as the study of violence inherent in post-partition India as it struggles to establish its identity as a democratic and secular nation state. Violence emerges as endemic not only at the local and national level, but also on an international plane. Riots within the nation and across the border, war with China, and London during Second World War are integral to the novel. Violence is a force to reckon with as it gains acceptance, validity and legitimacy. It regulates and determines identity construction of not only individuals, as can be observed in the militant nationalism of Thamma, the grandmother, but also collectivity as the construction of a nation. Why is it that violence with its association with the primitive and the barbarous has not been harnessed with the establishment of rationality and reason as guiding principles? Wherein lies its source of power to regulate every aspect of human transaction be it personal, religious, political, economic or social?

B.P. Singh in his work *Problem of Violence: Themes in Literature* points out that thinkers like Marx and Fanon refer to the constructive and creative aspect of violence when used to gain liberation by the oppressed and the exploited. Referred to as 'violence from below', Marx preached revolution to the proletariat, while Fanon held that the violence of the colonial regime is balanced by counter-violence of the natives. Mao too was supportive of war of liberation as desirable and just. Conversely, 'violence from above' results from the authority vested in the State which legitimized exercise of violence to maintain law and order. Religion too advocates usage of violence for redressal of perceived wrong as can be seen in the concept of Holy War in Christians, *Jihad* in Muslims, and *Dharamyuddha* in Hindus. It was the end that justified the means. In the contemporary world, the political and the religious converge to the point where politicization of religion reveals the reciprocal relation between the two. The resultant communalism draws its sustenance not only from the religious, but also the political and the economic, finding expression in sporadic outbreak of riots.

The subcontinent is intermittently shaken by communal riots which emerge as the substratum on which the novel stands. Reminiscent of riots that accompanied the partition, communal confrontation highlights the conflict of inter-group identities. A group's identity when determined by its alliance to one overweening identity, leads to the negation of personal affiliation to plural identities that go into the making of an individual. The borderlines that divide the subcontinent have given birth to three national identities which have over a period of time become more and more restrictive and exclusive. The trauma of partition has made territorial integrity the defining aspect of the health of the nation. Thamma is scandalized when she is told that there is no physical manifestation of border dividing India from Bangladesh. Though physically absent, yet the shadow lines have irrevocably sundered Bengal. The arbitrariness of boundaries created by colonizers has constituted national identities that define themselves in opposition to each other. The dialectic of 'self' and the 'other' emerges, which is further reinforced by intervention of religion and culture resulting in group identities prone to self affirmation through violence. Sudhir Kakar in *The Colours of Violence* commenting on group identity holds: 'Identity implies definition rather than blurring, solidity rather than flux or fluidity, and therefore the question of boundaries of a group becomes paramount' (200). It is to the belligerent group identity of the rioters that Khalil, Jethamoshai and Tridib are exposed to and succumb to during their visit to Dhaka.

The nameless narrator points out the irony inherent in the situation, where, with partition it was hoped that the hostilities on both the sides will be confined to the border and managed there. However the spillover of bad blood results in an almost simultaneous outbreak of riots, both in Calcutta and in Dhaka, uniting them more closely than ever in the bonds of violence. The narrator wonders at the way divisions are meaningless to a person:

> ... the simple fact that there had never been a moment in the four thousand-year-old history of that map when the places we know as Dhaka and Calcutta were more closely bound to each other than after they had drawn their lines – so closely that I in Calcutta, had to look into the mirror to be in Dhaka; a moment when each city was the inverted image of the other, locked into an irreversible symmetry by the line that was to set us free – on looking glass border. (233)

The glass and mirror imagery recurs in the novel and emerges as constitutive of identity through the act of comparison or contrast. Foucault in his article "Of Other Spaces" presents the mirror as a 'placeless place' which reflects society as perfect or else as a society turned 'upside down', reminiscent of Thamma's imaginative delineation of 'upside-down' (125) house of Jethamoshai. Foucault says, 'In the mirror, I see myself there where I am not in an unreal virtual space ... . Starting from this gaze that is, as it were, directed towards me, from the ground of that virtual space that is on the other side of the glass; I come back towards myself; I begin again to direct my eyes toward myself and to reconstitute myself there where I am' (24). The 'Self' gets constructed either in relation to or in opposition of the 'other' guided by either admiration or disaffection. The narrator observes that Nick Price had become '... a spectral presence beside me in my looking glass; growing with me, but always bigger and better and in some way more desirable' (50). Nick emerges as an ideal to measure up to, till the narrator is demystified after meeting him in London.

A historical reviewing of the traumatic events following the two partitions have been explored by a number of literary works. *The Shadow Lines* takes up the outbreak of communal riots on both sides of the border in order to question and examine the nature of the invisible lines that divide the three nations and yet construct and determine the identity of multitudes who reside there; how the rigid contours of the identity that predominates and is seen as defining one leads to situations of conflict and violence. The self as it emerges owing to the reviewing of the past, both personal and historical, when faced with violence in the crisis situation becomes the object of critical scrutiny. Journey, both physical and metaphorical, emerges as an important motif in the work. Urbashi Barat calls it a 'bildungsroman' since 'it traces the growth and development of the narrator from childhood to maturity' (114). The journey undertaken by the narrator, which Ghosh refers to as 'a voyage into a land outside space, an expanse without distance; a land of looking glass events' (224), is an attempt to understand Tridib's violent death in retrospect.

The act of remembering is foregrounded and problematized in the work. The unnamed narrator is confronted by the shifting boundaries of memory where past and present coalesce and ramify till it seems multilayered and multifaceted. In the process of remembering the past, the narrator constantly transgresses the boundary that lies between the real and the imagined. This fragmented memory stands in opposition to total recall. The narrator remembers how, as an eight year old, he had tried to imagine Tridib at the same age. Baffled, he had 'decided' that Tridib had looked like him. Factual details are coloured and at times manipulated by the narrator as he reconstructs the past aided by memory and imagination. Tridib's character gets constituted from the collage of competing impressions and responses based on memory of other characters, filtered through the consciousness of narrator. Referring to memory and its partial nature, Rushdie holds: 'The shards of memory acquired greater status, greater resonance, because they were *remains*; fragmentation made trivial things seem like symbols and mundane acquired numinous qualities' (12).

The narrator interweaves personal histories with the history of the nation in search of the meaning of the mystery of Tridib's death and the silence surrounding it. R. Radhakrishnan in *Theory in an Uneven World* comments on the use of history in *The Shadow Lines*. He holds, 'Histories are never discrete; in fact when any collectivity looks into mirror to obtain a reflection of itself, the mirror operates both as a mirror into one's self and a window into other selves' (28). The common thread running through all the characters is the relevance attached to freedom in the construction of their identity. The concept of freedom is problematized by Ghosh as the search for freedom becomes the root cause of violence in their lives. It can be traced in the society at large where search for freedom invariably results in perpetration of violence. Robi points out '… if you look at the pictures on the front pages of the newspaper at home now, all those pictures of dead people … people shot by terrorists and separatists and the army and the police, you'll find somewhere behind it all, that single word: everyone's doing it to be free' (246). For Ila, it is freedom from the constrains of Indian 'culture'.

Thamma's militant nationalism is born of the relevance attached by her generation to geo-political freedom in the ethos of nationalistic fervour. It rebounds on her with the tragic death of Tridib. On hearing about the renewed hostilities between India and Pakistan she screams out her fear: 'For your sake; for your freedom. We have to kill them before they kill us; we have to wipe them out' (237). Thamma is unable to transcend the ideology which legitimized violence for the cause of freedom, first to win it and then to safeguard it. Inversely Tridib freedom was an apolitical concept, free of the weight of history and familial obligations. Tridib, most comfortable in 'neutral' places, wishes to meet May in a ruin: a place without history with the freedom of strangers. The paradox lies in the fact that he decides that 'Victoria Memorial' will be this ruin. The inherent paradox is brought to light when May refers to the statue as 'an act of violence' (169) as it is a brutal reminder of colonial history and its continuities. Tridib's wish to be free of other people's invention finds fulfilment in his violent death which remains a mystery and is sunk 'in the chasm of silence' (219).

Ila's decision to live in London arises from her wish to be free from constrictive Indian traditions. Her marriage to Nick seems to be inspired by her wish to be accepted in a society where she had faced racial brutalization as a child. The game of keeping 'house' she had played with the narrator as a child was an enactment of her need for acceptance as fantasized through the doll Magda with golden hair, blue eyes, white skin and pink cheeks. In Toni Morrison's novel *The Bluest Eye*, a doll similar to Magda is the dream of every black girl. The doll becomes the measure of their 'difference' and symbol of unattainable perfection. Ila too works out her need to be accepted through the doll, her alter ego. Ila reveals the dilemma of the diasporic sensibility. Though she decides to pretend as if nothing had happened, the violence done to their marriage by Nick's betrayal is reflected in her relation with him. Robi, her protective uncle, wishes for freedom from the memory of Tridib's violent death. Robi himself, a part of state machinery acknowledges that he will inspire his men to use force and even kill, if need arose, as a price to be paid for 'unity and freedom' of the nation. Inversely, he is unable to free himself from the trauma of Tridib's death in a riot even after the passage of fifteen years.

May seeks freedom in acts of philanthropy. Her philanthropy follows the tenet that one has to be cruel to be kind when she 'jabs' at the jugular vein of the wounded dog to relieve him from a painful and slow death. Her impulsive decision to save Khalil and Jethamoshai from the rioters leads to Tridib's death as he rushes out and plunges into the mob. Tridib fulfils his wish to be carried 'to a place where there was no border between one self and one's image in the mirror'. (29) With his last act, referred to as 'sacrifice', he transcends the borders that divide, negating the divisions created by nation, religion, culture, class and even reason. He throws his lot with the people and a land known to him only by their difference.

Puzzling over the circle drawn by a compass on Barthlomew's atlas the narrator realizes '... that within the circle there were only states and citizens; there were no people at all' (233) and that 'it is the logic of the states that to exist at all they must claim the monopoly of all relationships between people' (230). Amitav Ghosh critiques the construction of identity on the lines of nation, religion or culture due to the dehumanizing effect they have owing to the tendency towards one restrictive identity gaining relevance over others. Tridib's violent death points at the need to overcome the 'story' of mutual suspicions and conflict that the three nations have 'chosen' to live in, regulated by the 'shadow lines' of violence, dividing not only land and psyche, but also hearts.

Works Cited

Barat, Urbashi. "Imagination and Reality in *The Shadow Lines*" in *The Novels of Amitav Ghosh*. Ed. R.K. Dhawan. New Delhi: Prestige Books, 1999.

Foucault, Michel. "Of Other Spaces" in *French Journal Architecture, Movement Continuite*. October, 1984.

Ghosh, Amitav. *The Shadow Lines*. New Delhi: OUP, 1988.

Kakar, Sudhir. *The Colours of Violence*. New Delhi: Penguin Books, 1995.

Morrison, Toni. *The Bluest Eye*. London: Vintage Publishers, 1999.

Radhakrishnan, R. *Theory in an Uneven World*. USA: Blackwell Publishing, 2003.

Rushdie, Salman. *Imaginary Homelands: Essays and Criticism 1981–1991*. London: Granta Books in association with Viking, 1991.

Singh, B.P. *Problem of Violence: Themes in Literature*. Shimla: Indian Institute of Advanced Study, 1999.

19 SIMRAN CHADHA

Ethnic Nationalism and the Pluralistic Space of the Nation in the Fiction of Michael Ondaatje

Things fall apart; the centre cannot hold
Mere anarchy is loosened upon the world,
The blood-dimmed tide is loosed ...
                "The Second Coming", William Butler Yeats

In seeking to explore the dynamics of change – social and political in Sri Lanka, this essay analyses ethnic separatism through the two novels of Michael Ondaatje often referred to as his Sri Lankan novels – *Running in the Family* and *Anil's Ghost*. Written when insurgency/terrorism/militancy was at its peak in Sri Lanka, not only did Ondaatje's fictive recreation of a highly politicized trajectory achieve international acclaim but highlighted the comparatively lesser known fact regarding the author's Sri Lankan origins. A naturalized Canadian citizen and an English immigrant, Ondaatje is also by birth a Sri Lankan Burgher – the Burghers being the miscegeneous offspring of the colonizing Portuguese (1505–56), the Dutch (1656–1815) and the British (1815–1848). While the texts drew attention for the radically postmodern modes of narration, the point-of-view of the author was nonetheless decried as that of an outsider, rendering his claims to a Sri Lankan heritage rather dubious. Moreover with the protagonists in the texts proclaiming their national identity as apart from either the Sinhalese or a Tamil identity, it was amply clear that the author's politics lay with the concept of a unitary as opposed to a divided nation – the primary agenda of the civil war. This essay attempts to unravel the ramifications of the term 'unitary' when applied to a multi-ethnic nation such as Sri Lanka. Moreover, in addressing the traumatic issue of terrorism and its effects on the civic life of a people, this reading leans on literature as the representational space where the grief of a people, caught in the quagmire of violence, finds lucid articulation, almost akin to a ritualistic mourning.

Ethnic origins at least in the Indian subcontinent are generally perceived as the racial/religious identity with which a person is born and this is inevitably linked to notions of continuity and ancestry. This confers a feeling of belonging to a particular community and of partaking of its linguistic and cultural heritage. However, over a period of time, ethnic boundaries can develop into rigid fundamentalist discourses especially when perceived as threatened, economically and culturally, by a community of a different ethnic denomination. As fundamentalist politics takes root, the rallying cry for self-determination finds recourse in violence often euphemized as militancy, insurgency and state suppression. While this essay raises broader questions regarding nationalism, electoral politics, and the multi-ethnic compositional character of Sri Lanka, the focus is on hybridity as an essential feature of pluralistic South Asian societies, especially the Sri Lankan.

Kumari Jayawardene's extensive sociological documentation and analysis on ethnic separatism show how race antagonisms between the two communities have been constantly bolstered by propagandist myths of origin and their rapid dissemination by revivalist groups, rampant in such a scenario.[1] Caught between the state and the rival militant groups, the uncertainty of life, the trauma of loss and the inability to perceive a solution to the problem is the one primary factor that has lead to the creation of a vast Tamil Diaspora. For the purposes of this paper, the implications of the term Diaspora are confined to an imagined community beyond the geographical boundaries of the official nation state. An active body of writing by the Sri Lankan Diaspora engages in this fraught act of *narrating the nation*, caught in the throes of violent conflict.

While Ondaatje's identity can be theorised on multiple levels, it is the hybridity of his Burgher origins that the novel *Running in the*

Ethnic Nationalism and the Pluralistic Space of the Nation 183

Family takes account of. The Burghers were/are a community emblematic of this cusp of history created in the crucible of colonization. The Burghers therefore exemplify the act of colonization as the conflagration of two very diverse cultures, each influencing the other. *Running in the Family* was published in the year 1982, a year before the Tamil genocide in Colombo. Tensions were running high and it was this that prompted Ondaatje's desire to intervene in the constructions of his homeland, as much as the urge to re-connect with a deceased parent – his father Mervyn – a bond severed owing to a family history of divorce and migration.

The text traces a line of descent or in politicized rhetoric, Ondaatje's ethnic origins. Ondaatje's family history, as other Burgher ancestries, is much enmeshed in the moment of Sri-Lankan colonization. Moreover, in the absence of direct access to the father, *his-tory* must be fabricated through scattered acts – family memories, the gossip of his aunts Phyllis and Dolly, a visit to the family home and the meeting with his stepmother and sister. The history of Sri Lanka, meanwhile is constructed through similar multiple sources both archival and popular. This methodology accounts for a richly imaginative text, often animatedly discussed as postmodernist and even fantastic. Inundated with different voices – often contradictory and cutting across time frames – the narrative perhaps intends to point to the fact that it is with similar such details and recollections, sometimes faulty, often misconstrued, that history too is constructed. This makes the acclaimed "truth" of historical re-construction, as Anil in *Anil's Ghost* comes to realize concomitant upon multiple factors, factors that often 'bounced between gossip and vengeance' (*Anil's Ghost*, 54).

The historical period that Ondaatje imaginatively recreates is the era of his parents and grandparents, the 'roaring twenties', the heyday of the Burgher community in Sri Lanka, before their mass exodus, following Prime Minister Bandaranaike's declaration in September 1956 of Sinhala as the national language. As he says: 'Those relations from my parent's generation who stood in my memory like frozen opera, I wanted to touch them into words' (22). Reconstructing this 'ex-centric' (to borrow Linda Hutcheon's phrase) community, involves the escapades of his grandmother Lalla who 'could read thunder' (113), his father's drunken escapades cavorting on the islands train system, among others.[2] The blatant exaggeration is a pointer that the past is often recreated in a frame that is larger than life: 'Men who had lost fortunes laughed frantically into the night ... a hand cupped the heel of a woman who wished to climb a tree to see the stars more clearly ...' (51–52). Similar such details of exotic locales, flora/fauna and the constant explication of cultural nuances, have prompted Arun Mukherjee's accusation that Ondaatje is 'exoticizing' the land of his birth and pandering to the tastes of a western reading audience (*Towards an Esthetic of Opposition* qtd. by Sugunasiri). Suwanda H.J. Sugunasiri, in "Sri Lankan Canadian Poets: The Bourgeoisie That Fled the Revolution", asserts that Ondaatje: 'was (through his class and community) the colonizer!' (64). To situate culturally and politically the Burgher community, Ondaatje stresses their separateness from both: the colonizers and indigenous population. Unlike the colonizers, who like the 'visiting' white spotted Karapotha beetles 'never grew ancient here' the Burghers did settle permanently in Ceylon. The name 'Ondaatje' which at best is a 'parody' of the ruling language, speaks of the cultural, social and racial distance of this community from the colonizers (64). Arising from intermarriages with the local Sinhalese and Tamils, Burgher – the pluralistic dynamism of the term itself, challenges the singularity and purity deified by myths of racial origin. Tracing origins unearths this sense of cultural spaces as syncretism.[3] As Ondaatje observes:

> Everyone was vaguely related and had Sinhalese, Tamil, Dutch, British and Burgher blood in them ... . Emil Daniels summed up the situation for most of them when he was asked by one of the British governors what his nationality was – 'God alone knows, your excellency'. (41)

Reflecting on the ambivalence of his ancestry, Ondaatje says: 'I am the foreigner. I am the prodigal who hates the foreigner' (79). Similarly the description of their home in Kuttapitiya as 'perched high above the mist which filled the valley below ... cutting us off from the real world' (144) symbolically refers to the distance of this community from the native population and colonizers alike.

Germane to a Burgher ancestry, is a taking stock of the colonization of Sri Lanka. Ondaatje points to the multiple transitions in name, rule and identity that the island nation of what is now formally known as *Sri Lanka Janarajaya* has undergone. Bearing testimony to the changing cartography of the island (depending on the colonizing power) are the 'false maps' in his brother's study in Toronto, so deviant in shape that they seem to be 'translations – by Ptolemy, Mercator, Francoise ...' (63). By foregrounding the contingent nature of historical re-construction, Ondaatje asserts that cultural/national representation is concomitant upon power structures:

> The island seduced all of Europe. The Portuguese. The Dutch. The English. And so its name changed, as well as its shape, – Serendip, Ratna Dipa ("island of gems"), Taprobane, Zeloan, Zeilan, Seyllan, Ceilon and Ceylon ... . (64)

At the same time Ceylon is also 'the wife of many marriages, courted by invaders who stepped ashore and claimed everything with the power of their sword or bible or language' (64). The deployment of violated female sexuality, to depict the act of colonization, effectively highlights the ravages that the process entailed. A similar sexual undertone is echoed by the intertextual interface between the Webster's *Duchess of Malfi* and the engrossing eight hour game of *Ajoutha* that Ondaatje insists, enabled the Portuguese to conquer Sri Lanka. What is equally significant, is the use of the words 'wife',' 'courted' and 'seduced' that convey the passive acquiescence of the woman/land in the act of her/its own appropriation. Identifying Ceylon with the woman's body and as the passive receptor of the colonizing gaze amounts to making a political statement. It enables Ondaatje to foreground the receptiveness of Sri Lanka to different cultures that contributed in a large measure to the creation of the multi-ethnic space of the island. A similar stance is conveyed through the intertextual use of Ondaatje's poem *The Cinnamon Peeler*. The woman's sexuality is here linked to the arresting aroma of cinnamon. This reference to the prized export of the island – cinnamon, makes explicit the lure of Sri Lanka for the imperial rulers. However by essentially exhibiting her sensuality: 'I am the cinnamon peeler's wife/Smell me' (97) she appears to be inviting the colonizers gaze and the consequent male invasion. As Ondaatje asserts, the island 'became a mirror. It pretended to reflect each European power till newer ships arrived and spilled their nationalities ...' (64).

The past as framed by Ondaatje imaginatively violates all attempts at coalition and most certainly at linearity, the ends are not all neatly tied up or framed with a beginning, middle and an ending. The reader is not presented with history in terms of causes and effects. In putting together a story that purports to be a history in this carnivalesque manner, the question that Ondaatje asks is: 'how does one knit the story together, each memory a wild thread in the sarong' (110). Poignantly aware of the fictionality of his endeavour, Ondaatje relates it to Shakespeare's *King Lear,* with Edgar and Gloucester on the edge of the imaginary cliff and says: 'I long for the moment in the play when Edgar reveals himself to Gloucester and it never happens' (180).

Extending the focus, concerning the politics of cultural representation, the text is splayed with references to Oriental travelogues: Sir John Maunderville, Robert Knox (73); journals of Edward Lear (78) and the epigraph by a Franciscan Friar:' I saw in this island fowls as big as our country geese having two heads ... and other miraculous things which I will not write of here'. And *Orientalism*, as Edward Said exposes, is the discourse produced on the East by the West, a discourse which confirmed the "Otherness" of the Orient for the Occident and became a potent factor in the colonization of the land. Given this thesis perhaps Ondaatje too is guilty of practicing a latent Orientalism. At the same time, it must be mentioned that far from silencing the native voices, in a manner akin to Orientalist discourse, *Running in the Family* makes space for the indigenous discourse, as shall be discussed below.

Sojourning through different time and space frames, from colonization to decolonization, the intertextual use of the poetry of Lakdasa Wikkramasinha in Ondaatje's narrative is significant. Disavowing a colonial past from which stemmed a "Matisse" culture the poem begins with a trenchant critique of colonial mimicry:

Don't talk to me about Matisse ...
the European style of the 1900
the tradition of the studio ...

The next stanza moves to encompass a postcolonial time frame of insurgency, rebellion and suppression. Protesting the ruthless suppression of the student insurgency of 1971 by the government Wikkramasinha says: 'To our remote/Villages the painters came, and our white-washed/Mud-huts were splattered with gunfire' (86). This refers to a contemporary history of the government suppression of an indigenous people. A history that Ondaatje must learn through secondary sources. *Running In the Family,* poignantly refers to the whitewashing of the walls of the Vidyalankara Campus, thus erasing the writings by the student rebels who had been imprisoned there: 'Quatrains and free verse about the struggle, tortures, the unbroken spirit, the love of friends who had died for the cause' (84). Wikkramasinha's poem, shows how an entire trajectory of Sri Lankan history was wiped out by a centralizing hegemonic power.

The dense intertextual layering of *Running in the Family* is significant in drawing attention to the heterogeneous, alternative versions to every story: colonization, insurgency, suppression as opposed to an essentialist, and official, singular version. This enables Ondaatje to highlight the possibility for transformation and change for 'no story is told just once in this way history is organized' (26). Moreover by confessing that despite the 'air of authenticity', the book is 'not a history' but more like a 'portrait or gesture', Ondaatje accentuates the subjectivity of not only his endeavour but of historical reconstruction (206). It is this contingent and provisional nature of truth that is foregrounded when it comes to scripting the past especially in terms of ethnic origins. The past is cloaked in doubt, obscurity and suspicion and to trace genealogies is, as Ondaatje discovers, to disappear into a labyrinth. A tombstone in St. Thomas's church had effectively disrupted a neatly chronicled family line of descent leaving uncertainty as the only refuge (66). What emerges of the past are not coherent pictures but fragments. In this regard, the fragmented form of *Running In the Family*, becomes a conscious effort on part of the author of taking the reader inside history or rather showing history in the making rather than narrating it from a vantage point of view.

In his next novel on Sri Lanka, *Anil's Ghost,* Ondaatje foregrounds a similar perspective of the 'long distance' gaze (11) with which his protagonist Anil Tissera, the forensic expert investigating into the violation of human rights in contemporary Sri Lanka can look at the country of her birth. Echoing Ondaatje's personal experience, Anil's present status as a migrant is related to the sudden demise of her parents. The trauma of the severance, from her homeland and her parents, has left indelible scars. The text takes into account the 'unofficial war' (17) in Sri Lanka and its effects on the 'unhistoric' lives on the ordinary people caught in the quagmire of violence. To capture a contemporary situation of damning strife and conflict which he has experienced only vicariously, Ondaatje compares it to those horrific moments of recorded history, 'the extreme actions of nature or civilization ... Pompeii. Laetoli. Hiroshima. Vesuvius' (55). Ondaatje layers his text with intertextual references, using past to explicate the present: '... same for Colombo as for Troy' (64). For Anil, 'Amygdala', the nerve bundle which 'houses fear' has a Sri-Lankan sound to it. The text deals primarily with the heights of terror during the years '88, '89 when the country is caught in the grips of a fear psychosis:

> In a fearful nation, public sorrow was stamped down upon by the climate of uncertainty. If a father protested a son's death it was feared another family member would be killed. If people you knew disappeared, there was a chance they might be still alive if you did not cause trouble. This was the scarring psychosis in the country. (54)

Sporadic incidents of violence have escalated into a full-fledged blood bath. Since 1983 the island has been in a state of continual emergency. Yet, who is the enemy? The state claims no knowledge of organized campaigns of murder on the island. As Anil perceives: 'murders are committed on all sides' (18). Yet the government is not the only one doing the killings, equally responsible are the insurgents, the guerilla separatists groups fighting for a homeland in Jaffna.

Articulating the multitudinous marginalized narratives of miners, artisans, children-voices silenced in the limbo of violence and perhaps not even figuring on official lists of the dead/disappeared the text is shot through with micro-narratives of social victimage. For Ananda Udugama, the *netra* artist, who in painting the eyes on the idols of Lord Buddha, keeps alive a tradition that dates back to the ninth century, each day is a painful reminder of the loss of his wife Sirissa. The child Lakma, having witnesses the massacre of her parents, is admitted into a child-rehabilitation center. The forty-nine school children beheaded and displayed for public gaze; the excavation of the mass grave and the 'vigil for the dead' with which the text opens, each gesture underpins the terrible human cost that fundamentalism entails. Without justifying the perspective of the guerrilla separatists, the text makes space for their narrative. In foregrounding the silence that resides in the camp, Ondaatje points to the breakdown of communication between different ideological camps that have fostered the language of violence. Violence, escalating at an alarming speed and directed against government authorities leads to the assassination of President Katungala by a human bomb. As Anil says: '... it was a Hundred Years War with modern weaponry ... a war sponsored by gun and drug runners' (43).

Exploring a sacred grave for Buddhist monks, in the Bandarawela region, dating back to the sixth century, along with Sarath Diyasena of the Archaeological Department, Anil chances upon a skeleton that is 'not pre-historic' (50). This gives the much-required lead to probe a human rights violation for none without a government permit could have access to the restricted area. Sailor, as she names the skeleton, is the truth she must resurrect 'to give him a name would name the rest' (56). The ray of truth that is brought to light entails the murder of Sarath – a victim of political espionage.

Pointing to the shifty nature of historical re-constructions of the past, is the narrative of Palipana, the famous national epigraphist. Constructing a nationalist historiography by translating Pali scripts and the sixth century rock graffiti of Sigiriya, which harks back to a pre-colonial past, Palipana is the 'main force of a pragmatic Sinhala movement' (79). However, as later historians prove, his work turns out to be a fiction. And this 'forgery by a master meant much more than mischief, it meant scorn' (82). Like historiography, molded by the (conscious/unconscious) prejudices of the historian, the artist too must work through similar filters. Sailor's face, as Ananda resurrects it, betrays the serenity he unconsciously imagines for his dead/disappeared Sirisa: 'in the heights she loved in the dark she feared' (307).

Reading into the metaphor of home, which is never far from the fiction of immigrant writers, Ondaatje uses the symbolism of a grave plundered and of the statue of Buddha desecrated and defiled to explicate the state of affairs. Sri Lanka, once a seat of Buddhism, is now a symbolic mass grave. Anil's final words on Sri Lanka 'the darkest of Greek tragedies were innocent compared to what happened here' (11), could well be Ondaatje's judgment as well. *Running in the Family* had expounded on the JVP violence: 'The average of the insurgents was seventeen and thousands were killed by the police and army ... the Kelani and Mahaveli rivers moved to the sea, heavy with bodies' (85), which was unlike the wars waged by the Tamil Tigers. This insurgency pitted a Sinhalese Security Buddhist force against a Sinahlese Buddhist uprising. The movement saw itself as a regenerative force, aiming to destroy in order to create anew. This harking back to a pristine pre-colonial past prompted the urge to erase all influences of the west and capitalism. The insurgents were against tourism seeing it as the root of all evil and like Noah's flood in the Old Testament, the insurgents, caught in the binds of fundamentalism, saw themselves as a cleansing tide, envisioning the future as a return to tradition, an idyllic Edenic past, and a Buddhist haven, a denial of capitalism, western influences and values. Unfortunately, violence, razing to the ground the very foundations of the system, was the singular means they perceived of realizing this change. As Charles Sarvan in the essay "A Chekovian Awareness" asserts: 'Sri Lanka has witnessed the rise of racism, known euphemistically as "ethnic nationalism" ' (51). What is destroyed in the process is the multi-ethnic structure on which rests the foundations of the national space.

Tracing a process that began with decolonization, followed by the mass exodus of the Burghers, revivalist movements (Sinhalese Buddhism), separatist movements (LTTE), the fault lines in the nation's history become increasingly inviolable and territorial. One cannot help but notice the inexorable connection between the immigrant and the homeland that perhaps may help us to understand the complex ambivalent attitude of the immigrant writer towards the land of origin. While memory plays a significant role with Ondaatje it is literary intertextuality that takes the lead. While a black and white photograph prompts Rushdie's quest in *Imaginary Homelands*, it is a dream that triggers off Ondaatje's narrative. Having left Sri Lanka at age eleven, it is as if memory has internalized sights, sounds and smells and creates an image of the homeland as a warm semiotic place. Ondaatje on his 'Last Morning' in Sri Lanka indulges in a similar task: 'My body must remember everything ... smell of wet fruit ... . Dark trees, the mildewed garden wall, the slow air pinned down by rain' (*Running in the Family* 202). Writing about Sri Lanka has been a process of re-learning as much as re-membering, which explains the detailed descriptions about *thalagoyas* in *Running in the Family* (69), or cultural nuances, such as the *netra mangala* in *Anil's Ghost*. Yet it is moments, such as the violent expulsion of Anil from Sri Lanka or the Burghers after the 1958 declaration that stand out like beacons in the memory. Bhabha in *The Location of Culture* describes this as the 'unhomely moment', a moment paradigmatic with 'cultural displacement and social discrimination' (8), a moment that relates a personal history to the wider disjunctions of political existence' (11).

This tension or ambivalence in immigrant writing can perhaps be traced to the paradox that while you can never return to your past, you can never quite escape it. As Rushdie says, the 'in-between space' of the immigrant confers on them a status of being: 'one and the same time insiders and outsiders ... this stereoscopic vision is perhaps what we can offer in place of whole sight' (19). However: 'If literature is part of the business of finding new ways of entering reality, then once again, our distance, our long geographical perspective, may provide us with such angles' (150). It is the act of writing that confers a certain transgressive freedom as the graffiti on the campus walls by the student rebels in *Running in the Family* demonstrates.

The texts discussed in this paper, in giving space to the voices of alterity: that of a *kolla*, a homosexual, a Burgher – voices blanketed by a dominant discourse, highlight the restorative/transformative powers of literature as an art form. Herein lies the possibility to effect changes, bridge cultural differences and disrupt essentialist ideologies. Immigrant writers, similarly, subvert all attempts to label or classify their art through essentializing categories, such as – "Third world" or "Gay" writing. The space of the immigrant artist, as Bhabha in *Nation and Narration* asserts, is not merely a celebration of marginalization but an: 'intervention into those justifications of modernity – progress, homogeneity, cultural organicism, the deep nation, the long past – that rationalize the authoritarian "normalizing" tendencies within cultures' (4).

Significantly, Ondaatje closes *Anil's Ghost* with the serene image of the artist at work – Ananda resurrecting the 120-foot high statue of Lord Buddha. The ancient tradition *of Netra Mangala*, transforms the 'lump of metal or stone' into 'a God' (97–99). From his vantage point, with the dawn silently breaking across the sky (the eyes must be painted at five a.m., the hour Lord Buddha attained Enlightenment), Ananda experiences an intuitive cognition of the beauty/"seduction" that the world holds for the artist (307). Scarred by the travails of life, he as an artist must resume his work: 'for the eyes he [Ananda] had cut and focused with his fathers chisel showed him this' (307).

Notes

1. Regarding the multi-ethnic formation of Sri Lankan society that forms an essential background for this paper, Kumari Jayawardene, asserts that Sri Lankan society is peopled by the Sinhalese (74%), Sri Lankan Tamils (12.6%), Indian Tamils, Muslims (7.4%) and the Burghers who employed in the colonial administration formed a privileged class on the island. Where race antagonisms are concerned, she has observed that asserting a Sinhalese identity and legitimizing Sinhalese control of the country's polity, the leaders of the Sinhala revivalist movement reconstructed an image of the Sinhala past using elements of the origin mythology. 'Such a revivalist ideology attempted to establish a Sinhala-Buddhist hegemony of the island, antagonist to non-Buddhist groups ... . At the ideological level, The response to Sinhala chauvinism was the emergence of Tamil chauvinism and extreme forms of national mythmaking ... each ethnic group today has a distinct identity with strongly held myths of origin; the Sinhala believe they are Aryans from Bengal, the Tamils claim pure Dravidian origin and the Muslims aspire to descent from the Arabs ... . Jayawardene rightly asserts the point that that in denying the syncretic culture of the island and asserting a 'refusal to recognize the rights of minority groups', the contemporary Sinhalese Revivalist movement and the fundamentalist separatist groups, deny the plurality of space that is part and parcel of the Sri Lankan society. (Lacnet.org/srilanka/issues/kumari.html)
2. Linda Hutcheon in *The Poetics of Post-Modernism: History, Theory Fiction.* (London: Routledge, 1988), defines the term as: 'The center no longer completely holds. And from the de-centred perspective, the "marginal" and what I will be calling the ex-centric ...' (12).
3. As defined in by Ashcroft, Griffiths and Tiffin, in *the Empire Writes Back: Theory and Practice in Post-Colonial Literature.* (London: Routledge, 1989) syncreticism is 'the process by which previously distinct linguistic categories and, by extension, cultural formations, merge into a single new form' (15).

Works Cited

Ashcroft Bill, Gareth Griffiths and Helen Tiffin. *The Empire Writes Back: Theory and Practice in Post-Colonial Literature.* London: Routledge, 1989.

Bhabha, Homi K., *The Location of Culture.* London: Routledge, 1994.

Bhabha, Homi K., ed. *National and Narration*. London: Routledge, 1990.

Hutcheon, Linda. *The Poetics of Post-Modernism: History, Theory, Fiction*. London: Routledge, 1988.

Jayawardene, Kumari. "Ethnic Conflict in Sri Lanka and Regional Security", internet reference: lacnet.org/srilanka/issues/kumari. html.

Ondaatje, Michael. *Anil's Ghost*. London: Picador, 2000.

—. *Running In The Family*. New York: Random House, 1993.

Rushdie, Salman. *Imaginary Homelands: Essays and Criticism 1981–91*. London: Granta, 1991.

Said, Edward W. *Orientalism*. New York: Random House, 1979.

Sarvan, Charles. "*Reef*: A Chekhovian Awareness and Mood" in *The Toronto Review*, Winter, 1998.

Sugunasiri, Suwanda H.J. "Sri Lankan Canadian Poets: The Bourgeoise That Fled The Revolution", in *Canadian Literature*, 132 Spring 1992.

Yeats, William B. *Collected Poems*. New Delhi: Rupa & Co., 1993.

20 MINI NANDA

Mending the Fault Lines: Same Culture, Separate Nation

Borders are geographical places, where rivers flow and mountains demarcate the terrain, and are often marked by differences of ideology, religion and culture. Borders are also gendered sites – the motherland – the essentially feminine spiritual being, nurturing and sacrificing, which constitutes the cultural and religious constructs of a nation. Borders become emotional and historical entities and play a very important role in the imagining of a nation. Individual identities are challenged at personal and political levels in nations torn by war and internal strife. My concern is with the metaphor of dislocation; the horrific violence created by ethnicity and its impact upon individual lives, and with ways of reaching across. Borders thus have both positive and negative aspects. When one focuses on the nature of conflicts, borders create dissent and division, and when one reaches across borders it can lead to an understanding and healing. For the purpose of analysis my focus is on Jean Arasanayagam's unpublished play *The Captain Has Come* and her short stories "The Journey", "All is Burning" and "Prediction", and the role of space – physical and emotional – and individual identity. Ethnic conflicts everywhere are violent and reprehensible, erupting like fault line disturbances, which hold the land at stake. In Sri Lanka the two sides – the Sinhalese and the Tamils – claim an unchallenged right to the land and the goal of one side is to liberate it from the occupation by the other, by killing or expelling, or by 'ethnic cleansing". Decades of internal violence have created a maze of fault lines in Sri Lanka, which disrupt time and again like seismic disturbances. This genocide is also abetted by difference in religion.

Huntington[1] writes that religion can be one of the most defining difference between people, and cannot be dismissed as 'narcissism of small differences' as dismissed by Freud (qtd. by Huntington 254). Fault line wars are enhanced by different belief system and Jean Arasanayagam writes sensitively about the people caught in this cultural and religious crossfire. She has made the personal choice of staying in the strife-torn country, she believes that it can be as dangerous or as safe as any other place. Her creativity sustains her to negotiate divisive borders. Her writing reflects the painful nuances of homelessness and isolation. As a Dutch Burgher she had crossed barriers from being an outsider to being co-opted in the land of her birth. Minoli Salgado, in her book on Sri Lanka, writes that Jean Arasanayagam's marriage into another minority Tamil group, was totally unacceptable to her in-laws, she was rejected out of hand by her mother-in-law in spite of the gendered experience they might have shared (Salgado 75). The civil war in 1983 reduced the entire family to the status of refugees in their own country and the question of her racial identity became crucial.[2] Salgado writes that being a writer meant a commitment not only to oneself, but also to the social and political changes around oneself.

The questions that interest me are the strategies that the creative artist employs to shape and reshape the identity in times of horrifying crisis, and the manner in which the writer creates and negotiates space for the articulation of the trauma of a community and a nation. In this connection, Chelva Kanasanayakam, a Sri Lankan now settled in Canada, observes that a social or political engagement and critical practice becomes a historical necessity, particularly in countries like Sri Lanka which has endured the most horrific forms of violence and anarchy in the last three decades. It has also been a period of intense literary activity both in English and in national languages, as writers are trying to come to terms with the mayhem around them. The experimental dimension in these narratives, Chelva Kanasanayakam argues, becomes a necessary aspect of the aesthetic dimension. It is through the 'Third Space'[3] that Jean Arasanayagam articulates the narratives, where the personal connects with the community. She critiques the narrow borders which define/confine nations and its peoples. It is an undisputed fact that volatile fault lines also create inequality and exploitation, where hundreds are killed and an equal number willing to die.

Jean Arasanayagam's affiliation is with the vast metaphoric expanse of land, anchored in the inner domain. The anguish of the 'unhomely' resonates in Jean Arasanayagam's works. In a speech delivered at the British Council in 1987, she articulated this strange unhomeliness, drawing from her personal experience in the refugee camps:

> I see the whole country, being divided into camps – some of the barriers being visible, others invisible .... Majority and minority ethnic groups find themselves in an ever widening territory of refugee camps ... as well as military camps .... (qtd. in Salgado 87)

In a civil war 'home' becomes a dislocated, ruptured or devastated place, reframed in a temporary shelter or a refugee camp. In the unpublished play *The Captain Has Come* (2007) the location is a refugee camp, where identities linked to the past, are under threat of erasure. The refugees are nameless. They exist simply as Man-1, Man-2 and so on. The camp is 'fenced off from the rest of the humanity' (1). An enclosure in itself, akin to a prison, it is Foucault's heterotopic site, which in a single real space juxtaposes several sites. The camp has its divisions as the hierarchies of caste and class separate the refugees further. There is a stockade of chairs and desks and new arrivals are resented and ignored. Here, Jean Arasanayagam's language is pared to the bare minimum to underline the erasure of identity. In clipped tones Man-1 tells Man-2 that he is here to escape from being burnt alive, as war is not a 'season of picnics', it is a time of 'exodus'. Their homes burnt, their life's savings and possessions looted, they are in a state of extreme trauma, and are required to share a rapidly shrinking space. Man-1 says that mass burials would have to be performed, as wood is precious and urgently needed in the camp. The refugee camp is covered in a miasma of fetid air, as dogs and cows surround the dead. There are bitter moments as the woman laments the loss of the 'safe enclaves' they had created. In a moment of reckoning the woman realizes that she has ceased to be human in these war times, concerned as she is only with herself and the security of her own family. Man-2 taunts Man-1 that though he had fasted and prayed regularly, he had never thought about his neighbour and had relegated his daughter-in-law from a different status to the position of an outsider. She was rebuffed both at temple rituals and at funerals, indicating that her presence would sully their superior social status as they sashayed in their gold and brocades from their cars into the temple. Man-1 had strutted through life, attaching value to riches and power, complacent about his upper caste status and denigrating his daughter-in-law for her simple origins. In the refugee camp, he is stripped of all his trappings – class, caste and wealth. In a way the camp is a great leveler. Man-2 also wonders from where did mankind learn the ideology of destruction and worship of wealth in place of humanity and compassion.[4]

The Captain in the play brings both the good and the bad news and serves both as a leader and a link with the outside world. As he moves all the refugees to another camp, the woman finds comfort in the thought that the flamboyant tree will be aflame with blooms, beside the gnarled and twisted branches of barren trees like the cross of thorns and the cross. The images of crucifixion and resurrection are deftly entwined at the close of the play. The suffering and bereavement which has been the fate of the refugees may now lead to the flowering of a better future.

"The Journey" is a powerful story, which describes the escape of sixteen Sri Lankans to Berlin. Homes, families, names are all left behind, as is the war and its dividing borders. The narrator is the sole Sinhalese in a group of sixteen, the rest are all Tamils. Each one is reduced to a number. Even the guide is nameless, he is the seventeenth person who is to be trusted implicitly. There is danger in knowledge. The narrator draws the ironic parallels between the journeys of the several lives of the Bodhisattvas, depicted on the temple murals, on the "Road to Perfection", till he reached Enlightenment and their own journey across various geographical borders guided by material demands. They are together as one community, sharing food and water, packed in a huge container truck and piled one on top of the other for hundreds of kilometres in sub zero temperature. As they disembark, they are asked to tear up their passports for which they had paid thousands of dollars. Trudging though dense forests in snow or crawling in mud and slush, the narrator recalls Europe's history of conquest of territory and he wonders that while

South Asians know the history of the European world, the European world has no time to learn their history (5). He remembers his country in 1983, when his parents had given shelter to a Tamil family. They did not share a language, but an unspoken bond had developed. The narrator feels the same warmth in Moscow as they are all huddled in one room with no heating. A strange kinship develops between him and the mother with a child, there is an exchange of warm gestures, since they don't share a language. This bond continues till the end, when the narrator with the help of the woman and her family is united with his own relatives in Berlin.

Ernest Renan in his essay "What is a Nation", writes that there is something in man which is superior to language and that is the human will. This human will negotiates geographical, religious, racial borders to constitute a nation. Renan writes that a nation is a soul, a spiritual practice which graciously leads to the surrender of the self to the welfare of the community.

The journey ends in Berlin, a city that has known the defeat of two world wars a city seeking a new identity, made up of many nationalities, not just pure Aryans alone (18). Here they would have to face the neo-Nazis, looking at the xenophobic graffiti scrawled on the walls. He wonders what kind of graffiti would they discover about themselves in times to come? The narrator feels that he too would be in a minority here and would he ever be able to find employment? Jean Arasanayagam encodes her text in spiritual parables. The important question is which place has escaped the scars of war? We can go back to Buddha's sage advice to the bereaved woman to find a house untouched by death.

The story "All is Burning" is inspired by Buddha's Fire Sermon, where everything is burning with the fire of hate, delusion, birth and death. Alice undertakes a different journey, as she steps out of her hut purposefully on bare feet, taking the 'death walk' to search for her abducted prospective son-in-law – Sena. The writer's sensitive depiction of the evening, describes the pall of fear that shrouds the village:

> She still felt her flesh raw, hurt by the events of the night. That sense of peace which came with late evening and the dusk that settled ... had been deceptive. The bathers had returned from the river, they did not linger very long these days. The water, silver shot with ripples of gold,

soon turned dark and opaque, vanishing into the dense clumps of trees .... (168)

She is just an ordinary woman, carrying on her extraordinary mission to look for Sena among the dead, with strange determination and persistence. The unhomely moment, as Bhabha has described it, had crept into her hut when *Yama* had come knocking and taken away Sena. In this sense of 'unhomeliness' the recesses of the domestic space – the hut – become the site of history's most invasive intrusion.[5] Alice realizes in this 'unhomely' moment that her life is suddenly reduced to the searching out the living, her only kin among the dead. She must take quick action because her life and her daughter's life depend on it. In the 'death walk' Alice turns the faces of strange men whom she would have never touched if they had been alive. Questions beseech her as she descends into the world of the dead like Dante. What would her village do without the men? What plants would grow here? Would there be any birds left in the village after the gunshots? In this eerie 'unhomed' state Alice provides maternal succour to a dying youth, easing his pain as she promises him a sip of water. She was a woman who had always wanted the certainty of truth. The truth was that all the men were dead, but life would have to go on. The borderline existence, poised on the stillness of time, bridges the home and the world (Bhabha 13).

Civil war creates the schism in a nation, splitting homes, families and all human links. The deep sense of detachment which makes the woman an 'outsider' sadly imbricates with Virginia Woolf's analysis (Woolf 201) that a woman has no country. She is an outsider in the realm of land, wealth and property. In this context, Ritu Menon poses this age-old question yet again in her essay, "Do Women have a Country?". Menon argues that the rise of militant, religious and cultural nationalism in South Asia imposes an idealised notion of womanhood and circumscribes their rights and space. In wars and partitions the three mediating agencies of family, community and state determine woman's individual and collective destiny. She warns that yet again 'community identities are being sharpened like knives', and history bears witness to the implicit consensus on permissible violence against women, who know that weapons of war are not very different from those of peace. Menon raises the pertinent question that will women ever be able to exit their communities and claim their countries? (61).

Another critic, Chandra Talpade Mohanty focuses on life story oriented narratives which are rooted in political consciousness. The written text in not created in a vacuum and oral histories and all forms of life stories are an important strategy of remembering. What is equally important is how they are recorded and how the reader reads and disseminates them.[6] Mohanty believes that writing becomes the site for the production of consciousness as it contests reality and forges new identities.

In another story of Jean Arasanayagam, "Prediction" we see how self representation can ease the legacy of a historical burden. Through the agency of the self, the passage through the present eases, there is an unburdening of the colonial stigma. It is a personal narrative where a remarkable lady with the symbolic name Sybil and endowed with an amazing gift of reading palms, predicts that the writer would have to make a choice between two ways and that she would always be a traveller. The writer makes a voyage to Pella in midwest America, where the nature of the colonization has been different from the one in Sri Lanka. Two hundred years ago her ancestors had laid the foundation of their family in Sri Lanka. She feels that peaceful or not the original inhabitants in both Pella and Sri Lanka had suffered displacement. A chance visit to a Dutch confectionary brings back the flavours of her home and childhood:

> Food was also remembrance, of recipes handed like genealogies down the line. Identity embodied in their flavours .... Memories clung like crumbs of flaky pastry to the fingers. A lingering touch on the tongue and lip. (118)

Members of her family, scattered in other countries, tried to retain a flavour of the past and in the mixing of the ingredients, the new flavours of the host country would mingle with the nostalgia for the country of their birth. The Burgher caterers carried their distinctive culinary skills to distant shores, just as the seamstresses carried their deftness in stitching wedding gowns. In new countries they could afford to be more lavish, but the longing to return always remained. They sought friends and familiar landscapes in the maps of the mind.

Bachelard poetically describes that our house is our corner of the world (4), and the diaspora, carries it in the corner of their hearts – the flavours, fragrances, families and friends, as they negotiate different borders. Homes where individual lives take root are imbued with a community of memories and images. Bachelard observes that in new places and newer homes, the memory of the old house leads to the moment of 'motionless childhood', a 'fixation of happiness' (6). The journey to the hinterland was undertaken to negotiate the historical identity 'of a colonizer' imposed on the writer, it was not an identity of her choice and she chooses to discard 'that archival documentation from an identity scrawled in hierographics of blood .... Dismissing the archaic language of that identity ... no longer duped by history's forgeries of name and lineage' ("Prediction" 121). She resolves to return to the country of the self, where no other flag would be hoisted, and resolves never to claim anyone's territory or set up boundaries. Her Sybil had stayed back but had inspired the writer to voyage out to gain this truth, willed by her own consciousness.

Bill Ashcroft, in the essay "The Emperor's New Clothes", is of the view that the contested issue of identity is linked to the very important process of 'postcolonial transformation'. Identities are not fixed. They are formed and transformed continuously by transcultural interaction, appropriation and transformation. Identities operate upon choice. The 'belief' that one has a choice in the changing and reshaping of one's life and society in which one lives is extremely empowering (Ashcroft 129). Man-1 in Arasanayagam's play, realizes the futility of hate and segregation in the name of wealth and status, the nameless Sinhalese narrator in "The Journey" had sloved off his past identities, the one he was born with, the other one he had bought and later discarded, he has now to reinvent himself, begin anew in a foreign land. Alice ("All is Burning") the lonely crusader has to work her way through the dead to a new resolve, to hold the community of lonely women together. The writer finds peace for herself in the story "Prediction" through making a choice of rejecting the imperial past weighing heavily on her, and asserting the freedom of her inner domain. Individual choices enable people to negotiate the volatile minefield across religious and cultural differences and some discover the core of humanism to mend and lave the fault lines.

Notes

1. The Tamils and Sinhalese had a history of peaceful co-existence. History alone was not responsible for the breakdown of peace. Huntington writes that demographic changes upsetting the balance were one factor. The numerical expansion of one group, put social, political and economic pressure on other groups. Gary Fuller (259) has shown in Huntington's book that the peaking of the Sinhalese nationalist insurgency in 1970 and of the Tamil insurgency in the late 1980s coincided with the "Youth Bulge". Fifteen to twenty-four years old exceeded twenty per cent of the total population of the group. A US diplomat in Sri Lanka noted that all Sinhalese insurgents were under twenty-four and the Tamil Tigers had a 'unique reliance' on boys and girls as young as eleven, and often those killed in the fighting were hardly over eighteen years. *The Economist* wrote that the Tigers were waging an 'under age war'. Huntington writes that fault line wars differ from other communal wars in two ways. First, communal wars may occur between ethnic, religious, racial or linguistic groups. Second, often communal wars tend to be particularistic and are unlikely to spread and involve additional participants. Fault line wars are between groups which are part of larger cultural entities. The diasporic kin groups, are enabled through technology to be aware of the latest development in the war zones. They provide moral, diplomatic, financial and material support to their ethnic groups.

2. In the article in *The Hindu* "Asylum for the Displaced", V. Suryanarayan, in the review of the book, *Ethnic Warfare in Sri Lanka and The UN Crisis* by William Clarance (Pluto Press: London, 2007), writes that when Eelam War II erupted in Sri Lanka, the United Nations High Commissioner for Refugees (UNHCR) officials were faced with a dilemma. They were under the moral obligation to protect the innocent victims of the conflict, who were not legally refugees – The Internally Displaced Persons (IDPS). William Clarance with his team were already present to care for the needs of reintegration of Sri Lankan Tamil refugees who had returned following the signing of the India-Sri Lanka Accord in 1987. It gained world wide recognition of its humanitarian endeavours, establishing open relief areas on both sides of the line. Through trust they moved freely in war zones. In 1991 Clarance and his colleagues prevented the conflict from going out of control an averted massive human destruction and displacement in Mainland Mannar. We witness the actual crossing of warring borders and creating an oasis of peace.

3. Third Space: described by Bhabha in *The Location of Culture* (38) as a space of enunciation of cultural differences. It has a colonial or postcolonial origin, which opens the way in the split space of enunciation of cultural hybridity. This in-between space becomes the site for construction or re-construction of people's history and identity.
4. Tagore (1917) much earlier had excoriated the 'national carnivals of materialism', which in its haste and its greed misses the 'ideal of completeness' (130). Tagore asserts his belief in the inner power, the essence of humanity, where poverty does not take away the richness of human values and the inner strength turns the hour of insult and injury to some measure of resolve.
5. Bhabha in *The Location of Culture* (1994), writes that 'unhomely' is a complex situation, where the unhomed is not necessarily homeless, the borders between home and the world get blurred, the public and the private imbricate and the vision is disorienting. It is a moment of deep significance where decision is to be taken which can change the course of one's life (13–14).
6. Chandra Talpade Mohanty talks about feminism without borders, a more expansive and inclusive vision which is transnational. She emphasizes women's solidarity, cutting across borders of nation, class and race. She makes a case of social justice and change, which cuts across demarcations, gives voice to the silenced, to highlight both the plurality and narrowness of borders and the liberalizing action of crossing them. The urgent need to recognize the repressive political, ideological, social framework, which aim to suppress and humiliate women (77–79).

Works Cited

Arasanayagam, Jean. *All is Burning*. New Delhi: Penguin Books, 1995.
—. *The Captain Has Come*. Unpublished Play, 2007. Page references to the manuscript.
—. *The Dividing Line*. New Delhi: Indialog, 2002.
Ashcroft, Bill. "The Emperor's New Clothes", *Nation in Imagination: Essays on Nationalism, Sub-Nationalisms and Narration*. Eds. C. Vijayshree, Meenakshi Mukherjee, Harish Trivedi & T. Vijay Kumar. Hyderabad: Orient Longman, 2007.
Bachelard, Gaston. *Poetics of Space*. Trans. Maria Jolas. Boston: Beacon Press, 1963.
Bhabha, Homi. *The Location of Culture*. New York: Routledge, 1994.

Foucault, Michel. "Of Other Spaces", *Diacritics,* Spring 1986.

Huntington, Samuel P. *The Clash of Civilizations: And the Remaking of World Order.* New Delhi: Penguin Books, 1997.

Kanaganayakam, Chelva. "The Poverty of Postcoloniality: Reading South Asian Literature and Culture". Keynote Address at the IRIS Seminar, February 2007. Unpublished.

Menon, Ritu. "Do Women Have A Country?" *From Gender to Nation.* Eds. Rada, Ivekovic, Julie Mostov. New Delhi: Zubaan, 2002.

Mohanty, Chandra Talpade. *Feminism Without Borders: Decolonising Theory Practicising Solidarity.* New Delhi: Zubaan, 2003.

Renan, Ernest. "What is a Nation?" *Nation and Narration.* Ed. Homi Bhabha. London: Routledge (1990). Rpt. 1991.

Salgado, Minoli. *Writing Sri Lanka: Literature, Resistance and the Politics of Place.* London, New York: Routledge, 2006.

Tagore, Rabindranath. *Nationalism* (1917). New Delhi: Rupa, 2002.

The Hindu. Tuesday, September 11, 2007, p. 15.

Woolf, Virginia. "Woman and Nationalism". *Literature in the Modern World: Critical Essays and Documents.* Second revd. edition Ed. Dennis Walder. New York: OUP, 2004.

21 E.V. RAMAKRISHNAN

Poet as Witness: Ethnicity and the Discourse of the Nation in the Poetry of Jean Arasanayagam and Agha Shahid Ali

I

South Asian countries have gone through similar phases of historical experiences such as those of colonialism, nationalist movements, state formation and efforts at decolonization. The politics of South Asia still bears the marks of colonial legacy. The boundaries which were politically drawn often contradicted the cultural boundaries that took shape over centuries. The nation building in these countries has been influenced by collective memories but the same logic did not inform the state formation. The minorities came into being through political processes of exclusion which were often the result of the policies prescribed by the state. Electoral politics made them increasingly self-conscious about their distance from centres of power. They were forced to defend their cultural identity against the aggressive assimilationist policies of the state. Their cultural identity took on aspects of political identity. They were caught in a conflict between atavistic sentiments and the compulsions of civil politics. The cultural givens that constitute the ethnic identities can mobilize people in times of crisis. Both Kashmiri Muslims and Sri Lankan Tamils can be described as ethnic communities since they are objectively different from other communities in customs, rituals and beliefs and they subjectively accept these differences as the basis of their distinctive identity. The prolonged civil strife in Sri Lanka and Kashmir has its roots in the conflict between ethnicity and nation state. Here we will study the poetry of Jean Arasanayagam, a Sri Lankan poet and that of Agha Shahid Ali, an Indian poet, both writing in English, to see how they respond to the crisis in their respective communities.

Let us examine the case of Sri Lanka. When Sri Lanka secured independence in 1948, it was the Sinhalese Buddhist elite which constituted the ruling class. Here it is worth mentioning that of the 26 per cent of Sri Lankan population that belongs to minority communities, 18.5 per cent are Tamils and 7.4 are Muslims. The divisive politics followed by the Sri Lankan state in the 1950s progressively alienated the Tamil minorities who are largely concentrated in the North and North East parts of the country. The dialectic of the monolithic, unitary state and its deliberate suppression of differences, linguistic and religious, led to the demand for a separate nation by the ethnic group. It should be remembered that the Buddhists have no special claim to Sri Lankan territory. There are strong cultural and racial similarities between the Sinhalese and the Tamils, the linguistic and religious differences notwithstanding. It is impossible to differentiate the Sinhalese and the Tamils from their physical appearance. Most of the Tamil speakers arrived in Sri Lanka centuries before and have contributed substantially towards the country's economic and cultural wealth.

After the formation of independent Sri Lankan state, the Tamils were systematically marginalized by the state apparatus. The Sri Lankan national flag shows a Sinhalese lion. The secular national discourse of the state became increasingly irrelevant as Buddhist culture and Sinhalese language became markers of Sri Lankan nation state. In 1956 Sinhalese was made the official language of the nation. The rhetoric of cultural nationalism ('Sinhala Only' was their slogan) was used by Bandaranayake's Sree Lanka Freedom Party to mobilize the majoritarian forces into a formidable political formation. Tamils who were a highly educated minority gradually lost their access to opportunities in higher education and representation in government jobs and the oppression of Tamils united them across religions. Gradually, as the relation between Tamil ethnicity and Hindu religion got severed and 'Tamil ethnicity replaces Hinduism as the focal point of nationalist pride among Tamils. As a result, some of the most active participants in the Tamil separatists movement have been Christians, even Christian clergy.' (Juergensmeyer 102). It is to be noted that the resistance movement of the Tamils has primarily targeted the Sri Lankan state.

The poetry of Jean Arasanayagam gives us an inside view of the Sri Lankan ethnic strife. By birth she is a Dutch Burgher. The Dutch came to Sri Lanka in the 17th century and the Burghers constitute a microscopic minority of Sri Lanka. During the colonial period they were a privileged group and this had alienated them from the mainstream. Jean Arasanayagam's marriage to a Sri Lankan Tamil, despite the disapproval of her family, meant embracing another minority identity. 1983 was a turning point in the history of Sri Lankan Tamils. In response to the killing of thirteen Sri Lankan soldiers on 23 July that year, riots erupted all over the country in which more than 2000 Tamils were killed. President Jayawardane did not condemn the rioters. This was the beginning of the long drawn out civil war which is nowhere near a peaceful settlement. Arasanayagam's volume of poems *Apocalypse 83* records her trauma as a refugee because, being married to a Tamil, she was also a victim of the political violence. In the poem titled "1958 ... '71 ... '77 ... '81 ... '83" she traces the recurring history of ethnic strife in the country and concludes:

> It's all happened before and will happen again
> and we the onlookers
> but now I'm in it
> it's happened to me
> at last history has meaning
> when you're the victim
> when you're the defeated
> the bridges bombed
> and you can't cross over. (*Fusillade* 26)

Some of her major poems from this period deal with the trauma of dislocation and displacement of the Tamil community in the context of ethnic strife. Several poems such as "Innocent Victim – Trincomalee," and "Eye Witness – Nawalapitiya" give first person accounts of the inhuman violence perpetrated on innocent people who had no inkling of the magnitude of the tragedy that was to befall them. The poem "In the Month of July" describes the scene of a man being chased by a mob and brutally killed. "It's Got to End" speaks of the need to speak out against violence. Several of the poems in the volume deal with the plight of refugees who are unable to come to terms with the sudden collapse of the familiar world they lived in. In the poem "'I Watch My Own Death' – Refugee Camp 1983" she writes:

> It is easier now to die than live,
> One waits for the burning to be over
> One waits for the final conflagration
> To end, seeing death and murder face to face
> In the eyes of enemies, stranger, predators,
> The degradation of the fugitive, the hunted
> Fleeing from the burning mazes, threats and death. (*Fusillade* 67)

In the poem "The Dalada Bombing" she shows how violence is routinized in the civil-war-torn Sri Lanka. She says:

> Who were the first to die?
> A family come to give their early offering
> Of milk, caught in the crossfire
> A woman on fire runs demented along the street
> The flames surging out of a singed glass
> Body-globe. (*Fusillade* 46)

The Nallur poems, in the same volume, are a poignant record of the temple town's slide into violence and chaos. Nallur houses a famous Murugan temple around which a minority culture of devotion and worship had grown. In "Nallur," she says that the 'thirtham' which tasted like nectar is now bitter and at the entrance of the town 'the silent guns are trained upon a faceless terror' (3). Smoking ruins, blackened stones, empty roads and trails of blood mark the landscape outside. The pilgrim town now has turned into a ghost town:

> The land is empty now
> the pitted limestone
> invaded by the sea
> drowns, vanishes,
> waves of rust swell and billow

beating into hollow caves and burial urns
filled with the ash of bodies
cremated by the fire of bullets. (107)

In "Remembering Nallur-1984," she recalls the annual festival of Nallur temple which used to attract lakhs of people. Now 'the conch blast echoes/over the veedhi of Nallur/summoning the penitents/to sacrifice, no one comes.' (ibid., 109). She also remembers the wandering singers who once travelled through the villages and bound them in their enchanting devotional music:

Where have they vanished,
The Bhakti singers in their trance,
Bodies bent backwards leaning against
Wind, borne by its surge
Across the empty plain singing thevarams,
Clashing cymbals, ringing their death knells
As they dance and sing traveling
From distant villages for miles and miles
Seeing only the gods behind the blind eyes
Of the world. (109)

The memories of devotion and communion which form a counter-narrative to the dominant one of arson, murder and dispossession constitute a site which assumes significance in her subsequent poetry. "Remembering Nallur-1984" ends with the lines:

This time the poojas are not made
With laden trays of flowers, tulsi, camphor,
Fruit, kumkum and thirtham,
The poojas are made with their bodies,
As they come thousands and thousands
Traveling from distant villages.
Nallur is now a battlefield
and the hands upraised
storming heaven
all bear arms,
all bear weapons. (115)

The context of ethnic violence forces Jean Arasanayagam to review the content of her minority identities. She offers a critique of the nationalistic discourse by producing self-critical narratives of her

Burgher and Tamil identities. In *A Colonial Inheritance and Other Poems* she recovers her past and in the process, takes stock of the colonial past. This is, by no means, an easy task because now she has to recognize that her ancestors have left her a dubious legacy of violence and shame:

> In the garden of museum
> a cannon rests. Within glass cases
> artefacts of time. Minted coins abraded
> silver larins, golden guilders, stuivers,
> ancient swords stained with rust
> and blood. Firearms antique,
> and in my face – a semblance. (*Colonial Inheritance* 5)

The minted coins are stained with blood. This is a moment of epiphany. The present violence was inherent in the colonial conquest of the natives and their brutal subjugation.

To own up to this dubious legacy is to be self-critical about her community:

> We were once invaders
>
> On our brows eating into skull
> We bear branded the mark of Cain. (*Red Water*: 85)

In a long poem called "Exiled Childhood" in the volume *Shooting the Floricans*, Arasanayagam confesses to her privileged status in the colony as a Burgher (9–10). To situate her own legacy is to accept that her relation with the mainstream is historically determined. The critical distancing she achieves in her narration of the past is a pointer to her awareness of the complications of history informing the present. In the middle of the poem she compares herself to a migrant bird which has overstayed its summer and has chosen to stay behind to cohabit with the native kind and has now grown 'into a rare genus' (13). Here she achieves a stasis of sort without any final resolution of her problem of belonging. The nationalist discourse, by its very nature, demands assimilation and the critical distance she acquires through her examination of her own location within Sri Lankan history, enables her to realize the inherent vulnerability of minority identities. In an article, Elaine Ho and Harshana Rambukwella have argued that Arasanayagam's writing is heavily invested in the idea of 'national belonging'. They suggest:

> It is from within the Sri Lankan nation and as an individual who desires to belong that Arasanayagam writes, but she is also acutely aware that in this national space, she is persistently marked as alien. The desire to belong co-exists with an equally urgent process of rewriting her own alien-ness, and to reinvent alienation as critical irony and poetic agency. (Ho and Rambukwella, 66–67)

I would like to argue that this is not borne out by her poems. She questions narrow notions of belonging. She has come to recognize that each discourse of belonging creates its others. She understands that choices are made by one's birth and one's location in a community which are historically determined. Today it is recognized that a nation state may contain more than one nation. Anthony D. Smith says in his study, *The Ethnic Origins of Nations*: 'Quite simply many individuals today belong simultaneously to two "nations" – Catalan and Spanish, Breton and French, Croat and Yugoslav, Scots and British, even Yoruba and Nigerian, perhaps' (167). The nationalistic discourse, as it has been defined by the Sri Lankan state, has no space to accommodate minority identities like hers. The nation state bestows equality whereas it is the nation which endows one with identity. She is caught between the state-seeking Tamil nationalism and the state-sponsored Sinhala Buddhist nationalism (See T.K. Oommen's article "New Nationalisms and Collective Rights"in Stephen May et al., 2004: 132–140. for details regarding the postcolonial nationalisms of South Asia.). It is not easy for her to endorse either of the two as it involves making painful choices. The metaphor of the migratory bird overstaying its summer and choosing to cohabit with the native kind and eventually evolving into a 'rare genus' does underline the fact that she will remain alien and different. Can she find her own space within the nation without getting assimilated? She will remain a vulnerable member of a minority community ever marked and singled out for differences. This burden of self-consciousness also will prevent her from being part of a dominant imagined community.

Arasanayagam is trying to find an alternative to the colonizing model of nation-building that characterizes the colonial and postcolonial nation states. This becomes apparent in the manner in which she negotiates differences with her Tamil identity. The insular nature of her mother-in-law's Tamil Hindu (Vellala) culture denies her entry into it. The culture and customs that constitute Tamil identity can also make it hegemonic in its own way when it excludes other identities from its day-to-day life. In the long narrative poem "The Women Goddesses and their Mythologies" the narrator describes how she is allowed to enter the pooja room of the matriarch only to be made aware of an intractable symbolic logic of the Tamil cosmology that excludes her and constructs her differently. Here we are made to feel the matriarch's centrality in Tamil culture. As a daughter-in-law from another minority culture she feels both unwanted and threatened. She has to subscribe to the codes of this new culture to gain entry here. As she says:

> Yet I entered, treading uncertain and wavering with
> Naked sole, my feet, now unpolluted, washed and bathed
> In turmeric, first having shaken off the dust of many
> Journeys on roads and streets I trod .... . (*Red Water* 30)

The dialectic of purity and pollution that is at the root of this narrative of the sacred clearly speaks of the essentializing tendency at work in the Tamil culture. The writer feels the need to resist this hegemonic element because it is the very same factor that is at work in the construction of the majoritarian discourse of the nation state. In her poem "Mother-in-law" she points to the hollowness of all claims to purity:

> "Aachi you have Sinhala blood.
> You drank milk of a Sinhala woman"
> "Who told you that? A Sinhala nona
> gave me milk. They all were
> respectable Sinhala nonas." (Wijesinha 71)

Nona means 'an honourable woman'. She wants to preserve the purity of her 'blood'. But we are all 'polluted' in one way or other. The ironic comment in the above lines points to an inclusive vision of the idea of identity and the need to resist fictions of purity. In a plural society one has to be wary of essentialist claims to insular spaces of identities.

II

The poetry of Jean Arasanayagam compels us to reconsider the 'modernity' of modern nations. In his study, *The Ethnic Origins of Modern Nations,* mentioned earlier, Anthony D. Smith argues that the core of ethnicity resides in the quartet of 'myths, memories, values and symbols' and in 'the characteristic forms or styles or genres of certain historical configurations of populations' (Smith 15). Ethnic communities carry the potential to emerge into nations as shown by the struggles of several such communities during the twentieth century. Citing the example of East European nations, A.D. Smith says that such transformations meant a triple movement: 'from isolation to activism, from quietism to mobilization and from culture to politics' (154). We have seen above how Sri Lankan situation forced the Tamil community to stake claim for a separate nationhood. The Kashmir context is equally complex. During its history, Kashmir has gone through Hindu, Buddhist and Islamic phases and has remained a confluence of cultures. The political crisis of modern Kashmir is, however, traceable to the partition of the subcontinent and the emergence of two nation states namely, Pakistan and India. It is also linked to the strong sense of *kashmiriyat,* the Kashmiri identity deeply implicated in the history and culture of Kashmir. This cultural ethos got politicized during the 80s due to the interference of the Indian nation state in the affairs of the state. The government in Delhi was deeply suspicious of Kashmir people's loyalty which created mutual antagonism (Ajit Bhattacharya 1994; Madhumita Srivastava 2001).

Agha Shahid Ali spent his childhood in Srinagar but moved to Delhi and then settled in the United States. He became more acutely aware of his ethnic roots once he became an exile. His poetry is not concerned as much with the routinized violence of Kashmir as its politico-cultural identity which he invokes through myths, metaphors and memories. While Arasanayagam documents the trauma of ethnic violence, Agha Shahid Ali embodies the trauma of Kashmir in the embittered elegiac poetic discourse he went on to perfect with chiseled precision.

Both Arasanayagam and Agha Shahid Ali know that there are larger ethical questions behind ethnic conflicts. Their poetry is an attempt to negotiate the homelessness inherent in their contexts. While Arasanayagam distances the tragedy with ironic examination of the very processes of exclusion in the construction of all identities, Agha Shahid is more concerned with memories as a source of cultural identity. T.K. Oommen's formulation of 'ethnie' may be applied to both of them. He observes:

> In order to get rid of the prevailing confusion, we need to conceptualize ethnicity as an interactional, as against, an attributional notion. We must view ethnicity as a product of conquest, colonization and immigration and the consequent disengagement between culture and territory. It is the transformation of the "outs" into "ins" that leads to the process of ethnies becoming nations. (Stephen May et al., 131)

In the case of Sri Lankan Tamils and Kashmiris the question of internal colonization is relevant. Both Arasanayagam and Agha Shahid have experienced the disjunction between 'culture and territory' Oommen speaks of. As an exile, Agha Shahid's alienation from land is more acute and this is reflected in his recollections full of anguish.

In his *Half-Inch Himalayas* (1987) Agha Shahid shows how the Kashmir of his childhood is now untraceable. As a homeless exile, he is condemned to his memories which unspool from the hallucinatory images of violence in the valley: 'This is home. And this is the closest/I will ever come to home. When I return,/the colours will not be so brilliant/the Jhelum's waters so clean,/so ultramarine. My love/so overexposed' (1). The Kashmir of his childhood has shrunken to the size of a postage-stamp. The over-exposed memory turns his memory into 'a giant negative, black and white, still underdeveloped' (1). He turns to the mythical images of the snowman to capture that elusive identity which is a haunting absence. In the poem "Snowmen" he says how his ancestors came from Samarkhand with a bag of whale bones. He still travels with generations of snow men on his back: "They tap every year on my window. Their voices hushed to ice" (8). In this surreal vision Agha Shahid recognizes his own otherness and homelessness. To recover his voice he has to speak from within the marginal space of an exile. It is by going back to the cadences of Urdu that he retraces the collective memories of his community. "In Memory of Begum Akhtar" uses memory as a source and resource to map a layered view of Kashmir:

> Ghazal, that death-sustaining widow,
> sobs in dingy archives, hooked to you.

> she wears her grief, a moon-soaked white,
> corners the sky into disbelief.
> You've finally polished catastrophe,
> The note you seasoned with decades
> Of Ghalib, Mir, Faiz:
>
> I innovate on a noteless raga. (*Half-Inch Himalayas* 28)

It is significant that his memory is mediated by the aesthetic form of ghazal and its classical heritage. In "Homage to Faiz Ahmed Faiz", he again invokes the ghazal as the form that speaks the language of exile:

> Your lines were measured
> So carefully to become in our veins
>
> The blood of prisoners. In the free verse
> Of another language I imprisoned
>
> Each line – but I touched my own exile. (ibid.: 32)

In poem after poem, the figure of the stranger appears in various forms: the previous occupant of the apartment, the riverside jogger, the 'someone' who lives in the house. The interiors of the poems become haunted as the poet feels unable to relate to a living community.

The crisis in Kashmir was precipitated by the insensitivity of the nation state which abdicated its responsibility of ensuring the people's right to dignity and identity. When the nation state delegitimates the demand for identity, the collective identity takes on an aggressive political role. T.K. Oommen in his article mentioned earlier on new nationalisms and collective rights, observes:

> But in the case of the new multicultural polities of Africa and Asia, there is a shift of emphasis from sequentiality to simultaneity. That is, the nations, ethnies, and minorities in the federal polities of these continents are increasingly insisting on equality and identity simultaneously. (Stephen May 131)

For 'ethnies,' region and nation are contiguous. The 'disengagement between culture and territory' (131) Oommen talks about, render both Jean Arasanayagam and Agha Shahid Ali as 'public poets' speaking as members of ethnic communities who voice concerns of a larger collectivity. It will not make sense to read their poetry in a strictly personal, individual context. The displacement they have suffered cannot be accounted for in individual terms. Agha Shahid reclaims a fragment of the inward-looking Kashmiri society through his scattered memories which range from those of Begum Akhtar to saffron farmers.

The poems in his *The Country Without a Post-Office* employ the metaphors of mourning to come to terms with the trauma of displacement and loss in the wake of Kashmir violence. The postcolonial state in India has become highly unitary and in the process, the marginal cultures have become increasingly invisible. Ali documents Kashmir, its geography, myths and rituals from the fragments of his memories. This 'region' he constructs is a site of resistance to the monolithic, unitary nation state. The nation state as a centre of power operates through codes that strictly define the boundaries of allegiance politically. Words like 'domicile', 'citizen', 'immigrant' or 'foreigner' are creations of these codes. Our liberal nationalistic discourse failed to recognize the ethnic, linguistic and regional identities as legitimate categories in themselves as it has become highly exclusivist and essentialist.

Ali constitutes his ethnic identity as a site of loss, hurt, injury and denial. It feeds on memories of embittered exiles and apocalyptic epiphanies. The discourse of mourning becomes the dominant way of dealing with life and its experiences. We have seen how poems about the snowman and the gypsy invoke the other. Here we may also recall that one of his early poems, "Eurydice" from *A Nostalgist's Map of America* (1991) which retells the myth of Orpheus from the perspective of Eurydice. It is set in a concentration camp in Nazi Germany where a crippled Eurydice limps past 'howl-choked dogs' to disappear 'in a sudden tunnel of mustard twilight'. There is a suggestion of homelessness in these portraits. In his epigraph to the poem "A Footnote to History" he writes: 'Gypsies ... coming originally from India to Europe a thousand years ago ...' (43). In his references to Begum Akhtar and the classical tradition she stood for, we have another clue to the separate cultural identity of Kashmir. In the concluding lines of the poem, "I Dream I Am the Only Passenger on Flight 493 to Srinagar," we can see a deep sense of hurt that is at the core of the Kashmir crisis:

He holds my hand speechless to tell me if

those smashed golds flying past those petrified
reds are autumn's last crimsoned spillage

rushing with wings down the mountainside
or flames clinging to a torched village. (*A Nostalgist's Map* 20)

Rooms Are Never Finished (2004) uses Hussain's sacrifice at Karbala and its commemoration in Muharram as a central metaphor. Memorializing is the poetic mode which Agha Shahid Ali perfects in his final collections. Memory and mourning become inseparable here. In working martyrdom and memory into the musical structure of the English ghazal he explores the possibility of community as an exile who cannot return to his homeland. Karbala becomes Kashmir and Palestine. Mother becomes both Zainab and Kashmir. The pain becomes physical and its overwhelming burden can be captured only in gestures. He uses translation as a verbal gesture of containing and communicating pain. One of the poems here is a translation from Ghalib who says: 'Grief crushed me so/again and again it became the pain that pain erases' (46). Translation is a mode that his poetry internalizes right from the beginning. We have seen his references to Begum Akhtar, Ghalib and Faiz Ahmed Faiz in his earlier poems. It is important to know that his use of ghazal form also involves translation. Rajeev Patke has argued that there is a homology between translation and migration in his poetry. He says:

> The unavailability of communion (with God) or connection (with parent, community, friend, home or country) is like the impossibility of full translation. Reversed, it becomes a denial of univocity, and thus a sanction for plurality of speech as dialects, of poetry as translation, of exile as migration, and guilt as restitution. (Patke 234)

The need to translate and the impossibility to achieve it go together. While translating Faiz Ahmed Faiz he touches 'his own exile' as the free verse of English turns his hand 'to stone' (*Half-Inch Himalayas*, 32). His efforts to transplant the ghazal into English has to be seen in this context. The free verse of English was not free enough to embody the larger pain of his private context. Ali says that 'suffering is seldom, perhaps, never, private' (ibid.). It is this aspect of suffering which is public and private at the same time that he is able to articulate through his English ghazals.

Agha Shahid Ali moved closer to the metropolitan poetic discourse in the later part of his career. But this is also the time he experiments with the ghazal form in English. Here I would like to emphasize the fact this use of the ghazal form creates a dialogic space in his quest for identity as a displaced exile. Traditionally ghazal has spoken about love and desire. In their essay on the English ghazal, Chandrani Chatterjee and Milind Malshe show how the traditional male gaze inherent in the traditional ghazal is redefined in the ghazals of the American poetess, Phyllis Webb (Ramakrishnan and Dasgupta 197). In the English ghazals of Agha Shahid Ali, he subverts the form from within by investing the tone with a collective voice. His use of ghazal in the context of the metropolitan tradition of American poetry is both an act of resistance and affirmation. It involves a border crossing that questions the assumptions behind such boundaries. He was opting out of the normative strategies adopted by hegemonic discourses and majoritarian languages. The ghazal as he reinvents it in English comes closer to the idea of 'minor' literature as defined by Deleuze and Guattari in their book *Kafka: Towards a Minor Literature* (1986). Minor literature contests the norms that constitute the normative codes of the literary. It renders the world and the word provisional.

What mattered in the ghazal for Agha Shahid was its paradoxical nature as reflected in its restraint and freedom, rigour and release and reticence and eloquence. It could be both personal and political at the same time. It could talk of the divine and the earthly love simultaneously. As he says in a small note on the ghazal form, the second line of each couplet 'delivers on the suspense by amplifying, dramatizing, imploding, exploding' (*Final Selections* 19). Ghazal gets deterritorialized as it moves out of its context. In its English version, it embodies the voice of an exile who cannot identify with any of the given identities constructed by hegemonic structures of power. Writing of Kafka's use of Prague German, Deleuze and Guattari comment:

> He will tear out of Prague German all the qualities of underdevelopment that it has tried to hide ... . He will turn syntax into a cry that will embrace the rigid syntax of this dried up German. He will push it toward a deterritorialization that will no longer be saved by culture or myth, that will be an absolute deterritorialization, even if it is slow, sticky, coagulated. To bring language slowly and progressively to the

desert. To use syntax in order to cry, to give a syntax to the cry. (Deleuze and Guattari 26).

This corresponds to what Agha Shahid Ali does in his English ghazals. He is able to find the syntax of a cry. His ghazals are 'in-formed' by his lamentations for the loss of his mother, his home, community and Kashmir. Ghazal allows him to find a midway home, an in-between space between the shadow lines created by nation states and his own present location. It renders the borders porous making it easy for the exile to be in and out, to be at home in his homelessness. He creates a 'minor' language within the majoritarian language of English by eschewing its affiliations and normative cosmologies. This also enables him to release the bodies that are mapped into objects by the nation state. We may remember here that English is the associate national language of India. It is the nation state's privilege to interpellate an individual as citizen, refugee or outsider. The 'minor' language neutralizes this power by transforming itself through the deterritorialized collective voice which is detached from a unified subject or body. Thus, the English ghazal becomes the speech of a person who has lost his speech. In "Arabic" Agha Shahid Ali says: 'The only language of loss left in the world is Arabic' (*Final Selections* 24). In another couplet in the same poem he addresses Amichai and says: 'I too Amichai saw the dresses of beautiful women. And everything else, just like you, in Death, Hebrew and Arabic.' The poem ends with the lines: 'They ask me to tell them what Shahid means ... Listen: it means "The Beloved" in Persian, "witness" in Arabic.' (ibid., 25). This is the paradox of which the ghazal becomes emblematic of: of belonging and not belonging, of defying prescribed affiliations and loyalties. He says this with clarity in the ghazal, "Land": 'If home is found on both sides of the globe,/home is of course here – and of course a missed land' (ibid., 50). It is the geography of this missed land that his ghazals map with great verbal precision.

To conclude, both Jean Arasanayagam and Agha Shahid Ali refuse to endorse the terms and conditions set out by the nation state to secure a sense of belonging. Arasanayagam has lived in Sri Lanka, but as a witness to the tragic divisions that has extracted a heavy human cost, she documents the violence inherent in all discourses of identity. Both remain exiles, acutely aware of the traumatic consequences of essentializing one's sense of identity. They take their ethnicity as a matter of fact and refuse to celebrate it. As they stand witness to the tragic divisions in their societies in their separate ways, their poetry questions and affirms, even as it contests and consoles.

Works Cited

Agha Shahid Ali. *A Nostalgist's Map of America*. New York: Norton, 1991.
—. *The Half-Inch Himalayas* (1987). Delhi: Oxford University Press, 1993.
—. *The Country Without a Post Office*. New Delhi: Ravi Dayal, 2001.
—. *Rooms Are Never Finished*. New Delhi: Ravi Dayal, 2002.
—. *The Final Selections: Call Me Ishmael Tonight; Rooms Are Never Finished*. New Delhi: Permanent Black, 2004.
Arasanayagam, Jean. *Apocalypse 1983.*, Colombo: International Centre for Ethnic Studies, (1984) 2003.
—. *A Colonial Inheritance and Other Poems*. Kandy, Sri Lanka: Privately Published, 1985.
—. *Trial by Terror*. Hamilton: Rimu Books, 1987.
—. *Red Water Flows Clear*. London and Boston: Forest Books, 1991.
—. *Shooting the Floricans*. Kandy, Sri Lanka: Samjna,1993.
—. *Fusillade*. New Delhi: Indialog Publications, 2003.
Bhattacharjea, Ajit. *Kashmir: The Wounded Valley*. New Delhi: UBS Publishers' Distributors, 1994.
Bose, Sumantra. *States, Nations, Sovereignty: Sri Lanka, India and the Tamil Eelam Movement*. New Delhi: Sage Publications,1994.
Colebrook, Claire. *Gilles Deleuze*. Routledge Critical Thinkers, Indian Reprint, 2007.
Deleuze, Gilles and Felix Guattari. *Kafka: Toward a Minor Literature*. Minneapolis: Minnesota Press,1986.
Ho, Y.L. Elaine and Harshana Rambukwella. "A Question of Belonging: Reading Jean Arasanayagam through Nationalist Discourse", *The Journal of Commonwealth Literature*. Volume 1 (No. 2), 2006: 61–81.
Juergensmeyer, Mark (1993). *Religious Nationalism Confronts the Secular State*. Delhi: Oxford University Press, 1993.
May, Stephen, Tariq Madood and Judith Squires, eds. *Ethnicity, Nationalism and Minority*. Cambridge: CUP, 2004.
Patke, Rajeev S. *Postcolonial Poetry in English*. Oxford: OUP, 2006.

Ramakrishnan E.V. and Subha Chakravarty Dasgupta, Guest Editors. *Translation Today* (Special Issue on Indian Translation Traditions), Vol. 3, No. 1 and 2, 2006.

Rothschild, Joseph. *Ethnopolitics: A Conceptual Framework.* New York: Columbia University Press. 1981.

Smith, Anthony D. *The Ethnic Origins of Nations.* Oxford: Basil Blackwell.,1986.

Srivastava, Madhumita. *International Dimensions of Ethnic Conflict: A Case Study of Kashmir and Northern Island.* New Delhi: Bhavana Books and Prints, 2001.

Wijesinha, Rajiva, ed. *An Anthology of Sri Lankan Poetry in English.* Colombo: English Association of Sri Lanka, 1998.

22 NISHAT ZAIDI

Centre/Margin Dialectics and the Poetic Form: The Case of Agha Shahid Ali

'Centre/Margin' – the metaphor itself implies a power relationship. However, in diasporic epistemology, as Homi Bhabha[1] and many others have shown, margins are no longer spaces marked by deprivation and powerlessness. They, on the contrary, are sites where culture is formed, marked by hybridity and multiplicity. 'Rootless? Certainly not', these words of Agha Shahid Ali unmistakably define his unique perspective towards the diasporic space he occupied.[2] An Indian-American, a Kashmiri-Indian, a Shiite-Muslim, the hyphenated existence to Agha Shahid Ali did not entail an existence on the fringes or a depriving force. He, instead of succumbing to the status of a refugee, became the cultural ambassador of his country. Agha Shahid Ali's poetry[3] is a sincere attempt to make this culture available to the world.

Answering a self posed question, 'What are the implications and consequences of writing between national paradigms, bilingually or multilingually?' Azade Seyhan in his book *Writing Outside Home* replies:

> Transnational writing can potentially redress the ruptures in history and collective memory caused by unavailability of resources, archives and recorded narratives. By uncovering obscure poetic traditions, discovering forgotten idioms and grammars, and restoring neglected individual and collective stories to literary history; it introduces the

---

An earlier version of this paper was presented at an International Seminar at Jaipur.

riches of hitherto neglected cultures into modern literary consciousness. (13)

This is best exemplified in Agha Shahid Ali's use of the ghazal form in English. Ali's experiments with form included his own mastery of 'canzone', a form which requires extreme repetitions, his use of the ghazal form in English (at times even using lines by American poets and developing them into ghazals) and his ability to persuade many American poets to write ghazals. By doing all this, Agha Shahid Ali not only introduced an entirely new idiom in English poetry but also exploited poetic form as a site where the 'in-between' space, the hyphenated identity could be posited. In the present paper, I have concentrated on Agha Shahid Ali's innovative use of the ghazal form of poetry as a bridge between the two civilizations that Ali traversed and as a means to retain identity in foreign surroundings. The paper aims to study Agha Shahid Ali's exploitation of the poetic form in the light of transnational poetics and attempts to establish that for Agha Shahid Ali the poetic form itself was transformed into a site where the oppositional cultural discourses of diasporic experience could negotiate and points of affiliation could be worked out.

Agha Shahid Ali (1949–2002) was born in India in a Shiite Muslim family. His ancestors came from Central Asia. Ali's mother, Sufia Noumani, came from a family of Persian origin and was connected to Sufi Saint Abdul Quddus Gangohi of Rudauli. Ali grew up in a culturally and linguistically rich environment where the entire family read and appreciated poetry and literature in Persian, Urdu and English. Shahid Ali's poetry can best be termed as an elaboration of the subcontinent's own mixed history. Agha Shahid Ali draws from the rich cultural resources of the country of his birth where plurality, compositeness and eclecticism mark cultural patterns, as he says:

> The point is you are a universe; you are the product of immense historical forces. There is the Muslim in me, there is the Hindu in me, there is the Western in me. It is there because I have grown up in three cultures and various permutations of those cultures.[4]

Border crossing to Agha Shahid Ali is not synonymous with a break or rupture; he rather perceives it as a continuum. History transpires Shahid Ali's poetry and he transforms it into the mythical one, whence personal, local and communal experiences are translated into a universal phenomenon. He does not use the linear time frame of history but prefers the elliptical movement using contrapuntal mythical terrain where one voice echoes several voices across time and space, where Karakoram ranges transform into Hindukush and Arizona, where rain infests Kashmir, Lahore and Amherst together, and where simultaneity overshadows sequentiality. From Ali's personal history, which takes us back to the time when his ancestors came from Kashmir to Samarkand ('Snowmen'), and communal history of Hussain's martyrdom and Zainab's desolation and grief as she was taken from Syria to Damascus to the contemporary reality of his people in Kashmir – Ali's poetry explores it all. Speaking of the diasporan citizens' duty towards their homeland, R. Radhakrishnan writes, 'As diasporan citizens doing double duty (with accountability both here and there) ... we have a duty to represent India to ourselves and to the United States as truthfully as we can' (212). Shahid keeps revisiting his homeland, 'this country/where a minaret has been entombed' (*The Country* 25). He not only displays a very clear and close understanding of the politics in his homeland Kashmir, but also raises a strong voice of protest against the political repression, the weak political will on part of the Government and the plight of innocent people dying in the valley. On the cultural plane, his poems are suffused with images that reaffirm the composite culture of India – images that range from those of Radha, Krishna and Laila Majnoo to Hussain and Zainab – and an equally diverse literary inspiration ranging from Ghalib, Faiz Ahmad Faiz to James Meryll and Lorca.

The ghazal, informs Ali, can be traced back to 7th century Arabic literature. In its canonical Persian (Farsi) form arrived in 11th century, it is composed of autonomous or semi-autonomous couplets (called Bait in Arabic meaning 'house' and she'r in Persian and Urdu tradition which means 'something composed or versified') that are united by a strict scheme of rhyme (*qafia*), refrain (*radif*) and line-length (*bahar*). The opening couplet (*matla*) sets the scheme by having it in both lines (*misra*) and then the scheme occurs only in the second line of every succeeding couplet (*Call Me Ishmael* 19). As regards the meter, the Perso-Arabic quantitative meter is rigorously defined. In Urdu prosody the phonetic length of syllables is taken into account while in English, stress is the criterion, the long and short syllables of the former corresponding to the stressed and unstressed syllables of the latter. A ghazal must have a minimum of five she'rs; there is no maximum limit. There is a paradoxical unity in disunity in the ghazal form. Formally each she'r of ghazal is connected by *bahar qafia and radif*, but thematically each one stands independently as an autonomous unit. The noted Urdu critic Shamsur Rehman Faruqi informs:

> In fact, all poetry in the Indo-Persian literary culture is seen as synchronic, and in the world of ghazal, there is no concept of a 'poem'. Ghazal consists of a number of individual verses, most often unconnected with each other by theme or mood. Even in performance, the poet may not recite all the she'rs of his ghazal or may change their order or even add a few on the spur of the moment, or incorporate she'rs from another ghazal in the same rhyme and meter. (*A Stranger in the City* 197)

The Persian form of ghazal poetry underwent a change when the form travelled to India, thus the Persian ghazals written in India are said to have followed what is known as "Sabk-i-Hindi".[5] When the form was adapted in Urdu, it drew from the Indian style of Persian ghazal i.e., Sabk-i-Hindi which is defined by its metaphoricity, intertextuality, word-play, separation of theme (*mazmun*) and meaning (*ma'ani*) whereby a poet could use the same *mazmun* for multiple *ma'ani*.

But in spite of this autonomy, there is an overarching unity that envelops the Ghazal universe. Faruqi and Pritchett elaborate upon this:

> Yet the small two-line verse is not left entirely to its own devices, for it inhabits the long-established, well-developed ghazal universe. The ghazal universe is founded on the figure of the passionate lover, and faithfully mirrors his consciousness. The lover, while longing for his inaccessible (human) beloved or (divine) Beloved, reflects on the world as it appears to him in his altered emotional state. To him its highs are infinite heavens, its lows abysmal depths, its every scene and every moment charged with intense and complex meanings – meanings to which non-lovers, the ordinary 'people of the world,' are appallingly blind. The ghazal universe exists in the consciousness of ghazal poets and their audiences, who construct it by knowing verses, and constantly refine it by making, hearing or reading, accepting or rejecting, yet more verses. ("Lyric Poetry in Urdu")

When it comes to writing ghazals in English, there are problems involved at the level of lexicon, syntax, semantics and the cultural context. To elaborate the same, since the form of ghazal seeks precision, it mostly depends on vocabulary taken from the lexicon of language which is pregnant with cultural context and thus does not need any elaboration. Thus Urdu words like *saqi (*the tavern keeper*), sharaab(*wine*), maikhana, paimana*(cask), *mai*(wine), etc., come from the same semantic domain but given the value of their occurrence they can be used symbolically in multiple contexts to invoke multiple meanings such as divine blessing, beloved's favours, preacher, metaphysical experience and so on. Lack of availability of such a tradition of diction in English handicaps the poet as he cannot depend on readers' participation in his metaphorical usages.

Similarly, cultural contexts metaphorically represented by this lexicon also facilitate the precision which the form is known for. Thus ghazal poets in Urdu have used lexical nodes such as *pyas* (thirst), *dar-badari* (nomadic), *maqtal* (battle ground), *qaidkhana* (prison), *hijrat* (migrancy), etc., to use history of Karbala as metaphor.[6]

Ghazal, by general consent, is a form that is deeply rooted in a certain classical tradition as its famous practitioner Faiz Ahmad Faiz suggests, '... it draws its sustenance from the storehouse of classical tradition. It depends for effective communication upon the readers' or listeners' emotive and cognitive linkage with this tradition' (Majeed 216).

Hence, to think of writing ghazals in English, involves the risk of using 'form for form's sake'. Why, then, did Agha Shahid Ali take this risk of not just writing and translating ghazals into English but also of inviting American poets to write ghazals in English? This question is best answered by none other but Shahid Ali himself when he says, 'What is someone of nearly two equal loyalties to do but lend, almost gift them to each other and hope that sooner or later the loan will be forgiven and they will become each other's?' ("The Rebel's Silhouette" 2)

Ali's experimentation with the ghazal form is an addition to his various other efforts to 'gift' the two equal loyalties to each other. If, on the one hand, Ali uses strict metrical forms of Europe such as 'canzone' and 'sestina' to express subcontinent ideas, Kashmiri themes and Urdu sentiment, on the other, he transplants the strict verse form of Indo-Islamic tradition, ghazal, in English language to fulfil the same purpose. Rukun Advani rightly points out, 'He had one foot in the realm of mushairas and Faiz Ahmad Faiz and other in the world of Western versification and translation activity. His own achievement was to blend the two' ("Agha Shahid Ali: A Few Memories").

Ali's "Introduction" to his edited collection, *Ravishing DisUnities,* explains his objectives in introducing this form to the western audience. He challenges Paul Oppenheimer's claim that sonnet is the oldest poetic form that started in 13th century Italy. The form of the ghazal, counters Shahid Ali, is by far older and thus the knowledge produced in the western academia tends to exclude everything that did not originate in the west. Ali sets out to amend this by obliquely questioning the disoriented Eurocentric epistemology and orienting it back to the east. Speaking of the dialectical centre/margin relationship that the diasporic community shares with the host country, with special reference to Indian-American community in America, R. Radhakrishnan writes:

> When someone speaks as an Asian American, who exactly is speaking? If we dwell in the hyphen, who represents the hyphen: the Asian or the American, or can the hyphen speak for itself without creating an imbalance between the Asian and the American components? (211)

Ali was always conscious of this possibility of imbalance. In his "Introduction" he expresses anger at the complete distortion that the form has met in the west. He expresses his displeasure at the way American poets have practiced the form in complete disregard of its formal structure, as he says, 'Free verse ghazal in America seems always a momentary exotic departure for a poet, nothing that is central to him or her, to their necessary way of dealing with the world of their poetry' (*Ravishing Disunities* 13).

This distorted, peripheral use of form obviously upsets the poet who is conscious of his twin loyalties. For this very reason perhaps, he declares in the beginning of his "Introduction" that he wants to take back the gift 'outright'. To him what matters, is the reciprocity of influence and not the unidirectional appropriative hegemonic interpretation of the 'other' by the centre on its own terms, or plane commoditization of the culture of the 'margins'. Ali's "Introduction" may seem to suffer from the anxiety of 'real' or 'authentic', which is so common in the diasporic consciousness, but it can better be understood as a reaction against the attempt of the west to accommodate third world cultures in its marketplace pluralism. Therefore, while Ali harps on questions like 'What is the true Persian form?' which sound essentialist, he does not forget to remind his American fellow poets, the advantages of writing this real 'Ghazal':

1. English can employ full rhymes, even the most cliché ridden, as *radif* saves them through a transparent mask.
2. Ghazal also offers English a chance to find a formal way, a legal way out to cultivate a profound respect for desperation (*Ravishing Disunities* 11).

What hope does the form offer to marginalized subjects? The non-linear, contrapuntal structure of ghazal, where couplets though independent in terms of theme are held together by 'a profound and complex cultural unity, built on association and memory and expectation' (2) allows the diasporic subject non-hegemonic, non-subordinate space. Ali says, 'If one writes in free verse-and one should – to subvert western civilization, surely one should write in form to save oneself from western civilization' (13). Therefore, writing in strict formal structure was his way to discover self and retain his identity.

Agha Shahid Ali manipulated the ghazal form at three different levels in his poetry. He himself composed ghazals in English; he translated ghazals of famous maestros such as Mirza Ghalib and Faiz Ahmad Faiz into English, and inspired many American poets to write 'Real Ghazals' in English.

Ghazal in Persian literally means 'talking to/of the beloved'. In one of his couplets Agha Shahid Ali explains the meaning of his name:

They ask me to tell them what Shahid means
Listen: it means "The Beloved" in Persian, "witness" in Arabic.
(*Call Me Ishmael* 25)

Thus overlap of the two meanings must have drawn this "Beloved Witness" to the ghazal form. Agha Shahid Ali wrote many ghazals in English which were later put together in the volume titled, *Call Me Ishmael Tonight*. Thematic concerns of these ghazals are no different from the thematic concerns of the rest of Agha Shahid Ali's poetry i.e., love, longing, loss, separation and search for home, for lost relationships for life for identity and even for death. However, what stands out in these ghazals is the complete new idiom of poetry drawn from the Indo-Persian tradition which Ali introduces in English poetry. The texture of his language is rooted in eastern poetic traditions more than it is in English. Some of the *mazmuns* in his ghazals are very close to the ones used in Urdu and Persian poetry for e.g. the *mazmun* of dust in the following couplet:

> I am mere dust. The desert hides itself in me.
> Against me the ocean has reclined from the start. (42)

This couplet immediately reminds one of Ghalib's famous verse:

> *Hota hai niha.N gard mein sehra mere hote*
> *Ghista hai jabi.N khaak pe dariya mere aage*
>
> (The desert hides itself in dust in my presence. The waves break their heads before me.)

Similarly, one also finds the poet trying to explore new *ma'ani* in the old *mazmuns*, a feature that was the hall mark of 'Sabk-i-Hindi' and was later followed in Urdu poetic tradition. Here is a couplet by Ali where Satan is projected as God's lost love:

> Who but Satan can know God's sorrow in Heaven?
> God longs for the lover He undermined from the start. (43)

This conceptualization of God and Satan in lover-beloved relationship where the beloved is always disregardful of the offerings of the lover is quite innovative. Ali also often used one *mazmun* for multiple *ma'ani*. This is best exemplified in his multiple usage of the *mazmun* 'Beloved':

> Now Friend, the Beloved has stolen your words-
> Read slowly: the plot will unfold in real time. (33)

Here 'Beloved' seems to refer to the repressive autocratic government which represses freedom of speech. At other places, the same is used for its literal meaning, to refer to God etc., as in the following couplet:

> The Beloved will leave you behind from the start
> Light is difficult: one must be blind from the start. (42)

Word play, which the Indo-Persian ghazal form revels in, is also found in abundance in Ali's poetry. Here are a few examples:

> Crucified Mansoor was alone with the Alone
> God's loneliness – just His – compiled by exiles. (28)

Here the two 'alones' and 'loneliness' are words drawn from the same semantic field, but all evoke different responses. Another couplet in the same ghazal which addresses Mehmoud Darwish, the famous Palestinian poet, says:

> Will you, Beloved Stranger, ever witness Shahid –
> Two destinies at last reconciled by exiles? (29)

This couplet stands as an example of what Shamsur Rehman Faruqi calls the 'art of congruity' where words are connected with each other in many different ways in Indo-Persian style of poetry. Metaphors are also an outstanding feature of ghazal poetry and as Faruqi points out, '... the chief achievement of Indian style poets was to treat metaphor as a fact and then go on to create further metaphors from that fact.' ("A Stranger in the City" 214) The syntagmatic use of metaphor is found in Ali's English ghazals too. Notice the metaphoric usage of fire and water here:

> In a mansion once of love I lit a chandelier of fire ...
> I stood on a stair of water; I stood on a stair of fire. (*Call Me Ishmael* 34)

Again the simultaneous use of metaphoric and literal meaning of the word 'exile' in the following lines where the poet addresses Mahmoud Darwish:

> In Jerusalem a dead phone's dialed by exiles
> You learn your strange fate: you were exiled by exiles. (28)

Apart from these stylistic features of traditional ghazal form which Agha Shahid Ali introduced in English poetry, one also finds in these ghazals, a pronounced awareness of the international politics in particular an awareness of the political scene in Indian subcontinent. There is a unique contemporaneity alongside side metaphysical anguish that marks these ghazals:

> The birthplace of written language is bombed to nothing
> How neat, dear America, is this game for you? (26)

Again referring to the politics of Kashmir, Ali says,

> And who is the terrorist, who the victim?
> We'll know if the country is polled in real time. (32)

Besides, references in these ghazals range from Mansoor, Shammas, Kali, Lorca, Ishmael, Majnoo etc., indicating the sweep of civilizations that the poet has been a part of. Ali has also religiously written 'Makhta' (the last couplet of ghazal where the poet introduces his own name or *takhallus* i.e., pen name) in almost all his ghazals, except a few. Ali also introduced another practice of ghazal tradition in English poetry whereby poets write ghazals on the *zamin* or ground of other poet's writings. Thus a *mirsa* or *qafia* or both *qafia* and *radif* used by any other poet is taken and improvised, adding new possibilities to it. Ali wrote ghazals taking lines of other poets such as Wislawa Szymborska. Ali's ghazals thus not just brought forth a new poetic form on the scene of English poetry; they rather introduced a new idiom of expression, a new vocabulary, semantic range and metaphoric and rhythmic possibilities in English poetry.

Ali not just wrote ghazals himself but also translated some by masters such as Mirza Ghalib, Ahmad Faraz and Faiz Ahmad Faiz. In his Introduction to *Ravishing DisUnities,* Ali justifies why it is not possible to stick to formal restrictions in translations as Ali admits, 'it is impossible to sustain convincingly' (11). Thus there are formal liberties that the poet takes in translation. However, unlike the poet's own ghazals, here the constraints of language makes the poet introduce lexical nodes which are not there in the original in order to make it work in the Target Language, invert the order of lines in order to create some semblance of rhymes etc., the casualties in all this being suspense/resolution schema which the two lines of ghazals have. Notice the examples:

> World, should Ghalib keep weeping you will see a flood
> drown your terraced cities, your marble palaces. (2003: 52)
>
> *(yuN hi gar rota raha 'GHalib' to e-ehle jahaaN*
> *deKHna in bastiyoN ko tum ke weeraaN ho gayee. n)*

(Literal Translation: If Ghalib continues to weep like this, O fellow beings Watch out your dwellings, they will soon become deserted.)

Here the translator uses lexical items such as flood, drowning, and marble palaces etc., which are not explicitly mentioned in the original Urdu she'r thus restricting the scope for interpretations. Again Ahmad Faraz's lines:

Kis kis ko batayenge judai ka sabab hum
Tu mujh se khafa hai to zamane ke liye aa

(Literal Translation: Who all will I explain the reasons for separation. You may be angry with me, come back for the world's sake)

Rendered by Ali as:

Not for mine but for the world's sake come back.
They ask why you left? To whom all must I explain? (48)

Here the sequence of lines has been reversed, thus again impacting the 'suspense-resolution schema. However, if these ghazals are read as independent pieces, no body can deny their poetic worth and beauty. This perhaps explains why Ali himself does not use the word 'translation'. He only says 'After Ghalib or Faraz'. Here are a few couplets for perusal:

Just a few return from dust, disguised as roses.
What hopes the earth forever covers, what faces?
I too could recall moonlit roofs, those nights of wine –
But Time has shelved them now in Memory's dimmed places.
She has left forever, let blood flow from my eyes
till my eyes are lamps lit for love's darkest places. (52)

As a member of the diaspora Asian-American community, Ali was always all too conscious of his two-way debts and his duties both to his host country and his homeland. This double allegiance led him to invite American poets to contribute to his anthology of ghazals. In doing so, he insisted that they should be 'real Ghazals' not those 'arbitrary, near-surrealistic exercises in free verse' which Ali found amusing. But this insistence on form does not simply imply structure but rather the poetic possibilities that this structure opens up. He assures American poets that this formal restriction may lead to 'further refinement of thought' (13). Thus, what results is a new range of expressions. This is best exemplified in a ghazal by John Hollander which is about the ghazal form itself. Here I quote its opening and closing couplets:

For couplets the ghazal is prime; at the end
Of each one's a refrain like a chime: "at the end."

Now Qafia Radif has grown weary, like life,
At the game he's been wasting his time at. The END. (76)

These couplets are remarkable not only for their formal structure and their beautiful pseudonymizing at the end, but also for their ability to expand the semantic range of words and their metaphysical content. There are many more such ghazals in the collection. Notice some of these couplets where the same word-play, discovery of new themes etc., are tried out by poets who have been alien to the tradition which the ghazal form is rooted in:

Here is a couplet by William Mathews:

By the people. For the people. Of the people. Grammar:
But politics is an incomplete sentence after all. (105)

And one by Teresa Pfeifer:

Pausing for ecstasy at the shore tomorrow?
Love, you will find quicksand for a floor tomorrow. (131)

It is this feature that Sara Suleri refers to in her "Afterword" to the collection when she says, 'There are poems in this collection that touch upon precisely that point of translation that converts the simple imitation of form into an opening ... cultural transitions take place' (180). This is what Agha Shahid Ali always aimed at – 'gift' his two loyalties to each other, that too on an equal footing, without any hierarchy. Thus he attempts to break the 'exotic' notions of ghazal and make it real.

Agha Shahid Ali explored dialogic possibilities in the poetic form whereby tensions and contesting claims of diasporic identity could seek synthesis and co-habit. He situates his diasporic identity on the site of the ghazal form where the twin identities could negotiate without any appropriation of one by the other. In this he also influences the centre by expanding their realm of linguistic and semantic possibilities. Speaking of the role of diasporic writer as a cultural visionary, Azade Seyhan points out:

The participation of diasporic subject in the cultural life of the host country registers the moment when other literary and artistic forms of expression enter (Western) history. Through this dialectic (in its original sense as a dialogue), the distance between ports of departure and arrival appears to collapse; the migrant, exile or voyager not only crosses the threshold into another history and geography but also steps into the role of an itinerant cultural visionary. (14)

Ali's innovative use of the ghazal form reaffirms the dialogic possibilities in the dialectically juxtaposed cultural spaces. In sharing his experience of multiple – linguistic, geographical, historical – islocations, and allowing his contemporary American poets the same experience of border crossing by offering them to write in an all new poetic form, Agha Shahid Ali invites his readers to see culture not as a static, fixed or a given entity but as something dynamic, in its interaction with other cultures. He exposes performative processes of cultural engagement.

Notes

1. See Homi Bhabha, *On Location of Culture*, (London: Routledge), 1994.
2. Refer "The Rebel's Silhouette", paper presented in 1992 at a translation workshop, New Delhi.
3. Ali's rich poetic corpus includes several volumes of poetry such as *Call Me Ishmael Tonight: A Book of Ghazals* (2003), *Rooms Are Never Finished* (2001), *The Country Without a Post Office* (1997), *The Beloved Witness: Selected Poems* (1992), *A Nostalgist's Map of America* (1991), *A Walk Through the Yellow Pages* (1987), *The Half-Inch Himalayas* (1987), *In Memory of Begum Akhtar and Other Poems* (1979), and *Bone Sculpture* (1972). He is also the author of *T.S. Eliot as Editor* (1986), translator of *The Rebel's Silhouette: Selected Poems by Faiz Ahmed Faiz* (1992), and editor of *Ravishing Disunities: Real Ghazals in English* (2000).
4. See "Calligraphy of Coils", 1998.
5. For a detailed scholarly study of 'Sabk-i-Hindi' see Shamsur Rahman Faruqi, "A Stranger in City: The Poetics of Sabk-i-Hindi', *Literary Theory: Perspectives from Asia*, Ed. Syed Naqi Husain Jafri, (New Delhi: JMI & Creative Books), 2004, pp. 180–285.
6. For the detailed study of Agha Shahid Ali's use of Karbala metaphor in his poetry see, Nishat Zaidi, 'Karbala as Metaphor in the Poetry of Agha Shahid Ali', *Indian Literature*, Vol. L1: No.1, 237:Jan-Feb, 2007, pp. 154–167.

Works Cited

Advani, Rukun. "Agha Shahid Ali: A Few Memories" *tehelka.com*, December 8, 2001. Tehelka, New Delhi: December 8, 2001 http://www.tehelka.com/channels/literary/2001/dec/8/lr120801 agha.htm, 2003.

Ali, Agha Shahid. "The Rebel's Silhouette: Translating Faiz Ahmed Faiz", Presented at the Workshop on 'Language, Culture and Translation' at IIC from 3rd October to 1st November. 1992.

—. "Calligraphy of Coils", in conversation with Rehan Ansari and Rajinderpal S. Pal, p. 2, availability, http://www.himalmag.com/march98/encounter.htm, 1998.

—. *Call Me Ishmael Tonight: A Book of Ghazals*, New York & London: W.W. Norton & Co. 2003.

—. *The Country Without a Post Office*, Delhi: Ravi Dayal 2000.

—., ed. *Ravishing DisUnities: Real Ghazals in English*. Hanover and London: Wesleyn University Press. 2000.

Faruqi, Shamsur Rahman. "A Stranger in City: The Poetics of Sabk-i-Hindi', *Literary Theory: Perspectives from Asia*. Ed. Syed Naqi Husain Jafri, New Delhi: JMI & Creative Books. 2004.

Faruqi, Shamsur Rahman and Frances W. Pritchett. "Lyric Poetry in Urdu: the Ghazal", Originally published in *Delos* 3, 3–4 (Winter 1991), pp. 7–12. cited here from <http://www.columbia.edu/itc/mealac/pritchett/00fwp/published/txt_lyric_poetry2.html>

Majeed, Sheema. ed. *Culture and Identity: Selected English Writings of Faiz*, Karachi: OUP. 2005.

Radhakrishnan, R. *Between Identity and Location: The Cultural Politics*, New Delhi: Orient Longman. 2007.

Seyhan, Azade. *Writing Outside the Nation*. Princeton University Press: Princeton, 2000.

23
VIJAYA SINGH

Hell is the Absence of the Beloved: Agha Shahid Ali and the Poetry of Impossible Mourning

I borrow the phrase 'impossible mourning' from Vijay Mishra's excellent essay, "Diasporas and the Art of Impossible Mourning" and conflate it with the 'absence of the beloved' in the last collection of Agha Shahid Ali's book of poems *Rooms are Never Finished* published in 2001, for the title of this paper. *Rooms Are Never Finished* for all practical purposes should be considered his last collection of poems even though his *Call me Ishmael Tonight* is published posthumously in 2002. *CMIT* is a collection of ghazals on which he was working before his death and is a compilation of new and old ghazals.

It was immanent that the phrase 'impossible mourning' should draw my attention to Roland Barthes's extraordinary treatise on memory and loss, *Camera Lucida* and indeed as I was reading Shahid's *Rooms are Never Finished* I could not help but draw a parallel between the two. There is an uncanny similarity, not only between the two books but also the persons: in their remarkable attachment to their mothers; and the outpour of inconsolable grief by both Shahid and Barthes over the deaths of their mothers, as reflected in their last works. In fact, even in the unusual circumstances of their death there is an eerie parallel. Where Barthes, after the death of his mother can only wait for his 'total, undialectical death' (72) and indeed dies merely three years after her death. Shahid too succumbs to the disease, his mother was suffering from: brain tumour – four years after her death.

Thus, I use parallels drawn between the act of impossible mourning and the condition of exile by Mishra; and Barthes's *Camera Lucida*, a valedictory meditation on his mother's death and thereby on memory and the nature of photography as the scaffolding for my paper. This is not a wilful juxtaposition of three disparate texts but an attempt to understand not only the aesthetics of such an 'impossible mourning' but also to underscore the deeply personal narrative of loss ingrained in the discourse of exile. Where for Barthes, the loss of his mother becomes the condition of an internal exile and gets translated into a deeply moving exposition on the art of photography, the lucidity of camera; for Shahid the loss of his mother coalesces with the trauma of the happenings in Kashmir highlighting his double exile from the mother and the motherland and is an example of how personal pain is woven into the aesthetics of poetry.

There is, as Mishra tells us, something of a tradition of 'impossible mourning' in contemporary western scholarship, he quotes Derrida's *Memoires for Paul de Man* and his *Specters of Marx,* Lyotard's essay "The Jews" to elucidate his point. Freud, Adorno, Benjamin, Arendt, all he says, 'wrote and rewrote according to this mourning' (33). 'Diaspora', for Mishra, is essentially a condition of 'impossible mourning' 'structured as a trope of absence' (30). he quotes Derrida to explain his use of the trope of impossible mourning:

> What is an impossible mourning? What does it tell us, this impossible mourning, about an essence of memory (of amnesia, of remembrance)? And as it concerns the other in us ... where is the most unjust betrayal? Is the most distressing, or even the most deadly infidelity that of a *possible mourning* which would interiorize within us the image, the idol, or ideal of the other who is dead and lives only in us? Or is it that of the impossible mourning, which leaving the other his alterity, respecting thus his infinitive remove, either refuses to take or is incapable of taking the other within oneself, as in the tomb or the vault of some narcissism. (as quoted in Mishra 30)

For Shahid the moment of trauma is his mother's death and becomes that unspeakable moment of melancholia from which there is no respite. Time cannot eliminate for him the emotion of loss and expands into the parallels in the daily killings and desolation of the

Valley caught in the crossfire between the Indian state and militancy. Mourning, as Mishra tell us, is 'bequeathed to us only as memory' (30) and thereby given a voice. For Shahid, however:

> "Memory" – two years later after your death they tell me – has no translation.
>
> ... You wait, at the end of memory, with what befell Zainab – from Karbala to Kufa to Damascus. You are wearing black. The cry of the gazelle ... fills the night. It is Zainab's cry. You cry it for us so purely that even in memory it lets memory cease .... On memory's mantle – where summers may truly shine – all, as never before, is nothing but translation. (*RANF* 29–32)

Karbala, Kufa, Damascus, examples of expulsion, persecution and suffering of the exile become that moment of mourning which memory cannot fully translate. To that extent, every nation has it own narrative of 'impossible mourning.' For Shia Muslims, the battle of Karbala crystallizes into such a moment. For Punjabis the event of partition and the exodus of people from both sides of the subcontinent is such a moment. For Kashmir too the continual violence, repression, persecution by both, the state and the militants makes it a place of 'impossible mourning'.

In poem after poem Shahid pours his heart out refusing to come to terms with the death of his mother (a condition of melancholia according to Freud) and can only result in the wounded cry of the gazelle, desolate without his mother. In his farewell poem, "I dream I am at the ghat of the only world":

> Mother will I lose you again, and in this
> the only world left? Won't the world, ashamed without
> you, find its shrines bereft of any premise of God?
> ... which world will bring her back.
>
> <div align="right">(<i>RANF</i>, 103)</div>

Just as *Camera Lucida* is an extraordinary exposition on the art of photography emerging from an intensely personal loss and the desire in Barthes to recreate 'Not just an image of the mother ... but a just image, an image which would both be justice and accuracy-justesse ...' (70), which he does eventually find in the 'winter garden' photograph of his mother: not her mere identity but the 'impossible science of the unique being' (71). Shahid's *Rooms are Never Finished* too is a poetic outpouring on exile, emerging from the traumatic event of his mother's death, which crystallizes in his book as the inner law of absence and the impossibility of its substitute.

If Shahid's earlier work is concerned with what Bruce King in his *Modern Indian Poetry in English* calls, 'the themes of exile, memory, loss of home, culture and history' (264–265) '... in an American idiom' (259), his *RANF* inaugurates a new aesthetics of loss, an overflow of grief and pain in poetry lines that cannot contain. Excess does not scare him, nor is he unduly perturbed by the claims of modern poetry that reality is too elusive to be formally represented and effortlessly embraces the more rigourous forms of ghazal, sestina and the canzone. He is not in the least self-conscious of his pain, which refuses to transcend into a universal condition of suffering, inconsolable he cries out: for compared to my grief for you, what are those of Kashmir, and what (I close the ledger) are the griefs of the universe when I remember you – beyond all accounting – O my mother? (*RANF* 19).

Barthes draws a similar parallel and echoes the sentiment of Shahid in the loss of his own mother and explains poignantly why his is the impossible mourning:

> It is always maintained that I should suffer more because I have spent my whole life with her; but my suffering proceeds from *who she was;* and it is because she was who she was that I lived with her ... 'I did not insist only upon suffering, but upon respecting the originality of my suffering'; for this originality was the reflection of what was absolutely irreducible in her, and thereby lost forever. It is said that mourning, by its gradual labor, slowly erases pain; I could not, I cannot believe this; ..... For what I have lost is not a Figure (the mother), but a being; and not a being, but a quality (a soul): not the indispensable, but the irreplaceable. (75)

RANF too is relentless in its anguish, of separation from the beloved. It contains what Barthes calls in a different medium (photography), *Punctum:* Which is a 'wound' (26), a 'detail' with a metonymic 'power of expansion' and that which annihilates itself as *medium,* to be no longer a sign but the thing itself? (45). In *RANF* the mother's death is the *Punctum* that 'impossible mourning' which expands metonymically into all the poems written thereafter and becomes the prism through which is filtered the narrative of pain and loss from

Amherst to Kashmir, from the hospital in Lenox Hill to the rock cliffs in Pir Panjal.

For this paper I am primarily looking at "Lenox Hill" and "I Dream I am at the Ghat of the only world" the first and the last poem from *Rooms are Never Finished*. The first poem is a farewell poem to his mother who died of brain tumour in Amherst, USA – as mentioned before. The last poem is Shahid's own farewell poem to the world before he too succumbed to the same disease.

The book is framed between these two deaths and farewells. In fact, the structure of the book is somewhat like that of a Mandala. The first poem, "Lenox Hill" which incidentally is not numbered, is the circle that surrounds all the four sections of the book. Shahid's mother is the presiding deity of the book and Shahid himself is the devotee, identifying so completely with his mother that he took on her disease – as mystics are known to do – to move into the other world, one would imagine, to be with her and some of his favourite people, Begum Akhtar, James Merrill, Eqbal Ahmad among others.

Mourning his mother he lovingly resurrects her through the memory of her last days in a hospital in Lenox Hill. During her last days in the hospital in Amherst the sound of the sirens fused for her into the tortured cry of the elephants falling off the Pir Panjal rock cliffs. The image of the elephants falling from the cliff merges with that of his mother dying, and extends into that of Kashmir being pushed over the cliffs by the 'punishing khaki'. Her footprint, 'the greatest of all footprints' is the valley of Kashmir, the universe, now turned into a tomb. And he, the son, the poet, the one elephant who returns to the jungle:

> ... where each year, on the day his mother
> died, he touches with his trunk the bones of his mother.
>
> (*RANF* 18)

In a reversal of roles in the penultimate stanza of the poem Shahid becomes the mother of his mother and turns her into his daughter, so that:

> I imagine her: a bride in Kashmir,
> she's watching, at the Regal, her first film with Father.
> I'd save you – now my daughter – from God. (*RANF* 18)

Thus, engendering her, 'he experiences her as his inner law, as his feminine child'. Risking the monotheism of Islam he elevates the image of his mother into that of God. In another poem in the same collection, she is:

> Farther than any god. And
> God? He's farther, farther from us, forever
> Far. We lift the shrine. (*RANF* 42)

She is a god with a capital G and is in fact, not only God but also the mother of God, Shahid himself is crowned Krishna by her in Lenox Hill. In another poem she is Zainab, the sister of Hussain grieving over the death of her family and nation. She is also Hussain, the martyred. She is Kashmir, the paradise. In fact, in the figure of his mother is inscribed, the very image of Kashmiriyat and its eclectic traditions. The mythology he creates around her figure contains the synthesis of the mystical Shaivism of Lal Ded and Islamic Sufism of Shaikh Nurruddin. She is also the talisman against a militant Islamic identity threatening to hijack the composite culture of Kashmir. But, she is also Zainab grieving over the death of the martyrs of Karbala and by extension over those brutalized and killed by the state apparatus in Kashmir.

In this final collection of poems the image of his mother fuses completely with that of Kashmir. The trauma of her death expands into that of Kashmir's. Kashmir the beloved paradise becomes 'separation's geography' as he says in "Above the Cities":

> ... For
> where there is farewell,
> you are there. And where there's a son, in any
> language saying Adieu to his mother, she is
> you and that son (there by the gate) is me, that
> son is me. Always. (*RANF* 36)

'Separation's geography' is charted out in the exile of mother by her death, as he says in "From Amherst to Kashmir", '... for she too was tired, fighting death, from hospital to hospital, from city to city' (*RANF* 26).

Similarly in "The Fourth Day":

> Four days: And eternities have so quickly slowed down.

> Only a few – disguised as roses – return from ashes ...
> for what is Doomsday but the Beloved's departure?
>
> Doomsday begins. It keeps on beginning.
> and the Beloved leaves one behind to die. (*RANF* 48–49)

One is tempted to read in this fusion of mother and motherland a nationalist agenda as indeed some scholars are wont to do. Indeed as Mishra too says, '... diasporas are also bastions of reactionary thinking and fascist rememorations' (29). Nishat Zaidi in her essay, "Karbala as metaphor in the poetry of Agha Shahid Ali", reads the metaphor of Karbala as not only central to his poetry but to his person as well. In fact, she goes on to grant an emotionally liberatory role to the metaphor, which she says helped Shahid 'resign to his deep personal loss by memorializing Hussain' (159). For Zaidi, it is not the personal loss of the mother, which is central to the narrative of Shahid's poetry but the metaphor of Karbala, which she says, 'reinvents his association with his surroundings' (160). In the same essay she goes on to say: Thus by connecting the blood of Kashmir with Hussain's Agha Shahid Ali registers his faith in the cause of Kashmiris and expresses his anger against the unjust atrocities wrought by the state machinery in the state (164).

This reading of the metaphor of Karbala almost reads like a purist desire for an ethnic state. But, Shahid above all is the poet of Kashmiriyat and not of a narrow nationalism. In his book, *The Country Without a Post Office,* in his first poem, "Farewell" he is haunted by the image of the Kashmiri pandits expelled from the Valley:

> In the lake the arms of the temples and mosques are locked
> in each other's reflections
>
> ... if only somehow you could have been mine, what wouldn't
> have happened in this world?
> I'm everything you lost. You won't forgive me. (8–9)

Amitav Ghosh, in his essay " 'The Ghat of the Only World': Agha Shahid Ali in Brooklyn" confirms this in a conversation he had with Shahid:

> 'I wish all this had not happened', he said. 'This dividing of the country, the divisions between people – Hindu, Muslim, Muslim, Hindu – you can't imagine, how much I hate it. It makes me sick. What

I say is: why can't you be happy with the cuisines and the clothes and the music and all these wonderful things?' (346)

Again, later in the same essay Ghosh writes, 'In the broadest sense, his vision tended always towards the inclusive and ecumenical' (355). He goes on to add:

> I once remarked to Shahid that he was the closest that Kashmir has to a national poet. He shot back: 'A national poet, maybe. But not a nationalist poet; please not that.' If anything, Kashmir's current plight represented for him the failure of the emancipatory promise of nationhood and the extinction of the pluralistic ideal that has been so dear to intellectuals of his father's generation. (355)

It would however be fair to say that Zaidi in her essay also points out that Shahid's poetry performs the 'unique task of highlighting the composite culture of India' (237). However, one is at variance with Zaidi over her granting the metaphor of Karbala the role of liberating Shahid from the deeply personal loss of his mother. And though the event of Karbala itself may indeed be read as a moment of 'impossible mourning' and the universal dimension of the event may not be denied. In Shahid's own case it is the death of the mother and the impossibility of mourning her loss that leads him to frame Karbala as a moment of similar emotional intensity and not the other way around:

> Thus I swear, here and now, not to forgive the universe
> that would let me get used to a universe
> without you. She, alone, was the universe
> as she earned, like a galaxy, her right not to die (*RANF* 17–18)

It is "Lenox Hill" the poem that is the opening poem of the book, "Karbala: A History of the 'House of Sorrows'" follows Lenox Hill. It is Lenox Hill that frames the history of Karbala and of Kashmir and the poet. Zaidi calls the inconsolable grief of Shahid, 'self-indulgent moments of overwhelming personal grief caused by the death of his mother' (158), with which he only comes to terms, as mentioned above, 'by memorializing Hussain'.

The melancholia of Shahid for his mother is not 'self-indulgence' but the essential condition of his poetry. It is a loss with which he never comes to terms with indeed he does not even want to come to terms with it. Ghosh attests to this:

For Shahid the passage of time produced no cushioning from the shock of the loss of his mother: he re-lived it over and over again until the end. Often he would interrupt himself in mid-conversation: 'I can't believe she's gone; I still can't believe it'. (359)

Indeed, the emotional quality of his poetry derives from this special emphasis and stands out in the oeuvre of Indian English poetry in its refusal to create a distance between his pain and his poetry. The rational intermediary of a political reading as provided by Zaidi reduces the emotional affect of the poetry. Shahid's poetry is of the order of *loving* and in that sense comes tantalizingly close to the tradition of sufi and bhakti poetry. It is when you recognize with your whole body the impact of the poem that it acquires an emotional dimension of the magnitude of *punctum*. As Barthes would say:

> A detail overwhelms the entirety of my reading; it is an intense mutation of my interest, a fulguration. By the mark of *something*, the photograph is no longer 'anything whatever'. This *something* has triggered me, has provoked a tiny shock, a *satori*, the passage of a void. (49)

The *intense immobility* of Shahid emotionally to come to terms with his mother's death allows his poetry the 'possibility of a rhetorical expansion' into the metaphor of Karbala and all suffering emerging from such exile. The impossibility of mourning her engenders for him the condition of Kashmir and of exile. Exile thereby becomes also the condition of truth, of alienation with a universe that allows the loved one to die. Exile is also the condition that engenders truth and the consequences thereof. So if Shahid himself refuses to go on living after the death of his mother, the death of a certain kind of truth, literally letting go of his life, others who proclaim truth too are not spared as he says of Mansoor al Hallaj, the great Muslim mystic who was crucified in Baghdad for saying, I am the truth, an a-al-haq:

> Crucified Mansoor was alone with the Alone:
>
> God's loneliness – just His – compiled by exiles. (*RANF* 72)

It is pertinent to point out that Mansoor Hallaj has a special place in Kashmiri sufi poetry. Exile for Shahid is not only the condition of being displaced from home but essentially the condition of loneliness, the condition of separation from the beloved. In fact, he does not spare even God from the pain of separation in his poetry, in "Hell", he says:

Pity? Yes, for Heaven (to us what music,
we who trade in love) and for love, first story:
God as only he could have known him. "God's so
Lonely ... else would He", asks one fallen angel,
Emphasizing *lonely*, "else would He, *would* He
Punish man so? (64)

Shahid in *RANF* creates an inventory of all those who were deeply loved and forsook him 'by dying' and those who were martyred in the cause of truth and freedom. In his last poem, "I dream I am at the ghat of the only world", the valedictory that began in the first poem addressed to this mother now finds expression in his own leave-taking but not before invoking the names of all those whom he loved and whom he hopes to meet in the next world. The poem is a 'theater of dreams' in which loved ones come and go through their chosen mirrors even as the poet is rowed by Gula the boatman through the Lake to each island of memory while he says his farewells. His own mirror of departure awaits him as he rows one last time through the burnt waters of Dal, burnt chinars, bulbuls without song and the house in Amherst where his mother died.

The figure of Begum Akhtar at the start of the poem is yet another reminder of the 'impossible mourning' she slipped into, after the death of her mother and was close to losing her mind, if not allowed to sing. Shahid, as Ghosh says was '... haunted by this image of Begum Akhtar, as a bereaved and inconsolable daughter, weeping on her mother's grave; it is in this grief-stricken aspect that she is evoked again and again in his poems' (350). Her invocation at the start of the poem endows the original moment of trauma of the death of Shahid's mother with an added meaning. As does the death of other loved ones, James Merrill and Eqbal Ahmad. As Mishra too says, 'homeland is recollected through traumatic moments' (37).

Begum Akhtar's music and the aesthetics of ghazals which were such an integral part of Shahid's life become, in his poetry what Mishra, quoting Slavoj Zizek, calls the 'enjoyment' of the nation, 'the fantasy about a particular way of life' (27). I quote from his definition of nation from Mishra's essay:

> To emphasize in a "deconstructionist" mode that nation is not a biological or transhistorical fact but a contingent discursive construction, an overdetermined result of textual practices, is thus

misleading: such an emphasis overlooks the remainder of some real, nondiscursive kernel of enjoyment which must be present for the Nation qua discursive entity-effect to achieve its ontological consistency. (202)

But again this enjoyment is 'predicated upon melancholia and loss' (28). As Shahid so poignantly says, 'love doesn't help anyone finally survive' (101). Unable to reconcile to the irreplaceable loss of his mother, he awaits his final annihilation. As Ghosh so memorably puts it, '... there are traditions in which poetry is a world of causality entire unto itself, where metaphor extends beyond the mere inkling of words, into the conjugation of a distinctive reality' (360). The impossible mourning thus results in the merger of Shahid with his mother, refusing to be cured of his 'open wound' but in the event assimilating, just like his mother, in the image of Kashmir. In his death he becomes one with his mother and his motherland.

Works Cited

Ali, Agha Shahid. *The Country Without a Post Office: Poems: 1991–1995.* New Delhi: Ravi Dayal Publisher, 1997.
—. *Rooms Are Never Finished: Poems.* New Delhi: Permanent Black, 2002.
Barthes, Roland. *Camera Lucida.* London: Flamingo, 1980.
Ghosh, Amitav. *The Imam and the Indian: Prose Pieces.* Delhi: Permanent Black, 2002.
King, Bruce. *Modern Indian Poetry in English.* New Delhi: OUP, 2001.
Mishra, Vijay. "Diasporas and the Art of Impossible Mourning". *In Diaspora: Theories, Histories, Texts.* Ed. Makarand Paranjape. New Delhi: Indialog Publications, 2001.
Zaidi, Nishat. "Karbala as Metaphor in the poetry of Agha Shahid Ali." *Indian Literature.* 237 (January-February 2007): 154–167.

24 ANSHOO SHARMA

Transcending Borders of Patriarchal Hegemony: Dattani's: *Where There's a Will*

Creating borders, contesting borders both ever continuous processes, invariably linked to one another, are rooted in the basic nature of human beings. Seen from the political perspectives, it becomes clear that the concept of nationhood is incomplete without the red/black lines drawn across white paper. It holds people together, defines cultures and creates communities, and the idea of oneness keeps out the 'other' who is different. But borders are not always present as concrete margins alone, they are also present in the abstract as in the case of psychological, emotional, ideological and interpersonal human relationships. Borders imply enclosures, exclusivity and ownership. When translated into relational borders, they throw up distances, possessiveness and hegemony, and result in creating barriers. Patriarchy, like the concept of nation, is another abstraction, but one which is manifested acutely in human relationships. It implies a descending line of authority and a centre that controls. V. Geetha defines it as 'the rule of the father not only over all women in the family, but also over younger and socially or economically subordinate males' (4).

The written word as text is also framed within the borders of the book but it escapes from this framework the moment it finds a reader. Literature throws open a wide variety of texts which are replete with examples of borders, borders that construct and those that divide, and individuals who contest or cross them and sometimes also completely erase them, or at least attempt an erasure. The present paper specifically focuses on Mahesh Dattani's play titled *Where There's a Will*, which carries a pun on the 'will' in its very title and simultaneously targets both money power and subversive strategies. It goes on to raise significant questions about the legitimacy of power as well as that of subversion.

In this play the framework of borders can be perceived at various levels. In Dattani's own words it is primarily 'an exorcism of the patriarchal code'. Clear defining borders exist delineating patriarchy, the gender division and also the stage vis-à-vis the audience. Mahesh Dattani takes up the upper class urban milieu, where personal relationships are stressed and under strain, where home is depicted as a place of resentment, confrontation and barely suppressed violence, as his principal dramatic subject. The domestic settings, marriage, parent-child conflicts and generational shifts or to put it more comprehensively 'the psychodrama of family relationships' is Dattani's modus-operandi (Dharwadker 269).

Authority, power, dictatorship or as in the present case 'patriarchal hegemony' is a force which always gives rise to an opposite and equally forceful reaction. The resistance taking birth as a result of a parent's excessive imposition of authority is seldom unsuccessful in creating fault lines, margins or borders. In *Where There's a Will* the patriarchal head of the family, Hasmukh Mehta, stands on one side of the unseen border and the rest of the family – his wife Sonal, son Ajit and daughter-in-law Preeti – on the other. Each of them illustrates a separate individualistic form of resistance towards the patriarch.

Ajit is aged twenty-three and married to Preeti who is expecting their first child. Considered from the Indian socio-cultural perspective he is old enough to shoulder all these responsibilities including the financial ones, but his father does not think so. For him it is essential that Ajit learns to follow his footsteps first. Ajit, on the other hand, from the very beginning, is depicted as the 'errant' son who is trying to forge an independent identity for himself. He wishes to put his ideas of modernizing his father's factory into action. The major catch, however, is that he needs his father's financial support for this purpose. He is not the kind of person who despite his desire to do so can carve an independent role for himself. At this juncture it is important to question whether the change desired is merely at the material level or does it stand as a metaphor for something deeper. It is in fact a continuous struggle for a separate identity. He does not want to be a mere extension or a mirror reflection of his father.

Throughout the interaction between the father and the son it is made obvious that they never see eye to eye. Each of them is trying to make the other 'listen'. Hasmukh wants his son to remain within the parameters that he has created (or so he thinks) and adhered to throughout his life. But Ajit on the other hand wishes to escape these same borders and chart out an independent territory for himself. His question 'Don't I have any rights at all?' is met by a very dictatorial answer 'you have the right to listen to my advice and obey my orders' (458). This answer is rather significant because it is an echo of what Hasmukh had himself done all his life, that is 'listened to' and 'obeyed' his father. An important point that needs to be emphasized here is that Hasmukh is unknowingly fettered to his past, and the relationship that he shared with his own father. That father who 'took great trouble to make sure' that his son worked hard; that father who expected his son to listen to him and make him happy; and that father who bore him to be able to 'live life again' when he himself grew old. It proves to be a chronicle of the narcissistic principle where one tries to continue existing through their progeny, who are compelled and trained to possess the same qualities as themselves.

The myth of Yayati is also an apt citation where the father exchanges his old age with his son's youth in order to continue enjoying the pleasures of young age. It is symbolic of the desire that a father harbours to create a son after his own image. Dattani traces this hegemonic pattern through the three generations of grandfather, father and son which works repetitive patterns. It is through the comments of Hasmukh's ghost about his own picture that we come to know of the similarities between him and his father—'I look too grim. My father always looked so grim.' 'Those cheeks are too hollow. The lips are too tight. I don't have such little mean eyes, do I? My father had. Thirty years of living in the city and he got mean little eyes' (488). 'Grim', 'hollow', 'tight', 'mean', 'little', all these adjectives provide a stark contrast to his name Hasmukh, which carries the meaning of cheerful. These terms illustrate more than just the physical features, they reveal the real man within. One who was coerced into becoming like this by his own father, and is now unable to break the bonds. Both knowingly and unknowingly he is now acting in a similar manner, autocratically and unthinkingly. This same cyclic pattern would have continued had Ajit not decided to try and step out of his father's shadow. Ajit's resistance to the authority of his father is motivated by a constant fear of being annihilated. During one of his many arguments with Hasmukh, Ajit questions 'And what becomes of me? The real me, I mean, if I am you, then where am I?' (461).

Dattani reworks this identity crisis towards the end of the play when Hasmukh's ghost echoes the same words. The realization permeates his very 'soul' so to say that during his lifetime he never really lived LIFE, never really stepped out of the borders set by his own father. He was just a symbol of achievements of his father's aspirations for him. The framework, which he tried to put in place, seems to be finally crumbling away. He seems to be nowhere – literally as well as metaphorically. Dattani on the other hand upholds Ajit's position, who may have his own set of weaknesses, yet he is conscious enough and holds on to his conviction that he does *not* want to replace his father – to become 'him'. Ajit finally stands vindicated when Kiran Jhaveri, Hasmukh's mistress and the 'epitome of the Dattani woman', whose word holds good says – 'He may not be the greatest rebel on earth, but at least he is free of his father's beliefs. He resists. In a small way, but at least its a start. That is enough to prove that Ajit has won and Hasmukh has lost' (510). The overthrowing of the patriarchal manacles works through multiple perspectives. The gender divisions are worked out which run parallel to the neat divisions within the structure of the play.

It becomes imperative to mention here Dattani's strategic experimentation with the theatrical form. He is a playwright, a director and also an actor. This polydexterity allows him a performative control and a comparative degree of autonomy vis-à-vis the performance of his avant-garde plays. He creates his own theory by distinguishing between the 'form' which may be borrowed for example the use of the proscenium along with the English language; and the 'content' which focuses on the realist contemporary urban experience. There is an erasure of the traditionalist borders as far as the structure of the play is concerned with direct address to the audience through his characters which do away with the need of a *sutradhar*, the chorus or the more conventional mode of a soliloquy. Instead Dattani uses Hasmukh's ghost as a chorus, combining in him the advantages of personal narration, hindsight and distance. Dattani's use of the available stage space reflects these structural, innovative additions where the fractured reality of the middle class urban milieu gets depicted in the performance spaces split up into multi-levels. The characters are made to use this space in such a manner that it becomes a narrative strategy highlighting the complexity of the plot and at the same time unravelling the core issues that seem to be troubling the characters.

In *Where There's a Will* there are three spaces: the fancy dining-cum-living room connected to the kitchen, which is an extension of the living room as it is a space where most of the interaction between the females of the house seems to take place; the hideously trendy bedroom of Ajit and Preeti which reflects availability of material resources but dearth of genuine taste and class; and finally the bedroom of Hasmukh and Sonal Mehta which seems to be as colourless and insipid as is their conjugal life. Like the hegemonic centre the living space rules the first half of the play, where the family gets together. The bedrooms are places of exit and withdrawal. Later on in the play, with Hasmukh Mehta's death having taken place, the bedrooms with their secret lives creep in. It is in the bedroom that Preeti has been playing games with the pills, it is in the bedroom, which Sonal shares with Kiran, the mistress, that Hasmukh's life is dissected and the different viewpoints of the three women expressed.

Where There is a Will plays on the 'will' of the son which is weak; he is wholly dependent on money. Kiran gets him to work as his father had never been able to. And then there is the 'will' of the father, who bequeaths all power to his mistress and seeks to control the lives of his family members even after his death. In this game, the silent will of Preeti is more effective in getting her father-in-law out of the way. The play is a comic contest between different kinds of 'wills', effectual and ineffectual, as it puts accepted conventions under the scanner.

The subversion of existing stereotypes takes place at various levels. The three generations of which only two are present in the play, (the grandfather is only a memory and the fourth generation of the expected yet unborn child, a future), depict a traditional joint family but with an undercurrent of clashing values and ideals. They live under the patriarchal order which is finally displaced by the *female order*. Not only metaphorically but at the physical level as well there is movement from outside space into the inner space when Kiran Jhaveri refuses to stay in the outhouse, and is invited into Sonal's bedroom. Another important strategy that Dattani employs is humour which sometimes almost borders on black. The craft of humour is converted into an art form. It delineates not only individual vagaries but also the middle class milieu in general, to which Dattani also belongs. As the play progresses, the contrasts begin to emerge. The resistance, in the main, is to unthinking power and the 'tradition' it represents through its hierarchies of gender, class and age. Ajit succumbs to it as he begins to wear a safari suit like his father, even as he grumbles that he has been shoved (and has not stepped) into his father's shoes (500). Kiran represents the 'will' of the dead man. Ajit tells his wife:

> He is making me do things he wanted me to do. Through her! In the office. Without realizing it, she has replaced father and is replacing me with father.
>
> Everything she tells me to do is exactly what he would have wanted me to do. We are all living out a dead man's dream! (501)

As Ajit and his wife share their confidences, the different strategies each has employed come into the open – outward submission, inward subversion in Preeti's case, open resistance in Ajit's case. For Sonal, the mother, it has been a yielding to the accepted pattern while Kiran, the mistress, is manipulative. She allows herself to be used only in order to use Hasmukh for her own ends. Once the secret of the exchange of the blood pressure controlling pills is known to Kiran, the Kiran-Preeti relationship undergoes a change. In the end questions of class boundaries – the three women all belong to less advantaged households; of gender boundaries – Kiran uses power more discriminatingly than Hasmukh; of family boundaries – even the wife-mistress antagonism yields to friendship – are all addressed differently as the notion of a structured, close family is turned on its head. Comically the absent 'maharaj' and the gardener, no longer matter as Maggie noodles give way to paranthas. Even the absent (dead) Hasmukh does not matter; his 'will' has achieved exactly the opposite of what he had desired. Thus we see he has created his own distinctive brand of quasi-melodramatic urban tragicomedy intertwined with the aesthetics of modernity, the institution of patriarchy and the experience of women characters who 'may be strong or weak, vocal or silent, liberated or repressed, complicit or resistant, conformist or subversive, generous or self-seeking' (Dharwadker 329).

Where There's a Will has been clearly divided into two halves, one prior to the death of Hasmukh Mehta, the central character and another post his death. In the first half Hasmukh is located at the centre while the rest of the family is at the periphery. He occupies this space through use of power – both economic and hierarchical. But use of authorial power invariably gives birth to resistance as mentioned earlier and Dattani seems to have dealt with this issue throughout the play and his efforts can be viewed through the deconstructionist criticism of Foucault where he 'sees resistance (or) counter hegemonic views and actions – as a realistic possibility' (Bertens 154). In the next half of the play, post-Hasmukh Mehta's death, the revelation of his 'will' is juxtaposed with the revelation of the existence of the 'other' woman in his life.

He aims at controlling his family through his will through which the marginalized are pushed further to the peripheries. According to the sociologist Ram Ahuja the manner of punishing a profligate child can be economic and psychological – like denying money, restricting freedom and reasoning (Ahuja 106), all the methods that Hasmukh Mehta tried to exert during his life time and even after his death. Ajit's hopes of gaining authority after his father's death go up in a haze of smoke and the 'wilful will' (Chaudhuri 29), catapults Hasmukh's mistress Kiran Jhaveri right into the centre of the action as well as the familial space. Dattani succeeds in subverting the gender role, placing a woman at the centre who is empowered with the task of decision making and who proves to be more successful in the role than her male counterpart.

This dramatic transition works at multiple levels and compels the reader/audience to try and decipher the intent behind this O'Henryisque transition. John McRae who directed *On a Muggy Night in Mumbai* feels Dattani's 'special theatrical quality is to build tension in a social context leading to a classic dramatic confrontation which involves not only the characters themselves, but which also confronts the audiences with its own expectations and attitudes' (*Collected Plays* 46).

Kiran becomes the sounding board through whom all desires, aspirations and feelings of the family members are reflected.

Interaction with her throws light upon their real selves. According to Preeti – 'The will has left us all naked' (493). Here Dattani has used a double entendre because the will has not only stripped away the economic benefits; it has also stripped away the masks that Sonal and Preeti were wearing during Hasmukh's lifetime. Only Ajit comes across as a person who never hid behind pretensions. There is no marked change in his attitude towards his father after his death. He resented his domination before and he continues to do so even after his death. It's a different issue altogether that he is essentially a weak person who cannot imagine striking it out entirely on his own. He admits 'I am too fond of your money to give it all up and say to hell with you and your will' (487). But at the same time he is the most consistent character throughout the play. His mother Sonal on the other hand is essentially a weak person oscillating between the shadows of her husband and her sister Minal, never strong enough to draw her own parameters, always bowing under the pressure to conform.

It takes the 'smart, shrewd, calculating, wordly wise' but sensitive Kiran Jhaveri, embodying qualities that Dattani staunchly holds as positive and strong and necessary for a woman, to show Sonal the path to self empowerment. 'Like most women who play gendered roles, Kiran is a victim too, but one who refuses to stay victimized. She becomes part of Hasmukh's life with her eyes wide open, and aware of the benefits that she will derive from the relationship' (Chaudhuri 31). In Preeti's case too it was the benefit motto which made her marry the 'well-placed' Ajit but the parallel ends here. Preeti desires money with a 'passion' which goes beyond the mere needs of sustenance or living life comfortably. Perhaps the underlying desire is for power that comes along with it. But the boundaries that she is ready to overstep, the extent that she is capable of going to, is revealed only towards the end of the play in the trademark *who-dun-it* style of Dattani.

During Hasmukh's lifetime Preeti subscribes to the patriarchal structures by keeping silent but this silence is a mere facade beneath which lurks a more sinister design to overthrow the patriarchal hegemony by crossing all borders of morality and ethics. Her act of exchanging Hasmukh's blood pressure medicines with ordinary vitamin pills – a truly Machiavellian act is discovered by none other than Kiran which leads to the final reversal and denouement. But

Dattani does not rest upon a traditional ending. He creates a reversal within a reversal when Kiran decides to keep quiet and her complicity perhaps denotes another way of finally erasing the hegemonic boundaries completely. This stands parallel to the fact that the wife and the mistress have already crossed over the borders by bonding together during the process of dismembering the man who had constantly put them under the pressure to conform throughout his lifetime. Though Hasmukh's presence permeates throughout the play he is slowly but surely displaced. After his death he hangs upside down getting a different view of the world and his perceptions about himself too receive a jolt. His ploy to control the family through his will works only too well. It brings the family together but he is removed from the centre once and for all. He is displaced from the house, on to the tamarind tree outside, but there is no respite for him yet, as Ajit plans to have the tree 'chopped off' at the earliest given opportunity! Thus, the diametrically opposed are brought together, the marginalized brought into the centre and the borders of patriarchal hegemony finally transcended as new equations fall into place.

Work Cited

Ahuja, Ram. *Society in India*. Jaipur: Rawat Publications, 1999.

Bertens, Hans. *Literary Theory: The Basics*. London: Routledge, 2001.

Chaudhuri, Asha Kuthari. *Mahesh Dattani*. Contemporary Indian Writers in English Series, New Delhi: Foundation Books Pvt. Ltd., 2005.

Dattani, Mahesh. *Collected Plays*. 2 volumes. Vol. I, New Delhi: Penguin Books, 2000.

Dharwadker, Aparna Bhargava. *Theatres of Independence: Drama, Theory and Urban Performance in India Since 1947*. New Delhi: Oxford University Press, 2006.

Geetha, V. *Patriarchy*. Calcutta: Stree, 2007.

25 PAYAL NAGPAL

Alternative Sexual Constructs in Mahesh Dattani's *Seven Steps Around the Fire* and *On a Muggy Night in Mumbai*

In this paper I propose to study the way in which Dattani draws attention to the marginalized sexual categories by placing them within an alternative construct. I would be using Judith Butler's idea of gender as a performative category as a continuous reference point to study the viability of this construction. I also wish to examine briefly the implications of Dattani's insistence on focusing only on the middle class in a naturalistic setting for his plays.

Dattani's plays concentrate on fixed boundaries that have been created by the social system. His plays are rooted in the Indian middle class and grapple with the margins within which this section of society operates. In his plays Dattani tries to unfold to an Indian-English sensibility the real ramifications of their social placement. Dattani's plays deal with issues ranging from child abuse within the family to homosexuality to gender discrimination. Even as we choose to believe that this takes place in some other part of society, Dattani ruptures this imaginary border in the modern sensibility, which keeps us feeling safe and intact from the gory realities around us. Through his plays Dattani seeks to cross this border and in ways unimaginable drags us as reader/audience with him to confront the real world in our own households and partly succeeds in the venture. According to Jeremy Mortimer,

Here was a playwright who was not afraid to work within a relatively conventional dramatic structure to tell a story that was bold and powerful without ever being melodramatic. (3)

In his play *Seven Steps Around the Fire* Dattani uses the female sleuth Uma, the wife of the Superintendent of Police, Suresh Rao, who interacts with the hijra community[1] for her research. She ends up solving a case that reveals the clandestine marriage between Subbu, the son of the minister and the hijra, Kamla. Dattani uses the normative social frame of the *saat pheras* (an important ritual in a Hindu wedding: the bride and groom walking seven steps around the sacred fire) to inscribe the circle of heterosexuality. All those who fall within its circumference are legitimized and those that cannot be accommodated are placed in a void that does not fall within the social purview. The hijra because of the 'lack' of sexuality or rather its distorted form is situated outside the circle of society. Through Uma's interaction with the hijra community, Dattani demarcates a space from where they can interact with the dominant social rubric in a meaningful way. The relationship between Uma and the hijra Anarkali, becomes the site of intersection of forces of the state, compulsory heterosexual modes and attitudes, and the desire of the hijra to be looked at as human.

Uma's first meeting with Anarkali in the prison reveals the callous attitude of the state authorities towards this marginalized community. The failure of the determining state powers to place the hijras within the continually enacted behavioural pattern ascribed to men and women in normative society allows them to do away with the human dimensions of this community. Uma refers to Anarkali as 'she' in the play but for Suresh she is either 'it' or a 'thing'. The nuances of the use of language are power strung as it refuses to accommodate the hijra within the binaries of 'he' and 'she' and places them as 'it' alongside the non-living objects dehumanizing the hijra. According to Suresh:

> They are as strong as horses .... Don't believe a word of anything it says. They are all liars. (*Seven Steps* 9)

Anarkali is placed within the male prison. Here she is made a target by the other male prisoners and the police authorities. She is beaten up and sexually abused by them. Suresh's apathetic response to Anarkali's presence in the male prison is a reflection of the dominant heterosexual conditioning that completely ignores the requirements of Anarkali. According to Judith Butler:

> Gender ought not to be construed as a stable identity or locus of agency from which various acts follow; rather gender is an identity tenuously constituted in time, instituted in an exterior space through a stylized repetition of acts. (*Gender Trouble* 140)

If gender is to be understood as the 'mundane way' in which the 'repetition' of certain acts constitutes the illusion of gender then this social sexual illusion is manifest in the performance of the *saat pheras* that ratifies or legitimizes the sexuality as the relation of Uma and Suresh. They belong to the upper rung of society and Suresh is part of the state networking as a Superintendent of Police. They are childless, a fact that resounds disturbingly in the other two plays of the detective series, *Uma and the Fairy Queen* and *Swami and Winston*. Suresh has political ambitions determined by the structure of power in which he is placed as both male and Superintendent. In this Suresh is both a victim and a perpetuator of this mundane social performance. His being a male in the biological sense is not enough to live up to the heterosexual norms. This in turn has to be ratified by the presence of a child. Uma has undergone her medical examination and is fit to be a mother but Suresh refuses to go for a check-up. A situation that is definitely not uncommon in our society. The easy way is to shift the blame onto Uma. At least this is how her mother-in-law perceives the situation. Suresh's refusal is a reflection of his insecurity in not being an active participant in the dominant social mode. This is also in conflict with his ambition to be a commissioner some day. In this triad of power, (male, commissioner and patriarch) he cannot compromise on his effective manliness, which would be subject to question if he goes in for a test.

As Butler adds:

> That gender reality is created through sustained social performances means that the very notions of an essential sex and a true or abiding masculinity or femininity are also constituted as part of the strategy that conceals gender's performative character and the performative possibilities for proliferating gender configurations outside the restricting frames of masculinist domination and compulsory heterosexuality. (*Gender Trouble* 141)

In the hijra Anarkali Dattani is able to bring out the performative aspects of gender and effectively displace the heterosexual matrix in the context of bourgeois relations. In imitating gender, Anarkali brings out the 'constructedness' of the stereotypes of gender. The performance of either gender allows the hijra to parody the 'notion of an essential sex' and the rigidity of a heterosexual society that restricts people to entrenched behavioural patterns. The alternative space in the play ruptures the otherwise fixed social matrices by revealing the concealed aspects of gender. The power wielded by heterosexuality is reinscribed by the state that in turn proliferates through it. The state forces legitimize heterosexuality making it a compulsory act. Kamla's relationship with Subbu defies such 'sustained social performances' and thereby contests this alliance between the state and the circle of heterosexuality. As a result Kamla is burnt and Subbu's wedding is expected to draw him within the normative heterosexual pattern in society. However at the wedding Anarkali and the other hijras engage in a performance expected of them. They sing songs and clap their hands loudly asserting their presence. But, the performance is no longer able to suppress the performative forces that are unleashed through the photograph of Subbu's wedding with Kamla. This leads to Subbu's breakdown and his killing himself. As Uma says:

> A picture of Kamla as a beautiful bride smiling at Subbu with the wedding garland around him. The poojari probably didn't know that Kamla was not a woman. Of course Mr. Sharma couldn't have it – totally unacceptable. So he arranged to have Kamla burnt to death. But Salim had to tell him about the picture. Mr. Sharma simply had to have that picture. He sent Salim to threaten Anarkali and Champa ... . He did get the picture eventually ... after losing his son. What a price to pay! (*Seven Steps* 41)

The alternative space counters the confluence of heterosexuality and state powers even as the case is finally hushed up and the people restored to their respective positions of power. The subversive potential of the space that Dattani presents is deployed only to expose the double standards of the visible bourgeois community. And to that extent Dattani is able to articulate their case with great clarity. But the play does not explore the invisible social entities that thrive in huge numbers in the country, or their possible relationship with the alternative community. The play urges the audience to address the hijra community in the context of humane relations and to recognize their sexuality as not a lack but one in its own right.

Dattani's *On A Muggy Night in Mumbai* delineates an alternative space within the suffocating confines of Kamlesh's flat. The *saat pheras* in *Seven Steps* transform into a 'wedding band' that keeps pressing onto the gay community ensconced in the heart of the city. The mugginess of the weather parallels the claustrophobia that characterizes gay relations in the play. The play centres on the gathering of a group of friends in Kamlesh's flat. Each one is established socially but has alternative sexual preferences that are in conflict with their socially determined identity. Kamlesh's flat becomes the place where each of these people tries to grapple with their unique sense of identity crisis. Kiran, Kamlesh's sister is engaged to his ex-lover known to his friends as Prakash and as Ed to his sister and is thereby considered to be two separate persons. As in the case of *Seven Steps* a photograph of Kamlesh and Ed, reveals that Ed and Prakash are the same person. Or rather, Kamlesh's lover and Kiran's fiancé is the same. *On A Muggy Night in Mumbai* dissects the sexual mores in bourgeois society to reveal the straitjacketed outlook generated by the overpowering heterosexual norms. The play unfolds the nexus between the state and its apparatuses that promulgate the heterosexual and activities around it as normative. Dattani through the struggles of this alternative community contextualizes the contradictions in the identity/social crises arising out the unavailability of space for expression.

Using different levels in the play that have a bearing on the psychological propensity of the characters the simple naturalistic setting is made complex. The levels are a platform to present the clash between the middle class individual and the society. On the level, *Shoonya*, the socially determined identities of the characters are placed along with positions that they seek, but ones that are not available to them. The characters never reach a particular essentialised zone but always remain in the fluid state unlike heterosexual norms that are always fixed and resist any fluidity. In her essay "Gender" Butler has observed:

> The discursive condition of social recognition precedes and conditions the formation of the subject: recognition is not conferred on a subject but forms that subject. Further, the impossibility of a full recognition,

that is, of ever fully inhabiting the name by which one's social identity is inaugurated and mobilized, implies the instability and incompleteness of subject-formation. (156)

The sense of claustrophobia that the play inscribes is a result of this 'recognition'. In it the social/sexual position as the set of choices that will be made by the characters is pre-determined. The identity is that of a heterosexual, and the set of choices probably lead to the 'wedding band'. However, the possibility of homosexual relations occurs in the space between the established conditioning and the 'impossibility of a full recognition'.

Sharad's entry into Kamlesh's flat inverts the normative gaze by re-positioning it from within an alternative space. As Sharad looks at the couple in the flat across through the binoculars the naturalistic gaze of heterosexual society that stereotypes the homosexual as aberrant is reversed. The homosexual is no longer being looked at but is looking both at him and the dominant social/sexual paradigm. Heterosexual relations, usually considered to be liberating are looked at as exploitative from the perspective of the woman who lacks any sexual compatibility with her husband the diamond merchant and seeks an alternative in the doodhwalla. This parallels Kamlesh's inability to out himself completely, leading to his relation with the guard or his fetishistic gaze at the couple in the flat across. The play deglamorises gay relations and looks at the possible hierarchies within it as Kamlesh pays the guard for being with him. But the implications of this relationship for the guard are only briefly touched upon. Dattani's ability to maintain a realistic tone prevents stereotyping gay relations. This also points to a general state of confusion where heterosexual norms cut across class and gender making it difficult to evolve positions that lie outside the boundaries of a homophobic community.

In this gathering at Kamlesh's flat the different positions in a bourgeois gay community are discussed. According to John McRae:

> It would be banal to see these characters as in any way stereotypical. They are a carefully balanced range of individuals with a depth of experience that exceeds traditional expectations. They are brought together in such a way as to bring out the conflicts, repressions and past secrets which are assailing Kamlesh and Ed/Prakash in particular. (45)

Sharad has no qualms about outing himself in his immediate context. But Ranjit, referred to, as the 'coconut' by his friends cannot sustain his gay identity in a Third World country that does not accommodate people like him. He has to go abroad to be who he is and is also socially equipped to do so. Bunny Singh, a television actor, poses to be straight. Bunny Singh's confession is a blow to the normalcy generated by the contemporary upper middle class heterosexual society that thrives on the convergence of power and sexuality as 'straight'. As Bunny Singh says:

> I have never told anyone in so many words what I am telling you now – I am a gay man. Everyone believes me to be the model middle-class Indian man. I was chosen for the part in the serial because I fit into common perceptions of what a family man ought to look like. I believed in it myself. I lied – to myself first. And I continue to lie to millions of people every week on Thursday nights. (*On A Muggy Night* 103)

His position encapsulates the easy way available to people of the gay community in middle class networking. He compromises on his identity as gay as he cannot face the ostracism that he would have to deal with because of his alternative sexual preference. In the guise of being straight he emblematizes the desire of the millions that see him as the ideal man, an image that is further reinforced by the media. Deepali's is the most sorted out position as she has a partner and is able to deal with its implications. The stringency of the heterosexual norms creates a sense of suffocation in society that prevents people from any kind of relationship that would harmonize their sense of identity.

Kamlesh's confession about his failed relation with Prakash inscribes the pain of separation that is caused by the intransigence of heterosexual norms. These are further reinforced by the apparently legitimate ways of the psychiatrist. Kamlesh visits a psychiatrist to overcome his sense of loss but is made to feel a deviant. The doctor analyses gay relations as a medical aberration that can be overcome using the 'aversion therapy'. Ed, however goes to the psychiatrist to condition his sexuality to ensure a secure place for him in society outside the claustrophobic spaces of the alternative community. This is a signifier of the general sense of suffocation in gay relations that find it difficult to establish a comfort level, as there is a gaze that continually castigates them as aberrant. The consequences are clear.

Ed decides to marry Kiran. He adopts the machoistic demeanor that makes him manlier than he was before. He uses his male aggression to draw Kiran into a relationship. In this overlapping space of heterosexual and homosexual identities the claustrophobia heightens posing the question of whether a homosexual can become a heterosexual. According to Asha Kuthari Chaudhuri:

> Much of 'mainstream' society, Dattani believes, lives in a state of 'forced harmony', out of a sense of helplessness, or out of lack of alternatives. Simply for lack of choice, they conform to stereotypes like 'homosexuals' that in some sense lead to a kind of ghettoisation within society, little spaces to which the marginalized are pushed. (*Mahesh Dattani* 47)

The play makes a case both for the alternative community and for the limited outlook of middle class heterosexual norms that suffocates marginal entities.

Sharad in parodying Ed's position generates questions both in the mind of Kiran and the reader/audience. In an interesting inversion, Sharad parodies not his own position as a homosexual, but Ed's as the reconditioned person who is soon going to be a part of the homophobic community. According to Butler:

> Paradoxically, but also with great promise, the subject who is 'queered' into public discourse through homophobic interpellations of various kinds *takes up* or *cites* that very term as the basis of opposition. This kind of citation will emerge as *theatrical* to the extent that it *mimes and renders hyperbolic* the discursive convention that it also *reverses*. The hyperbolic gesture is crucial to the exposure of the homophobic law that can no longer control the terms of its own abjecting strategies. (*Gender* 162)

In pretending to be Kamlesh's lover who now wants to become straight, Sharad brings out the limitations of the homophobic community that seeks a linear conditioning of social positions to maintain the status quo. As he says:

> You see, being a heterosexual man – a real man, as Ed put it – I get everything. I get to be accepted – accepted by whom? – well, that marriage lot down there for instance. I can have a wife, I can have children who will all adore me simply because I am a hetero – I beg your pardon – a real man. Now why would I want give it all up? So what if I have to change a little? If I can be a real man I can be king.

> Look at all the kings around you, look at all the male power they enjoy, thrusting themselves onto the world, all that penis power ... all it needs is a bit of practice. I have begun my lessons. Don't sit with your legs crossed. Keep them wide apart. (*On A Muggy Night* 101)

Sharad's parody of the enforced heterosexual pattern exposes the clichés on which its power is based. Being a 'real man' implies acceptability by the normative social code irrespective of sexual choice in the individual. This can be easily adopted by following the dominant and easily available behavioural pattern in society. In this being a man implies aggression and being a woman means to be docile. In the play the heterosexual matrix tries to appropriate the sexuality of the alternative community and resolves the conflict in Ed's mind by resorting to the binary positions of masculine and feminine. In it Ed would be the man leading Kiran to a blissful life. However in 'miming' conventional behaviour mechanisms Sharad dislocates them from their embedded social positioning making them available for scrutiny. The use of the 'hyperbolic' gesture by Sharad exposes the limitations of the position that looks at the heterosexual identity of people as an innate one.

The normative conditioning of social groups distorts social and sexual relations. After the revelation Kiran is able to see through her relationship with Ed and compares it with her previous relation. Ed however, cannot reconcile the pressing demands of the baraat outside the flat with his gay identity and tries to jump off the balcony. According to Nidhi Singh:

> Ed emerges as the most pathetic character. Once the mask of masculinity slips a weak, treacherous and hypocritical character is revealed who in his machinations to conform to heterosexuality, ends up becoming self-alienated. (*Contemporary Drama* 162)

The mugginess of the weather makes its way into the situation, and the two separate spaces are visible distinctly at the end of the play. The alternative community is under threat from the residents of the building who have seen Ed and Kamlesh's photograph. They will not allow them to stay in the building. This explains not only a lack of identity but also of space for the people of the alternative community in the society that has emerged in the contemporary scenario.

Dattani's plays draw their strength from the naturalistic setting focusing only on the middle class. However, this selective process leaves out certain important segments of the society where the parameters of an alternative community would be different. As the bourgeois standards exist in a definitive socio-economic relation with the other social groups the social and cultural norms also exist in conjunction with each other. This means that any analysis of the possibilities of alternative communities in terms of its inception and perception would be encompassing in perspective if it takes into cognizance the inter-relationships between different social groups. The purpose of theatre and its performative possibilities would be manifold if it is able to bring out the contradictions in the relationship between the different sections of society and their perceptions of normative paradigms of thought. Dattani ignores the dimensions of this dynamic space in the case of the other social groups and their relationship with the middle class. But, in both the plays Dattani is able to delineate the alternative community and pit it against the double standards of the bourgeois society. Dharwadker's observation is:

> In the plays Dattani has published so far, home is again a place of resentment, neurosis, confrontation, and barely suppressed violence, until a last minute reversal exposes some guilty secret from the past that has fueled the mundane family antagonisms. ... the condition of victimization extends to all the inhabitants of home who are trapped by cultural constraints and economic circumstances into an impossible coexistence. (*Theatres of Independence* 277, 282)

Dattani, a playwright of the post-independence era crosses the invisible but well defined and entrenched social boundaries that preserve the middle class and its stale value system. He brings out the decadent politics in urban India that has cocooned this social group in a way that makes it completely inert and passive. Through his plays he creates alternative structures that emphasize the need to acknowledge and understand the depraved condition of urban upper class society shielded by the comfortable habitat of the bourgeoisie.

Note

1. *Hijra* is a Hindi word for eunuch or hermaphrodite. The Hijra community, in itself, constitutes the third gender. Normal avenues of

employment are not easily available to them. They, for the most part, earn a living out of ritual performances at childbirth, marriages and other such social functions and festivals.

Works Cited

Butler, Judith. *Gender Trouble: Feminism and the Subversion of Identity*. New York: Routledge, 1990.

—. "Gender". *Gender: Readers in Cultural Criticism*. Ed. Anna Tripp. New York: Palgrave, 2000.

Chaudhuri, Asha Kuthari. *Mahesh Dattani: An Introduction*. New Delhi: Foundation Books, 2005.

Dharwadker, Aparna Bhargava. *Theatres of Independence: Drama, Theory and Urban Performance in India Since 1947*. Iowa: University of Iowa Press, 2005.

Dattani, Mahesh. *Seven Steps Around the Fire. Collected Plays*. 2 Vols., Vol. 1. New Delhi: Penguin, 2000.

Dattani, Mahesh. *On A Muggy Night in Mumbai. Collected Plays*. Vol. 1. New Delhi: Penguin, 2000.

Mortimer, Jeremy. "A Note on the Play". *Collected Plays*. Vol. 1. New Delhi: Penguin, 2000.

McRae, John. "A Note on the Play". *Collected Plays*. Vol. 1. New Delhi: Penguin, 2000.

Singh, Nidhi. "The Not-so-gay 'Gay' Plays of Mahesh Dattani". *Contemporary Indian Drama: Astride Two Traditions*. Eds. Urmil Talwar and Bandana Chakravarty. Jaipur: Rawat Publications, 2005.

Contributors

Anshoo Sharma worked for her doctoral degree on "Spatial Metaphors in Jane Austen" and is currently engaged in a postdoctoral project on the Aesthetics of Girish Karnad and Mahesh Dattani.

Avinash Jodha has worked on *Poetics of Exile*. He has also made a short documentary on disabled school children. Currently he is working on theory formation with special reference to nation states and nationhood with reference to South Asia Diaspora.

Charu Mathur is Assistant Professor in the Department of English, University of Rajasthan. She has researched on American drama and is interested in Indian writing in English. She has also worked on diasporic studies.

E.V. Ramakrishnan is a bilingual writer who has published poetry and criticism in English and Malayalam. His work includes study of modernism in Indian poetry, titled, *Making It New*. He has edited a volume of translations of Indian poetry, *The Tree of Tongues*. Professor of English at South Gujarat University, Surat his creative writing includes *Being Elsewhere in Myself* (1980), *A Python in a Snake Park* (1994) and *Terms of Seeing* (2006).

Jasbir Jain is an independent scholar with a wide range of interests. She has just completed a major project on Feminist Thought in India and is currently working on the discourse of forgiveness. Her other interests are in narratology and films.

Jean Arasanayagam is a prolific writer. While her writing reflects her own life and immediate experience, her short stories and poems also reflect the tragic ethnic, social and political conflicts of her native country, Sri Lanka. As a painter in words, Jean Arasanayagam allows the landscape, in its broadest sense, to come to the fore. She has written over thirty books including several plays. Most of her work deals with conflict and violence going on Sri Lanka. Amongst her latest works are *Shooting the Floricans, Peacocks and Dreams* and *The Dividing Line*. This year she has been awarded the State Award for Literature.

Keki N. Daruwalla, poet and fiction writer of rare refined sensibility combines a deep concern for language and life around him. The near epigrammatic beauty that he distills into his poems gives them intensity and condensation that simultaneously works through a combination of involvement and objectivity. Daruwalla began writing at an early age and has published several volumes of poetry such as *The Map-maker, Orion, Keeper of the Dead* and three volumes of short stories in addition to a travelogue of the Himalayas. His third volume of short stories is *The House of Ranikhet*. Currently he is working on a novel. Daruwalla has several awards to his credit.

Kinshuk Majumdar is a young scholar, located in Delhi and currently engaged in research for his doctoral degree.

Madhuri Chatterjee worked on John Updike for her doctoral thesis. Since then, she has diversified her interests to women's autobiographies, travelogues and diasporic studies. She teaches English at Subodh PG College at Jaipur.

Mini Nanda is Associate Professor in English at the University of Rajasthan. Interested in British Studies, she has moved onto Canadian and Canadian native traditions, Indian literatures and feminist studies. At present Nanda is working on Muslim women writers with special reference to partition novels and films.

Nayantara Sahgal is among the foremost Indian novelists who writes about political atmosphere of the nationalist movement and the changing social situation after independence. She has written nine novels and several works of non-fiction, radical in their approach and related to contemporary conditions. Sahgal has dealt with the political and cultural shifts of modern Indian society in novel after novel like *Rich Like Us, Mistaken Identity* and *Lesser Breeds*. Among her several awards are the prestigious Sahitya Akademi Award, Commonwealth Award, Alumni Achievement Award of the Wellesley College and the Doon Ratna Award.

Nidhi Singh teaches English at the University of Rajasthan. For her doctoral dissertation she worked on "The Mythic Reconstitution of Character and Place in the Novels of Rudolph Stow". Currently she is exploring writers from Egyptian and Arabic backgrounds.

Contributors

Nishat Zaidi is Associate Professor in the Department of English at Jamia Millia Islamia. Her main interests are in Indian writing both at home and abroad. She is a multilingual translator working with equal ease with Hindi, Urdu and English.

Payal Nagpal has researched on modern European drama and is currently teaching it at Janki Devi Memorial College, Delhi. She is also associated with the Institute of Life-Long Learning at Delhi University where she develops content for adult learners.

Purabi Panwar is a translator and teaches English in Delhi. Her work on *India in the Writing of Kipling, Forster and Naipaul* has been well received. She has worked extensively in the field of diaspora studies and is a reputed Naipaul scholar. Panwar has also done considerable work in Indian writing across languages.

Savyasaachi Jain is an independent documentary filmmaker and media trainer based in Noida. He studied at IIT, Kanpur, but chose a career in the media because he preferred to work with people rather than machines. He has worked as a newspaper journalist and as producer of the prestigious television current affairs programme, 'Eyewitness', in the first half of the 1990s. He has been independent since 1995, and has worked extensively in areas of conflict such as Kashmir. He produced *J&K Reporter,* a weekly episode on Kashmir for over a year. He is a recipient of the Commonwealth Vision Award, 2002.

Shyamala Narayan is Professor at Jamia Millia Islamia and has published widely. She is the co-author (with M.K. Naik) of *Indian English Literature 1980–2000: A Critical Survey* and of monographs on *Sudhir N. Ghose and Raja Rao*. Since 1972, she is also the contributor of the bibliography for the Indian section of the *Annual Bibliography of Commonwealth Literature.*

Simran Chadha is Senior Lecturer in English at Dayal Singh College, Delhi University and is currently engaged in research on the study of conflict and strategies for peace building with a special focus on Sri Lanka at the Jawaharlal Nehru University. Chadha is also interested in film studies, especially adaptations.

Somdatta Mandal is Professor of English at Viswabharati University, Shantiniketan. She is a well-known film scholar and has worked widely in feminist and American studies. Her recent publications include *Film and Fiction: Word into Image* and is currently working on South Asian diasporic cinema on a Rockefeller Foundation Award.

Sudha Shastri is located in IIT, Mumbai and has worked on intertextuality for her doctoral thesis. She has a wide range of interests and has done some work on dalit writing. Narratological studies are her major area of interest.

Suniti Namjoshi born in Bombay in 1941, a Canadian citizen and resident of England is a poet, fabulist and novelist. Her work infuses a deep engagement with issues of gender, sexual orientation, cultural identity and human rights. Her poetry, fables, articles and reviews are featured in various anthologies and journals in India, Canada, the US, Australia and Britain. Exploratory and experimental, Namjoshi's work is touched by autobiographical elements such as gender, politics and her Hindu background and is studied around the world for its transformed creations. Her more recent book *Building Babel* (1996) is an innovation in fiction, bringing together myth and cyber world.

Usha Bande, former Fellow, Indian Institute of Advanced Study, has a wide range of interests which extend to folklore, monuments and rural studies. Amongst her latest publication are *Writing Resistance* (2006) and *Ecology and Folk Traditions in Himachal Pradesh* (2007).

Vijaya Singh is a poet, short story writer and critic. She has a long-term interest in films having worked on them for her doctoral work and has explored the different nuances of the form. Her current project is on the role and significance of trains in films.